GENTLY
with the TIDES

Timeless advice from the first 15 years
of *Living Aboard* magazine

GENTLY with the TIDES

Timeless advice from the first 15 years
of *Living Aboard* magazine

Edited by MICHAEL L. FRANKEL

Living Aboard
Austin, Texas

Gently with the Tides

Gently with the Tides was first published in 1990 by the Center for Marine Conservation, Washington, D.C., and subsequently in 1993 by International Marine, a division of the McGraw-Hill Companies.

Living Aboard
P.O. Box 91299
Austin, Texas 78709 U.S.A.
(512) 892-4446 • fax (512) 892-4448
info@livingaboard.com • www.livingaboard.com

Printed in the United States of America

Cover photograph by Kathleen Norris Cook

Cataloging-in-Publication Data

Gently with the tides : timeless advice from the first 15 years of living
    aboard magazine / edited by Michael L. Frankel.
    xii, 220 p., 23 cm., charts
    Articles previously published in *Living Aboard* magazine.
    Includes bibliographical references, index.
    ISBN 0-9741991-1-7

    1. Boat living.   2. Houseboats.   3. Boats and boating.
    I. Frankel, Michael L.   II. Title   III. Living aboard

        GV777.7   797.1'2

Contents

Acknowledgments

THIS BOOK would not have been possible without the generous contributions of liveaboards and dreamers who have corresponded for more than 15 years with the *Living Aboard* journal of the Homaflote Association. This loosely formed association was conceived by Janice and Roland Smith in 1972. It started as a small band of sail- and powerboat liveaboards and steadily grew from a few neighbors and friends along the Eastern Seaboard to thousands of journal subscribers across the United States, Canada, and a few foreign countries.

Along the way Maureen and George Breen, Linda Grover and Tom Doherty, and Michael and Raf Frankel have manned the editorial helm and kept the *Living Aboard* journal on course. The stories and mail received by the Journal from active liveaboards, planners, and those still dreaming of this lifestyle have given me the opportunity to participate in this much-fantasized-about lifestyle. My thanks to the many individuals who have taken the time and effort to share their adventures in boat living. I am particularly indebted to those who have contributed articles to the *Living Aboard* journal and this book: Jill and Adrian Alpine, Sally Elizabeth Andrew, Janet Groene, P. J. Lantz, Hannah Merker, Captain R. D. Peterson, George Hostetter, Kit Armstrong, Beverly Bakes, Jim Chamblee, Dojelo Russell, Donna Schlosser, Janice and Roland Smith, Linda Grover, Steve and Lora Perry, Margaret Roth, Gail Swanton, Holly Shimizu, Joanne Zwernemann, and the staff of the Center for Marine Conservation.

Preface

THIS IS a book about people living on boats, who are often called "live-aboards" and sometimes less flattering names. The materials used to compile this book came from articles and mail contributed to the *Living Aboard* journal of the Homaflote Association, which has been published quarterly since 1972.

People have probably been living on boats since man discovered that wood floats. We have no specific records of prehistoric liveaboards in dugout canoes, but it's only reasonable to assume that some intrepid hunter or fisherman must have experimented with a covered log canoe "home" as an alternative to commuting back and forth to a mountain cave.

The Chinese have been living and working on their junks for thousands of years. Early European explorers lived on ships for years at a time as they ventured forth to discover our watery planet. New England whalers routinely spent two to four years on a single voyage, journeying from the North Atlantic to the northern Pacific in search of whales. And modern-day super-tankers, too large for ports, shuttle between offshore moorings with live-aboard crews. As a matter of fact, these modern colossi of the sea have replaced traditional crew quarters with "apartments," and the ship's complement often consists of the crew and their spouses.

Living aboard isn't a new phenomenon, and for most who live aboard today it isn't a counterculture escape from society. It is merely the recognition that three-quarters of the Earth is covered by water and for some, living on the water is convenient, natural, and an enjoyable alternative to more traditional land-based homes.

Since 1972 the readers of *Living Aboard* have been sharing their stories about their liveaboard lifestyle and their dreams through interviews, postcards, letters, and articles. Roland and Janice Smith started the Homaflote Association after leaving a professorship and librarianship at the University of Connecticut. It all started with a teaching sabbatical for a marketing trip along the Eastern Seaboard to study the burgeoning fiberglass boating industry. As they toured East Coast marinas and boatyards, the Smiths made many new boating friends. They were astonished at how many families were actually living on board year-round. Many of these friendly people invited the Smiths aboard to see first-hand the accommodations they had made to living afloat.

As the Smiths cruised southward they learned more and more about the liveaboard lifestyle. "We went aboard sailboats, houseboats, trawlers, and cruisers. We found everything from sophisticated electronic navigation gear for extended water travel to attractive deck gardens. Some boats in marinas were equipped with stereo, TV, and telephone. Others, anchored out, had generators and all the essentials for comfortable living—their own self-sufficient island. We thought it would be a great idea to have some means for all these water mobile families to get to know each other and to exchange experiences." The seeds for an association of liveaboards had started to grow.

The Smiths thought long and hard about the name of the new association, and although they objected to misspelled words, they finally settled on the unique name "Homafloat." "From the beginning we planned to make the journal of the association a clearinghouse for the self-expression of the members and tried to avoid materials that could be obtained easily from books and boating magazines. This was to be a unique exchange of ideas, experiences, and philosophies of those who were living aboard or contemplating the liveaboard life."

By now the Homaflote operation had become a floating home and office for the Smiths and their journal. "Everywhere we stopped we gained new ideas and suggestions from the innovative people living along the Intracoastal Waterway. There was the sailboat equipped with a heavy molded salt shaker over a 12-volt bulb, creating a fresnel lens for an anchor light. There was the cruiser with the string of bells on the lifeline to serve as a warning if anyone stepped aboard. A red plastic cereal bowl provided a serviceable night-light. A nylon mesh bag for laundry helped prevent mildewed clothes. A piece of nylon net made an admirable dishcloth that could be wrung out and dried in a flash. A small piece of masking tape, pointed at one end, became an efficient, easily moved marker to indicate a position on a chart. Small ideas but a great help when living in tight quarters. We heard recommendations for marine equipment that had proved its worth and brickbats for equipment that failed. We gathered information about marinas that welcomed liveaboards and those that were not cordial. We learned about good spots for anchoring out and about places to watch out for that were not marked on charts."

As the Smiths continued their journey they kept notes on this wonderful lifestyle. "We met families whose children attended local schools and were upstanding members of the community, and families who moved from place to place and provided a correspondence school education for their children. There were retired families living on pensions; others were employed in local businesses; and some conducted their business off their boats. A few lived aboard while the breadwinner flew to work on Monday mornings and rejoined the family on Friday nights. One family had established an at-home boatbuilding company in which they all participated." By now the Smiths had established a quarterly journal to link the liveaboard community.

In 1982 George and Maureen Breen took over publication of *Living*

Aboard. The Smiths felt that the association should be continued by younger and more active boat lovers. The Breens published the journal until 1985 when the helm was handed over to Linda Grover and Tom Doherty. Linda, who had given up a fast paced life in New York City writing TV soap scripts, and her friend, fisherman Tom, kept up the journal's traditions of providing a clearinghouse for liveaboard correspondence and a vehicle for extolling the liveaboard lifestyle.

In 1987 my brother and I took over publication of *Living Aboard.* With the advent of new home publishing technologies, the journal became beefier and more professional looking. But at its heart were still the generous offerings of liveaboards and dreamers who took the time and effort to write us about their inner thoughts, experiences, and the "how to" of boat living. This tireless correspondence and the endless survey questions we asked made up the profiles, lifestyles, boat descriptions, voyage accounts, and the daydreams of living aboard. Almost two decades of liveaboard correspondence reflect the happiness and frustrations, serenity and fears, loneliness and bonding relationships . . . it is "The Best of Living Aboard."

Preface

Michael L. Frankel
aboard Sabra

For more information on the Center for Marine Conservation contact:
The Ocean Conservancy
1725 DeSales Street N.W., Suite 600
Washington, D.C. 20036
(202) 429-5609
www.oceanconservancy.org

1
Fantasy or Reality?

The Demographics of Living Aboard

Living aboard is more than a unique and often-fantasized-about lifestyle—it's a state of mind. For the most part, people who live aboard have modified the "American dream" for ever larger dwellings and "upward mobility" in favor of simplicity, self-reliance, and "a more meaningful existence."

However, it is impossible to generalize the liveaboard community with a few cultural or socioeconomic terms. The communty, like the rest of society, encompasses a wide variety of individuals, from those who live on the likes of the *Trump Princess* to the local "wharf rat" living on a derelict homemade raft.

Liveaboards. They can be found at marina slips and moorings, at anchorages, or forever wandering the seas and waterways. Many migrate annually in search of the endless summer. And still others dream of someday turning this fantasy into reality. For liveaboards—whether on sailboats, motorsailers, trawlers, cruisers, or houseboats—life flows gently with the tides. It is the peaceful serenity of the water, the quiet beauty of shorelines, the camaraderie of fellow boaters, and the close communion with nature that draws them to a floating home. For many it is an opportunity to get away from overcrowding and to be adventurous, self-reliant, and in charge of their own small universe.

The term *liveaboard* is probably unfamiliar to most. Even the vast majority of day sailors and weekend recreational boaters probably have not come in contact with liveaboards. And for those who are familiar with the term, it may conjure up the image of a counterculture, Bohemian type, or, even worse, an illegal alien coming to this country on an overloaded boat from a Third World Caribbean island nation.

In some parts of the country, liveaboards have become both familiar and infamous. This has happened in areas of prime waterfront real estate where liveaboards are sometimes called "hideaboards" or "sneakaboards," "low-life anchor-outs," and other derogatory names. In these places the liveaboard is seen as a visual blight on the waterscape. These misconceptions and unflattering images hide the true character of the majority of liveaboards and the fascinating lifestyle of this small, misunderstood, and often-fantasized-about subculture within our society.

Who Are the Liveaboards?
Liveaboards fit no molds and defy most generalizations. They are endlessly

Descriptions of Lifestyle	Scariest Moments
Independence	Hurricanes Hugo, Klaus, Gloria, and Andrew
Quiet	
Peaceful	Ramming another boat in the dark
Togetherness	Finding the entrance to an unknown harbor
Solitude	
Freedom	Traveling at night
Time to read	Motor dying in a crowded, barge-filled lock
Tranquility	
Meeting liveaboards	Pulling out the drainplug
Mobility	A crowded anchorage in bad weather
Being more aware	
Enjoying the weather	Typhoon in the China Sea
Being the master of your destiny	Fog and wind
	Tornado
Having choices	Electrical fire while asleep
Being unique	Putting myself in hock to be a liveaboard
Relaxing on the water	
Needing only one car	Feeling that I made a mistake
Privacy	Burglars
Self-sufficiency	Waterspouts
Contentment	Hauling the boat out
Simpler life	Getting lost on a cruise
Sense of accomplishment	Installing a through-hull fitting
Sharing experiences	The shock of moving aboard
One with nature	Lightning
Wonderful therapy	The thought of not doing it

interesting—and interested. Forever learning, liveaboards are undaunted by mountainous waves or creeping dry rot, by seasickness or subzero temperatures, or by social ostracism.

Age and ill health fail to stop them, and economic distress doesn't slow them down. Ingenious, intrepid, and indefatigable, they are gregarious loners, pioneers in an age-old quest, while helping and encouraging others along the way. Many liveaboards were practically born on boats, while others have just found their adventurous spirit in middle age, setting off for new horizons in their fifties and sixties. Living aboard or just dreaming about it, these mariners constitute a very special group with fascinating profiles.

In spite of the great diversity in this lifestyle, there is a remarkable consistency in many of their views about their boats, boating skills, occupations, mates, pets, fears, bureaucratic hassles, and the special rewards of living aboard.

Fantasy or Reality?

How Many Liveaboards Are There?

First, let's give some estimated dimensions to the liveaboard population. The U.S. Bureau of the Census and the Department of Housing and Urban Development estimated that in 1987 there were 3.2 million persons living

---

Drawbacks of Being a Liveaboard

Lack of space
Getting on and off the boat
Receiving too many weekend visitors
Not being rich
Government restrictions on liveaboards
Marina hassles
Heat and water in the winter
Keeping track of shoreside obligations
Confinement during foul weather
Having to minimize possessions
Docking within easy reach of shopping
Plentiful iced drinks
Dampness
Acceptance by shoreside neighbors
Separation from children
Getting spouse to go along
Rubbish disposal
The rest of the world
Lasting relationships
Reliable mail service
Finding a companion who likes it
No fixed address
Mosquitoes
Leaving the boat to go skiing
Not being able to see friends regularly
Difficult to entertain family and friends

What You Miss Most

Space
Unlimited fresh water
Flush toilets
Access to libraries
Telephones
Large showers
Spacious kitchens
Workshop
Nearby university
Cultural amenities
Two-car garage
Gardening
Trees and grass
Pizza
Bathtub
Woodstove
Darkroom

in boats and recreational vehicles. Unfortunately, they have no further breakdown of this large group to isolate those living on boats. Even though they take great pains to estimate how many Americans live with indoor versus outdoor plumbing, the Census Bureau's data do not reveal whether the occupants are living in trailer homes firmly rooted to highways and trailer parks or in navigable floating homes.

Looking at this from another perspective, the National Marine Manufacturers Association estimated that in 1987 there were approximately 500,000 state-registered and federally documented boats over 26 feet in length in the U.S. Assuming that very few people live on boats under 26 feet, this number seems to be an extreme upper limit for available liveaboard homesites. (However, it is important to note that some do live on smaller boats. Lin and Larry Pardey, one of the most famous and widely read about liveaboard couples, made their home on a 24-foot boat for 11 years before moving up to a palatial 30-footer! There's a story going around Key West about a fellow who was living on a 16-foot Sunfish. He had obviously been playing in the sun too long without a hat.)

Nevertheless, the over-26-foot boat seems like a reasonable minimum size for a liveaboard vessel. Most of these vessels are too large for everyday trailering so they require slips or moorings. Those that are not at slips are in boatyards, junkyards, stored on land, kept outside the U.S., anchored-out, or in constant motion, but the majority are tied up someplace along our coastline, lakes, rivers, and inland waterways. The 1987 International Marina Institute survey indicated that there are more than 8,000 marine facilities in the U.S., and of these, 5,500 reported more than 500,000 slips for sale or rent. Informal surveys of marina operators by the *Living Aboard Journal* suggest that anywhere from zero to ten percent of slips are occupied, officially or unofficially, by liveaboards. This estimate is difficult to verify because many liveaboards are reluctant to admit their status in fear of being asked to leave. Others want to keep the fact that their marina tolerates a few liveaboards a secret, lest the word get out and other boaters flock to the marina. Climate is another complicating factor in estimating the liveaboard population. Although there are quite a few year-round liveaboards in the frostbelt regions of New England and the Great Lakes, the majority favor the more comfortable southern climes.

The 1989–1990 *Living Aboard Journal* survey (biased toward the more comfortable southern climes) covered marinas throughout the country with a total of over 120,000 slips. Respondents reported approximately 8,000 liveaboard boats at these marinas, or about nine percent (when corrected for unreported marinas) of the total number of slips (see Appendix A for more on the marina survey). Applying this nine percent liveaboard slip ratio to the estimated 500,000 slips nationwide yields an estimated marina liveaboard boat population of 30,000. To this should be added about 2,500 liveaboards that are not accounted for by marinas. For example, in San Francisco Bay there are approximately 20,000 marina slips and about 100 to 200 permanent anchor-outs. If this half of one percent ratio is applied to all slips in the U.S., the result is about 2,500 liveaboard boats anchored-out nationwide.

Judging from cruising club memberships and the number of books and articles written about the cruising life, it would be safe to assume another 2,000 to 3,000 vessels owned by U.S. liveaboards are floating at any one time somewhere around the globe. Therefore, a final estimate, or best guess, of the number of U.S. liveaboard boats is around 35,000.

Remember, this number is only an educated guess, but it is growing steadily as more people learn about this attractive lifestyle.

Where Do Liveaboards Live?

As one might suspect, most liveaboards favor the warmer sunbelt climates and the more popular coastal and inland cruising areas. However, quite a few brave the frostbelt regions of New England and the Great Lakes. It's amazing what a bubbler, cabin heater, and a greenhouse covering can do to keep a boat toasty even in the harshest winter weather. The small interiors, good insulation, and the constant, above-freezing temperature of the water help considerably.

Many liveaboards try to avoid winter weather and migrate annually between north and south in search of the endless summer. Others are in constant motion for the adventure and thrill of travel.

Most liveaboards have found perfectly acceptable slip or anchorage accommodations around the country. However, some local governments and communities have made it difficult, if not impossible, for liveaboards. Several Florida communities, most of San Francisco Bay and San Diego Bay, the State of Hawaii, a growing number of marinas in Long Island Sound and Chesapeake Bay, many communities on Puget Sound, and several other areas around the country severely restrict liveaboards. The most common reasons given are that liveaboards represent a prohibited residential use of public trust resources, they pollute the water, their presence clutters up the natural vistas, they compete unfairly for scarce local jobs by accepting lower wages, they pay no local taxes, they spend little or no money for marina services, and, worst of all, the unspoken reason—they're different from other folk and therefore undesirable.

How Young or Old Do You Have to Be to Live Aboard?

More than half of the liveaboards are over 45 years old. Many have opted for a life afloat at retirement age, when the children have left the nest and the house just seemed too big for the two of them—and they've always wanted to see the sights at a leisurely pace. For many, living aboard has been a lifelong dream that they have finally been able to realize in midlife.

5

AVERAGE BOAT DIMENSIONS

	SAIL	CRUISER	TRAWLER	HOUSEBOAT
LOA (ft.)	35	36	39	40
BEAM (ft.)	11	12	13	13
DRAFT (ft.)	5	4	4	3
DISPLACEMENT (Lbs.)	20,127	23,833	34,875	18,000

LIVEABOARD ANNUAL INCOMES

	SAIL	POWER	DREAMERS
Under $24,999	13.3%	10.9%	20.0%
$25,000-$69,999	46.9%	56.3%	52.5%
Over $70,000	39.8%	32.8%	27.5%

AVERAGE BOATING EXPERIENCE

BOATING EXPERIENCE	17 years
LONGEST VOYAGE	1,042 nautical miles

CREW COMPLEMENT

SINGLE	25.7%
WITH MATE	74.3%
WITH CHILDREN	5.7%
WITH DOG	16.3%
WITH CAT	12.2%
WITH DOG & CAT	4.5%

YOUTH OF LIVEABOARD CAPTAINS

	SAIL	POWER	DREAMERS
Age 20-29	1.7%	4.1%	6.7%
Age 30-39	20.9%	13.5%	24.4%
Age 40-49	46.1%	41.9%	37.8%
Age 50-59	23.5%	29.7%	26.7%
Age 60-69	7.0%	6.8%	2.2%
Over 70	0.9%	4.1%	2.2%

DISTRIBUTION OF LIVEABOARDS

PACIFIC	13%	NORTHEAST	28%
MOUNTAIN	3%	SOUTHEAST	29%
		CENTRAL	27%

Sailboat liveaboards are slightly younger than their powerboat brethren. This is probably explained by the greater physical demands of sailing. However, one hears of plenty of agile sailors in their fifties, sixties, and even seventies.

Not surprisingly, the number of years of boating experience is very high among both sail- and motorboat liveaboards. Average boating experience is 17 years. The average longest voyage is approximately 1,000 nautical miles. In some instances, the years of experience represent the combined skills of captain and mate, in others only the captain's experience is noted. This suggests that the true level of experience of the ship's complement is probably even higher than these averages. As further evidence of this high level of boating experience, almost 20 percent of liveaboards hold a U.S.C.G. captain's license and 3 percent have U.S. Power Squadron and CPR certificates. (All this boating experience suggests that boat insurance, a frequently mentioned and expensive hassle, should be a good risk for insurance companies.)

Do Liveaboards Work?

For those who haven't yet retired, the liveaboard life has not restricted the variety of their occupations. Among the liveaboard set can be found cartographers, stockbrokers, lawyers, consultants, teachers, doctors, real-estate agents, engineers, law enforcement officers, fishermen, journalists, land developers, salesmen, fire fighters, U.S. Congressmen, priests, an incarcerated prisoner (at the moment), and many businessmen. There are a number with ties to the military and also to aviation. A large number of those who fly professionally also like to live on boats, thereby exchanging a 600 mph-plus pace for one at around 6 mph. Another very popular occupation among liveaboards is engineering. With all the onboard systems to watch over on a boat, engineering seems to be a useful occupation.

Among mates' occupations are marine insurance agents, microscopists, travel agents, attorneys, veterinarians, machinists, teachers, social workers, TV executives, and opticians. There seems to be almost as many types of jobs among mates as captains. Quite a few have characterized their occupation as "housewife" or "boatwife," but clearly that simple title hides a multitude of onboard skills.

Nevil Shute, in a foreword to Miles Smeeton's famous adventure book about a Cape Horn passage, *Once Is Enough,* described "housewife" Beryl Smeeton as follows:

> *Quite a number of yachtsmen have sailed round the world with their wives, for the most part running downwind in the Trades in the lower, more generous latitudes. How many of the wives, I wonder, could take a sextant sight from the desperately unsteady cockpit of a small yacht at sea, work out the position line with the massed figures of the tables dancing*

7

before one's eyes, and plot it on the chart?…What can one say of a woman who catapulted from the cockpit of a somersaulting ship into the sea and recovered on board with a broken collarbone and a deep scalp cut, worked manually like a man with her broken bone and did not wash the blood from her hair and forehead for three weeks, judging that injuries left severely alone heal themselves best?

One certainly wouldn't dare call Beryl a "housewife."

Liveaboard Incomes

As a group, liveaboards appear to be in higher income brackets than the national average. Notwithstanding the popular image of the Bohemian hippie liveaboard, most of those who live on the water are in the mainstream with incomes well in excess of $25,000 per year, with at least *one-third* with incomes of greater than $70,000 per year. By comparison, about half of U.S. households have annual incomes of less than $25,000 and only 17 percent have incomes greater than $50,000. (Source: 1989 *Statistical Abstract.*)

Supplemental incomes. Only a small percentage of liveaboards supplement their income with temporary cruising jobs. Supplemental jobs include boat surveying, yacht brokering, yacht delivery, nursing, artistry, canvas work, tax preparation, consulting, mechanics, and water-taxi driving.

Chartering and writing head the list of cruising jobs. This isn't surprising. Countless dreamers fantasize about a life of boat cruising paid for by travel articles. Unfortunately, supply is much greater than demand. For example, one leading boating magazine reportedly receives about 2,000 unsolicited manuscripts per year. It only prints about 60 of these each year and pays about 10 to 20 cents per word for 1,000-word articles. If you were lucky enough to have one story accepted per month, that would yield about $1,800 per year. Working as a supermarket check-out cashier or a burger slinger at McDonald's at minimum wage for a few months is financially—although not intellectually—more rewarding.

In spite of the above-average income levels, most liveaboards have opted for a downsized existence where income is concerned, replacing the frenetic lifestyle that accompanies a larger income with the serenity of the floating life. And most would admit that jobs are secondary to the freedom and adventure of life aboard.

The Ship's Complement

As you might expect, most who "go down to the sea in ships" do so in pairs, and in most, but not all of those pairs, the captain is male and the mate female. But the reverse is also found and seems to work just as well. There's a surprising number of singlehanders—about 25 percent of both sexes among

LICENSES & CERTIFICATES HELD

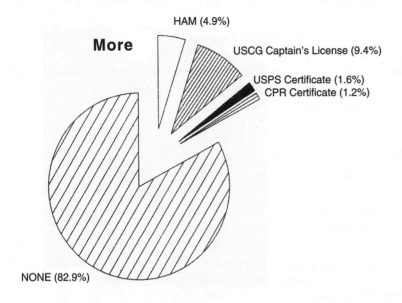

More

HAM (4.9%)

USCG Captain's License (9.4%)

USPS Certificate (1.6%)
CPR Certificate (1.2%)

NONE (82.9%)

NATIONAL LIVEABOARD MARINAS	
Total Number of Marinas Reported	493
Total Number of Slips Reported	110,062
Reported Number of Liveaboard Slips	6,657
Percent of Total Slips with Liveaboards	9%
Average Slip Rental Cost ($/Ft/Mo)	$5.37

LIVEABOARD OCCUPATIONS

Engineer	Consultant	Teacher
Accountant	Contractor	Administrator
Pilot	Machinist	Flight Attendant
Lawyer	Mechanic	Computer Tech.
Nurse	Salesperson	Realtor
Medical Tech.	Retired	

liveaboards—but again males predominate.

It is also interesting to note that many males who have recently become single have opted for the boat life, and are now searching for like-minded mates.

Approximately one out of 15 boats has children living on board. Many have grown children who visit and probably stay for short periods of time. One liveaboard jokingly reminds us of the shortest chapter in Reese Pailey's irreverently funny book, *Unlikely Passages*. The chapter is headed "Children Afloat," and it contains one sentence, "It's a damn sight better than having them aboard."

Pets Aboard

There is approximately one pet for every three boats. Cats and dogs appear to lead the list of pets heading for the high seas, but there are also monkeys, gerbils, tropical fish, a rabbit, a wildcat, and, would you believe—pet spiders! One responded to the pet survey question with an emphatic "Lord, no!" A singlehander said it best, "I lost my dog George last spring, and after 13 years of his constant company things just seem a little empty a lot of the time....I am not going to replace him right away (as if he could be replaced) mainly because of the hardships of maintaining a dog aboard. I had George first and got the boat second, so there was never any choice to make. However, if you have the boat first, I would advise giving careful consideration to the logistics of animal ownership afloat. Especially living on the hook or cruising, and especially a larger dog, and especially, especially if cruising to foreign countries."

Compared to the general population, according to a *Good Housekeeping* survey of 1986, boaters seem to have fewer pets and especially fewer dogs. Only 40 percent of the general population has no pets, while more than 60 percent of boaters have found no room for pets aboard.

Why Do They Seek the Liveaboard Life?

Why do they do it? For many, love of water and water-related activities is primary. One lengthy entry sums it up with, "Boats, sun, water, beaches, islands, solitude, nature, boat people, navigation, warm and hot sun, cruising, fishing, crabbing, oystering, floundering, jigging, beachcombing, birdwatching, boat parades, shelling, and sightseeing."

When asked to give three reasons for choosing the liveaboard life, several replied: "Love it. Love it. Love it." At the other end of the spectrum one liveaboard wrote, "She got the house, and I got the boat."

Travel, freedom, challenge, and adventure are recurring themes, as are escaping from smog, high real-estate taxes, telephones and television, traffic, boredom, and "getting away from the crazy mixed-up calamity they call society."

Some people have chosen a liveaboard life for change, independence, peace and serenity. Simplicity. "Like a vacation the year-round." "Closer to nature." "For the kids." "Reduced housekeeping chores." "Cheapest way to see a lot of places in reasonable comfort."

For some, love was the motive. "Husband is half-man, half-boat." "I like it, she likes it, I like her." One liveaboard reported, "Really great primitive sex when you're out there hundreds of miles away from everything...wildly exciting."

Several listed freedom from cutting grass and other Harry Homeowner activities. Others found the boat a great way to escape cold winters and broiling summers and take their house with them.

When asked what they enjoy most about living aboard.... "When Murphy stays ashore." "When anchored in a secluded scenic area with the porpoises and seagulls for company." "When we decide to move on or stay put. It's our choice." "Cool spring and fall with their bright, crisp, clear mornings and evenings and with the rest of the fair-weather boaters back ashore not knowing what they're missing." "Just after the anchor is dropped. Sounds of silence." "When the wind is at our back, the sails are wing 'n wing, and we're headed for an unexplored (by us) island for a new adventure."

What Are the Drawbacks to Living Aboard?
One liveaboard says, "The boat is your jailer as well as your liberator." Lack of storage is the most frequently mentioned drawback, with weather and laundry facilities also vying for top honors. Hauling supplies, water, and fuel down to the dock in winter and hauling clothes to the laundromat in the rain are frequently mentioned. No workshop aboard, mildew, limited access to family and friends (although this may be a plus), no space for a piano, the number of tasks that must be done to make things work, mail catching up with you, finding adequate medical attention, getting ashore for exercise, being at the mercy of marina operators, drunks along the piers, large wakes by idiots, and finally, people who cannot or will not accept this as a responsible way of life.

What Are the Scariest Moments?
Boating is generally considered a riskier activity than lawn bowling or mowing one's lawn. When asked about the scariest moment, liveaboards responded with a lengthy list of such moments. Heading the list was the weather, and particularly hurricanes. Next came groundings, especially during bad weather. Engine failure at inopportune times was also high on the list.

Several liveaboards reported that selling their homes and moving aboard was the scariest moment. Getting divorced when the wife refused to go cruising was cited as scary. Lightning, encounters with freighters and barges at night, leaving the boat unattended, the cat falling overboard, coastal inlets and tides, drunken boaters, and being boarded by Hell's Angels and the

11

Mexican Coast Guard were also among the scariest moments.

One cruiser with 47 years of boating experience boldly replied, "NONE!" He must be awfully lucky, brave, or oblivious to the dangers around him.

What Is the Greatest Source of Conflicts?

This question was frequently left unanswered, suggesting either no onboard conflicts or a great deal of denial. For those that did respond, the conflicts focused on the weather, lack of space, expenses, no attic, power versus sail, seagull droppings, making the perfect onboard martini, where to go next, choosing between work and cruising, rude boaters, spiders in summer....

The most prevalent source of conflict had something to do with the mate, and particularly the mate's lack of enthusiasm for "messing around in boats." Comments included: "Can't get the wife to share in skipper's duties." "Mate refuses to live aboard." "Shorebound girlfriend." "Finding someone to go cruising with." "Wife just not interested."

What Makes a Good Liveaboard?

An important characteristic for living aboard is a good sense of humor, closely followed by patience and adaptability. Other characteristics reported by liveaboards are consideration, curiosity, optimism, perseverance, an acute sense of safety, compatibility, and the ability to take what comes along without going to pieces. The perfect liveaboard appears to be one who likes small places, is self-sufficient, an upbeat problem solver, able to be unserious most of the time, and generally relaxed.

It's obvious from the responses that liveaboards have to have a combination of good technical skills as well as interpersonal skills. They're often managing a small and complex universe far from the serviceman, hardware store, or the psychiatrist. Skills and traits were often mixed together in lengthy responses that included woodworking, adventurousness, painting and varnishing, alertness, knowledge of the weather, and sanity.

What Does It Cost?

There is quite a range in the reported monthly costs for food, fuel, maintenance, slip rental, insurance, medical expenses, and incidentals. One of the big variables is the cost of the boat itself. Most respondents included the "mortgage" costs in their monthly totals, but, given the age of many liveaboard boats and the limited length of boat mortgages, the final costs may be understated for anyone contemplating starting out with a new boat mortgage. Sailboat owners averaged $3 per month per foot for maintenance and $41 per year per foot for supplies. For motor boats the averages were $2 and $24 respectively. Therefore, for the average 37-foot sailboat the monthly maintenance cost is about $237. Add to this the cost of a mortgage for an average $65,000 boat, about $800 per month, and the total approaches $1,000

WHAT DO LIVEABOARDS LIVE ON?

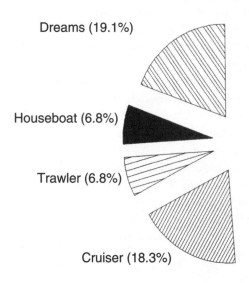

Dreams (19.1%)

Sail (48.9%)

Houseboat (6.8%)

Trawler (6.8%)

Cruiser (18.3%)

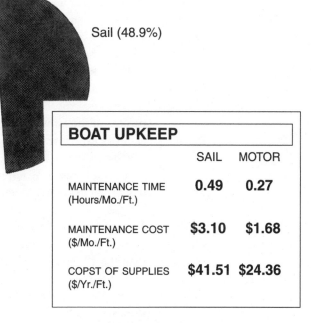

BOAT UPKEEP

	SAIL	MOTOR
MAINTENANCE TIME (Hours/Mo./Ft.)	0.49	0.27
MAINTENANCE COST ($/Mo./Ft.)	$3.10	$1.68
COPST OF SUPPLIES ($/Yr./Ft.)	$41.51	$24.36

ENGINE CHOICES

	SAIL AUXILIARY	MOTOR
GASOLINE	25.5%	63.2%
DIESEL	74.5%	36.8%

HULL MATERIAL

FIBERGLASS	74.3%
WOOD	7.3%
STEEL	7.3%
ALUMINUM	2.0%
FERROCEMENT	0.8%

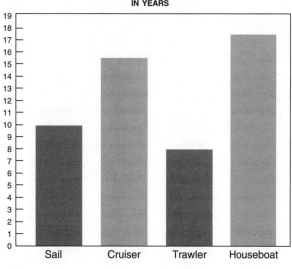

AVERAGE AGE OF BOATS
IN YEARS

per month.

Another variable in total boat costs is the amount of maintenance work contracted with the marina or service people. Liveaboards' inclination toward self-reliance makes it safe to assume that they alone perform much of the maintenance. This would tend to depress the estimated monthly cost of maintaining their boats. The average maintenance time was reported to be about one-half hour per foot per month.

There is no appreciable difference in slip rental fees between power- and sailboats. The average cost per foot per month around the country seems to be a little more than $5.

How do these costs compare with those for land-based homes? Considering average single-family house prices in the $120,000-plus range and the conventional wisdom that the maintenance and home costs run around one percent of the house value per month, it would appear that boat homes are about as expensive. If you compare real-estate investment appreciation with boat depreciation, you come to the conclusion that boating ain't cheap!

Several liveaboards responded to the cost question with: "Too much." "I don't want to know." "Afraid to calculate it."

What's Missed Most and What's Most Rewarding?

Responses to what's most rewarding were by far lengthier and more varied than those to what's missed most. In fact, almost 40 percent said that they missed nothing and others (jokingly?) replied, "Calling for a pizza delivery." "Being able to rearrange the furniture." Other items on the missed list were storage space, fireplace, garage, workshop, tub, washer and dryer, and piano.

The most rewarding aspects of living aboard were mobility, freedom, a feeling of self-reliance, closeness, and a unique lifestyle. Many of the reasons read like a thesaurus of feel-good terms: quiet, peace, tranquility, solitude, seclusion, simplicity, serenity, relaxation....

Simply living on the water, "messing about in boats," and communing with nature also were frequently cited as the most rewarding aspects of life aboard.

These statistics and anecdotes tell only a small part of the story. To fully understand liveaboards and their lifestyles one must hear them tell it in their own colorful and unassuming words.

2
Liveaboard Lifestyles

LIVING ABOARD is both an activity and a state of mind, and there are aspects of society that both encourage and restrict this envied lifestyle.

Several trends have taken place in the 1970s and 1980s that are having a dramatic and positive influence on the number of liveaboards and the quality of their lifestyles. Many more people have the financial opportunity to vacation more often and longer. Some are on permanent vacations or a low-work, reduced economic lifestyle that resembles a permanent holiday often accompanied by travel. For those who choose to live their vacations on the water, this means they have the time and opportunity to take extended waterway voyages or simply to stay put and enjoy the waterfront ambiance along coastlines and inland waterways.

Alternative lifestyles have become more accepted in society, especially as people forgo workaholic schedules in favor of quality time with themselves, their friends, and their family. And one particularly rewarding lifestyle is found in sharing a small "island" home, learning to give each other "mental space," communing with nature, and experiencing the confidence and self-reliance of managing a boat home.

Also, people are retiring at a younger and healthier age. This gives them the physical strength and motivation for a vigorous life long after their official retirement. Many retirees have chosen to abandon the responsibility of their large homes, now that the children are gone, and to follow their dreams of leisure travel or simply the serenity of the waterfront. A boat home offers the opportunity to see and live right in the midst of some of the most beautiful and sought-after scenery in the world.

Modern technology in the recreational vehicle industry and particularly in boating has made boat living very comfortable, convenient, and safe. One no longer has to be a daring adventurer or go without modern conveniences to consider living afloat. All the accoutrements of a land-based home can be reproduced on a boat—without having to mow the lawn. Boats are getting larger: As the lengths increase, the volumes increase by the cube. The modern liveaboard has the choice, at a price, of roughing it or living in style. Technology also has made possible the ability for a singlehander or a short-handed couple to manage a boat easily and safely, thus eliminating the need to arrange for a large crew every time they want to travel or move their home.

Technology, materials, and advances in boat designs also have made interiors less rustic and often much more attractive than a comparably priced apartment. Boat designers have given in to demands for luxury interiors ranging from double berths to built-in stereo systems to bright, decorative "wall" coverings. In the ads, some of the boats look more like luxury condominiums than seagoing vessels. Compare, for example, the rich feel and texture of finely crafted teak joinery and bronze portlights with dry-wall, cubicle construction.

Another technological development that has benefited liveaboards is the advent of computers and communications technology. Not only can liveaboards stay "connected" to land via cellular, radio, or satellite telephone hook-ups, they can also conduct their business from the boat. Stock ticker-tape machines, FAX machines, beepers, paperless files, modems, 12-volt laptop computers and printers easily can turn the boat into an office.

The crowding, crime, increasing dirtiness, and frantic pace of urban living have made people turn their thoughts to the peaceful beauty of the waterfront. This has resulted in conflicting trends. On the one hand, shoreline development has brought about new marinas and other marine facilities that contribute to the convenience of living aboard. On the other hand, highest and best use development pressures, the scarcity of shoreline property, and environmental restrictions over waterfront encroachment have driven up prices sharply and turned many rental slips into "dockominiums." This has made it more difficult for middle-income boaters, retirees on fixed incomes, and those who purposefully choose to live a simpler, economically reduced lifestyle to partake of the liveaboard dream.

Another economic pressure associated with waterfront development is the tendency for landowners, who have paid dearly for their shorefront homes, to want to be the last ones in an area in order to protect the privacy and surrounding natural beauty for the lucky few that are already "in." This trend has emerged in the form of community regulations and marina policies aimed at restricting liveaboard privileges for slips and anchorages.

One of the most intangible, but strongly felt, trends is the increasing isolation and economic class structuring taking place in neighborhoods on land. This trend is different on boats along the waterfront, where camaraderie and dockside neighborliness at a marina or anchorage are the norm. The common experiences, shared responsibilities, and shared environment bring people of all economic and social classes together. One liveaboard on the Detroit River said, "I'll bet the community relationships are five times better than in any neighborhood ashore....I walked up to a house recently trying to find somebody and asked if the people knew where he lived. They'd never heard of him; it turned out he lived in the house next door. That doesn't happen among liveaboards along the same pier."

THINGS MY MOTHER NEVER TOLD ME
ABOUT LIVING ABOARD

Sally Elizabeth Andrew, a liveaboard since 1982, cannot imagine living ashore again. After several years in the San Francisco Bay area, she and her friend have departed for parts unknown in the South Pacific.

In 1982 she graduated with high honors from the University of California, Berkeley. Her honors thesis was "Living Aboard" and showed how and why liveaboards are culturally different from mainstream Americans even though most are essentially middle class. Her thesis was written from an anthropological perspective and later excerpted for a more informal dockside article.

Houseboats and liveaboards have been a part of the San Francisco Bay environment since the 1880s, when a colony of floating summer homes, "arks," existed in Belvedere. After the great San Francisco earthquake in 1906, many ark owners were forced to live aboard all year round. With the worsening economic conditions of the depression and two world wars, the number of houseboats and liveaboards along the waterfronts of San Francisco and Richardson bays increased. By the 1960s, houseboats were concentrated in a few areas. Today liveaboards continue to be scattered throughout public and private marinas in the Bay Area, including Alameda, Sausalito, Redwood City, and Berkeley. In the Bay Area, many of the original liveaboard communities that sprouted up along the waterfront after the depression were composed of artists, loners, and bums squatting on public and private shorelines. Today, communities of artists still exist, but there are few squatters. Even so, liveaboards all too often face negative stereotypes despite the fact that most liveaboards hold (or have held) traditional jobs and have a wide range of incomes. They hold essentially middle-class values, send their children to public schools, have a high level of education, and they pay "liveaboard fees" for the privilege of occupying their vessels. They are not unskilled or poorly educated dropouts from society.

Liveaboards come from all walks of life. I know two liveaboard dentists, three carpenters, a sales manager, a project manager, a secretary, a painter, two harbormasters, an assistant harbormaster, a marketing manager, a physicist, a psychologist, a writer, a yacht club manager, a sailmaker, a credit union vice-president, a yacht salesman, and a canvas worker. The income per family varies from about $20,000 to more than $100,000 annually. Boat-related expenses range from as little as $300 per month for a couple without a boat loan to more than $2,000 per month. Boat values range from $15,000 to more than $150,000. Boat size is from 25 feet to more than 46 feet. Family size ranges from one to six.

Everyone has a different reason for moving aboard. Some people move aboard to get used to living in small spaces before going cruising; others want only to do something different. In some instances, economics play a large part. A boat consumes both time and money, and it is very difficult to maintain both a land- and a water-based dwelling. In an effort to streamline, one or the other must go. And although living aboard is not necessarily cheaper, it is often the preferred option.

I moved aboard in 1982 in response to an advertisement:

"Crew wanted for trip to Tahiti: healthy, intelligent, non-smoking, athletic woman with a great personality."

Although I jumped ship and never made it to French Polynesia, I spent an incredible six months cruising in the Sea of Cortez. Today, I am still living on a 33-foot sailboat, and I doubt that I will ever move ashore.

Some people move aboard in an effort to escape the "rat race"—traffic, telephones, television, the pressure of "The Job," and "keeping up with the Joneses." In so doing, they are forced to simplify their lives because there is no room for the clutter of a mainstream-American lifestyle based on unlimited consumption and uncontrolled consumerism. This abandonment of the American ideal of "upward mobility" and the accumulation of goods leads some people to believe that liveaboards must be "deprived" because they can't engage in unlimited consumption, or that they must be getting away with something since they are reneging their obligation to consume. But this is not the case.

As liveaboards, we are not able to accumulate lots of "things" because of space restrictions. But we enjoy this self-imposed condition. Whether we realize it or not, our conscious choice for simplicity and limited consumption allows a greater potential for setting and attaining life goals and for being satisfied. Freedom from the installment payments associated with "owning" lots of "things," goals to own the boat or to go cruising, and the importance of feeling free play a large role in the enjoyment of the lifestyle of living aboard. We try to take greater responsibility for our lives, and we try to make it a little more meaningful, a little less artificial.

Increased efficiency in the use of space after moving aboard is accompanied by a decreased consumption of both energy and material goods and an increased degree of self-sufficiency. Even so, a quality of lifestyle is achieved that is consciously appreciated. Statements such as "I like not buying lots of things!" "If I can't afford it, I don't need it," "We buy less stuff and feel less controlled by possessions," and "We don't have room for things that don't serve a definite purpose!" lead me to wonder if "downward mobility" in consumption and energy use can actually be as satisfying as (or more satisfying than) upward mobility. This enjoyment of a simple lifestyle that is voluntarily chosen shows that low consumption can be tied into high satisfaction. Isn't this a contradiction of the "American dream"?

Most moves aboard are voluntary, but occasionally external circumstances (such as financial strain or divorce) force a change in lifestyle. In such a situation, the change can be more difficult and more often than not, unsuccessful. Which leads me to wonder whether the San Francisco Bay Conservation and Development Commission (BCDC) really has to regulate the number of liveaboards or whether, in fact, the lifestyle itself is self-regulating due to its eccentricity. Opinion is divided. Some liveaboards feel that no regulation is necessary: "If liveaboard marinas provide proper and adequate facilities, regulation is unnecessary as well as a further infringement on personal liberties." Others feel that some regulation might be necessary: "I suppose I like the idea of a certain number (of liveaboards) per marina, if only to totally selfishly keep the marina quiet and not feeling like a condo complex!" "Individual marinas should provide basic regulation based on general state-specified guidelines (i.e., state-specified minimal environmental standards for water and air quality), and each marina set its own standards for cleanliness, number of liveaboards, etc."

Living aboard is a lifestyle fraught with contradictions. I own and buy fewer material possessions than I did when I lived on land, but the boat itself is a very expensive, very material possession that continually requires costly marine-grade gear and equipment. In addition, although some parts of my life become simpler, others (such as doing laundry, voting, getting mail and credit) become more complex. The sense of freedom that I get from living on the water is, in reality, accompanied by various political restrictions on my chosen lifestyle.

For example, voter registration in California does not accept a marina address as a bona fide residence. Consequently, liveaboards are made to feel like they are non-contributors to society and cannot vote because of the difficulty in establishing residency status—even if berthed in the same marina for years. They are classified as transients, limited by circumstance, not by choice. Unless you can beat the system or don't tell them where you really live, voting is not possible.

Banks and credit institutions also fail to accept this alternative lifestyle. "No street address, no phone number, no credit. Sorry, lady." Once I was refused a credit card simply because I chose not to have a phone on the boat. Why do they need to know where I sleep at night? So what if I can't or don't choose to have a home phone number? I have a daytime number at work.

People move aboard and remain there for more than economic reasons. The illusion of living more simply and of feeling closer to nature and its forces contributes to the enjoyment of living aboard, as does a sense of harmony with the varied wildlife—the white cranes, the night herons, the ducks, the coots, the sea gulls, the fish. I like to fool myself that I'm in contact with nature, especially when the ducks come by!

Liveaboards are drawn together as a group by friendships and shared common experiences, including pleasures and hardships. We share tales of small triumphs and disasters as well as advice from experience gained the hard way. We are bound by this sharing and by the insecurity that results from the current legal status of liveaboards. Eventually living aboard will be accepted as a responsible lifestyle. Until then, living aboard may remain a privilege for the few who persevere or "sneak aboard," and not an inalienable right.

Sally Elizabeth Andrew

IN SEARCH OF THE AVERAGE LIVEABOARD
Linda Grover is a former editor of the Living Aboard Journal.
*In one of her first editorials she discovers the essence
of an average liveaboard in her partner.*

A few years ago in New York City, between writing books and a temporary lunatic digression into the wacky world of TV serials, I managed to put food on the table for a time not only through the quite commonplace combo of taxi driving and short- and long-order cooking, but also by the perhaps more canny and certainly more direct route of reviewing restaurants, ordering everything in sight and trucking the leftovers home in a doggy bag for later distribution.

When, eventually (and inevitably) my kids mutinied against an excess of moussaka for breakfast and limp chow mein at lunch, I managed to mooch my way up the journalistic ladder to the next, more impressive level of "Interviewer." Embarking on a score or more of thoroughly enjoyable meetings with leading lights of grand opera and musical stage, City Hall and Seventh Avenue, getting to know Big Apple personalities from Theodore Sorensen to Moondog, I discovered that talking to unique, interesting people and writing down what they have to say is preferable most any day to working for a living.

Now, through a series of happy accidents, having found myself in the position of being able to run out and interview cruising folk as often as I like, I couldn't wait yesterday to get started. However, there aren't a great many liveaboards here at this sparkling new marina in South Carolina where we arrived last week with *Almitra*. I strode forth, notebook in hand, and returned about five minutes later just a bit daunted; my first intended quarry would not be available till evening.

I'd nearly resigned myself to the task of scrubbing away *Almitra*'s waterway smile, that ubiquitous Intracoastal Waterway (ICW) yellow banner of travel emblazoned on her bow, when, casting about for one last excuse to avoid the job, I flashed upon a scene from my past—actually multiple scenes from my past. I saw fuzzy images of various of my children, in small, medium, and large sizes, entering the apartment on Central Park West with clumpingly fierce intent, slamming the door behind them, and then cornering me in the kitchen with a terse "Mother, I have to interview you for my homework." "But why me?" "Because you're the only average citizen I can think of."

Now, in search of an average liveaboard . . . my eye fell upon my partner, Tom. "Captain Daugherty," I began (engine rooms being even easier places to corner victims in than kitchens), "I'd like to talk to you about boats...." Is Tom a typical liveaboard? Is there such a thing? Perhaps not, but it would seem there are some rather characteristic early manifestations of the malady, to wit:

"All my life I've loved the water and everything about it. Whenever we went on car trips when I was little and I'd be lying down in the back, my folks always knew all they had to say was 'There's water up here' to get me to sit up. Once I had a whole shoeboxful of fiddler crabs that somehow got loose in the back seat—my mother was standing on the dashboard shouting that she wasn't even going to think about starting the car again until every last one of them was found. I searched and searched but still ended up one short...." (That's Tom, the kind of little boy who would keep an exact count of fiddler crabs.)

"When I moved to Florida with my parents in 1959, the house we got was on a lake. Most of the kids that lived there seemed to have little rowboats and I didn't, so Dad finally came up with a little flat-bottomed pram. I dearly loved it—I'd go out and pull it up on the bank behind the house and just sit in it. Later on I'd take pillows and sleeping bags, go anchor out and spend the

21

night all by myself on the lake. A liveaboard at the age of nine."

"Did your boat have a name?"

"The *Pink Lizard*. That's what we christened her, myself and Mike and Rick, a couple of guys in the neighborhood. She pretty quickly became communal property. We kept her on the bank, and if you came out in the morning and the *Pink Lizard* was gone, you just looked out on the lake till you found where the guys were and you hollered for them, or you walked around to where they were. That was the good old days when the lake was full of fish. You could catch a limit of bass any time you went out. We were just the third or fourth house on the lake…everything else was white sand beach and bamboo groves and beautiful. The water was clear, and the neighbors were friendly.…Of course the good times don't last forever.

"After a couple of years the boat started leaking pretty badly, and the floorboards were falling out of it. We finally towed her back from the other shore, put a couple of concrete blocks inside, shoved her out onto the lake and let her go down. I could still find her though—I'd lined up two palm trees on my parents' property and a guy's dock at the other end of the lake to mark the spot, so for about 2 years afterward we used to go down to see if she was still there. In fact about 18 or 20 years later, when I was over at my parents' swimming, about, I don't know, a year and a half ago, I lined up the one palm tree that was left, the other one had been frozen and gone, and the guy's dock pilings, they were still there. I went out in the water—it's dark and murky now, loaded with algae, dove down and felt around. And underneath all the silt, I could still feel the bottom layer of fiberglass. It was very thin now but the *Pink Lizard* is still down there.

"There were other boats afterward of course. I've almost always had a small boat of one kind or another, but something about the *Pink Lizard*…it was only a five-acre world to explore on that lake, but it was quite a world. That's the thing about a boat they say, the freedom of being able to get out there on the water and just take off and go. Like now, when I get up in the morning on this boat and look around and feel the boat move under me, and I think, gosh, here I am, down inside of this big boat and it's floating. It's a different feeling, to know your home is mobile—that all you've got to do is untie it and give it a little shove and it's going to go somewhere. You don't actually even have to have all these engines and things. Just a pole and a sail, and it would go somewhere. Being a liveaboard, you can go and see what the world has to offer and still be able to take the things that mean a lot to you with you. Ever since I was nine years old there isn't a thing in life I've wanted like I've wanted to live on a boat. Now I do. We own her."

"So what did it feel like? The minute we got *Almitra* how did it feel? Or let me put it another way. When was the moment that you felt you'd actually fulfilled your dream, the moment she was finally ours?"

"When we ran her aground the first time."

"That's when she was yours?"

"That's when you realize that this is my boat, and now I've got to do something about it. We can't ask someone else to come over and help us; tell 'em we're tired of fooling with this now. It's no longer a toy; it's reality and it's yours and it's big and heavy and expensive and can frighten you sometimes with the things that it does, but you've got to figure out how to contend with it."

"Why don't you tell us about it?"

"Well, this was the day after we'd taken title to the boat and started north, and we had Peter and Mary, friends of ours from Ft. Lauderdale who came with us the first six hours or so to help us learn the boat. It was about 7:30 at night, right after dark (poor planning, mistake No. 1) that we came into Old Port Cove to anchor. I'd never gone into a crowded anchorage and dropped anchor with this boat before, or anything approaching its size...."

"Had you ever anchored any boat before?"

"No, as a matter of fact I don't think I had. Except for the *Pink Lizard*. But we had Peter along to help. It was tricky because the wind was blowing about 20 to 25 knots from the east and the anchorage was on the western shore right up against a tall concrete seawall with foot, foot-and-a-half choppy peaked waves—the place looked like the top of a banana cream pie, just a constant sea of moving meringue peaks. Plus there's a lot of windage on a boat like ours, so we had to set out two anchors and make sure they were good and tight.

"Then it was time for Peter and Mary to go ashore and get back to Lauderdale. We lowered the dinghy into that chop and started off to what we thought was a restaurant and a dock, but it turned out to be somebody's house, so we turned and had started to fight the current back when the motor died. (We'd forgotten to check the gas.) We shifted people around so one of us could row and then, on about the third stroke, one of the oars broke.

"So here we are, four people in this little round-bottomed dinghy, bouncing around, getting close to the seawall in the pitch black, taking on water alarmingly fast, and a flashlight on board that doesn't work too well. We decided we had to put onto the seawall. I shined a light over, and we spotted a culvert about halfway up, just an open concrete hole, but it could provide a foothold. Linda and Mary climbed up first (into a graveyard, it turned out); we took all the gear out, and Peter and I tried to haul the boat up over the wall. But with its weight and the wind we couldn't manage it, so I stood in the boat and held it off the wall while Peter pulled it along by the bowline. When we finally got around the corner and into a canal I handed my way down to the end. Peter and Mary and Linda had to climb a 12-foot-high chain-link fence with barbed wire to get into the area where I was with the boat. After they joined me, we carried all our gear out to the guard shack and arranged for Peter and Mary to get a taxi back to Lauderdale. (The whole adventure still had an air of unreality about it.) Then we had the task of finding fuel and oil for the dinghy motor at ten o'clock at night with a dollar twenty-nine in our pockets (error number which? of the proud new boatowners). We walked into a gas station down the road just at closing. He had a half bottle of oil left, and so we found an empty antifreeze bottle, put the fuel in, dumped the oil into it and for a dollar we were out of there, on our way back to the dinghy with 29 cents.

"Next morning we woke to a bright, sunny, windy day, found ourselves next to an old-world cruiser with rust and tattered sails and a South Seas name. We had breakfast, raised the anchors (a joint effort), and started off. We figured to go right out between the markers the way we came in. And I did—I split the markers exactly, and we felt so good, the sea was so bright and the sun so pretty; we'd made it through the night without any major disasters, and then all of a sudden, without any warning, our forward motion stopped. The boat just silently, sickeningly came to an utter and complete halt. And it wasn't till then, until that very moment, that I realized this wasn't just a trip up the Intracoastal in somebody's boat. This was us, this was ours—I had to start using my head and do the right thing for once.

"I tried rocking her forward and back, forward and back, but we were sitting well aground. Forty-eight thousand pounds of us was sitting aground. I thought maybe I was making a little progress loosening her up, when, right in the middle of the maneuvering, all hell broke loose with that deafening sound of the water alarm. I shut down the engine, turned off the bells, and went below, expecting to find the boat sinking or the Lehman totally melted down to a puddle. Things didn't look too bad, however, so I went back up and set out an anchor again—so in case we did drift off we wouldn't be blown into the marina. Then we sat down, got out all the books and manuals and instructions George and Maureen had left us, and started reading.

"The problem turned out to be a seawater filter—we'd churned up a bunch of silt and mud trying to get off that bank. It took about an hour total before the engine was running again and we felt secure enough to try to get her afloat. A great moment, feeling her rock free once more. Then rather than back her around and fill up the filters with mud again, we put the dinghy over, took the sounding lead, and ran back and forth across the area till we found a passage on the extreme right-hand side of the channel. We climbed back aboard *Almitra*, let her drift across to the right-hand side of the markers, took her over the bar, and steamed gloriously back into the Intracoastal Waterway to head north once more. I didn't know it then—not in so many words—but that was the moment she was ours, and this was my dream come true."

Linda Grover

THE WHOLE HARBOR BECOMES MY LIVING ROOM

*Hannah Merker is a writer who lives and works on board her
houseboat,* Bette Anne, *in Long Island Sound. She recently
married a fellow liveaboard on the sailboat,* Haimish. *The
houseboat now serves as office and getaway.*

Gavia stellata sits in the swells, riding the rise and fall of the incoming tide,
her dagger-like bill turned upward, her injured webbed foot falling at an awk-
ward angle atop her stubby tail feathers. Or is it a him? Can't tell with loons.

Mercury and Saturn are rising with the sun. Flutters of gray clouds are
leaning into lavender. It is almost dawn, yet still dark, with silver-steel light
stretching over black waters. Winter light, I call it, a cast of clear no-color
catching the last of night, etching the dying eelgrass, shaping the sharpness of
life out here from December to February.

Living on the water connects you to all kinds of living creatures. My
injured loon, in its winter plumage, is the color of winter light, gray of crown
and hind neck, sheer white undersides from throat to a belly lying low in the
morning waters. I am sitting outside on my porch (cockpit, to be exact),
wrapped in my electric blanket, the long cord connected to the invisible current that connects me to the world people think I have left. I am watching the
coming of morning. Skim ice catches the growing light. Fine frost clings to
the long dock that separates my home, the good ship *Bette Anne*, from that
other world, land.

My loon is close to my houseboat. I could net her now, as I have been trying to do for days—but it is too cold to emerge from my blanket. Later today,
I shall try to entice her close, and take her to a nearby veterinarian who, without charge, tries to aid injured wildlife.

These mornings of winter are mine. No one else seems to claim them. My
loon is alone on her wave. These last days she has separated herself, in her tra-
vail, in the pain and terror of her injury, from the extraordinary abundance of
wildlife on this inlet in Huntington Harbor, this place on the edge of things.
Since the fishhook pierced her foot she has been swimming alone, circling
and diving under the dock, rubbing against the homes.

Or, perhaps, the birds of these winter waters have separated themselves
from her. In this winter world of geese and gulls, mallards and mergansers,
swans, scaups, loons, brant, buffooning buffleheads, and occasional humans,
you've got to stand on your own two feet, webbed or toed.

On the water, in winter, life emerges into essentials that elicit survival. I
have learned a lot from birds.

Why? I am asked often.

And, How long?

And then, When?

Why did I decide to do this—live in a small space under conditions often harsh, frequently dangerous, always demanding vigilance? My sea stories tell all that. If there is a common bond, a source of beginnings for all my writings, it is the sea. To me the 10- by 20-foot space of my cabin is not small at all. Through wide windows on every side, the whole harbor becomes my living room. On the water the dimensions of living space are not measured by inches or feet. Instead, the elements define expanse. The size of my cabin surrenders to the stretch of heat and cold, clear skies or clouds, rain, fog, snow, wind.

Yes, most of all, wind—that live creature that is always my companion, even when still. The wind, on a willful pathway, can reduce my living space to almost nothing—twice it nearly has.

How long?

Six winters—I count time lived on the water by winters.

And when?

When will I give it up, this temporary aberration, and move back to land? That story may never be written.

Winter, in my mind, begins in late August, a glimmer of needs to come, more real in summer, when I think of them, than the hot, humid reality of that moment. There are always tremendous needs: warmth, security from wind and weather, repairing leaks, perhaps another step toward some specially desired comfort. That first winter, six winters ago, my greatest desire was to stay afloat.

I had always wanted to live on the water; I had thought about it for years. One day I heard about a houseboat that was for sale, and I bought it. I moved aboard in late October, with wild winds whipping even the protected waters of Centerport Harbor, where I would spend one year.

The roof leaked, the water system worked sporadically, the insulation was insufficient, and winter was early. I bought long underwear and an electric blanket. Ice hugged our craft for months, an arctic wonderland as far as I could see. Inside I watched winter, warmed by a kerosene heater, my dog and seven cats nestled at my feet.

Year two, I became greedy. I wanted to stay afloat, be super-warm and learn to take care of some of my own repairs; it seemed cheaper that way. I bought a hand saw, stared at it for two months, and decided we could live together. I had never used one.

Year three, I still had all my fingers and toes. My saw and I understood each other. I built real bookcases (instead of the bricks-and-boards things) to hold my more than 1,000 books. I learned to install water pumps, patch the hull, make temporary repairs on my forever-leaking roof. Still, I was not prepared for year four.

It was October, very cold. I was dressed in the sartorial splendor of my morning dog-walking outfit, which meant I had thrown a couple of sweaters over a flannel nightie and raced out at dawn to do some bird watching with Sheena, my hearing guide dog. In the foggy mist I tripped over a tree stump, breaking some ribs and ripping ligaments in one leg. I spent several weeks in a cast, unable to leave the boat.

My first week out, on crutches, while Sheena and I were being photographed in four-degree weather for an article I had written about her, I fell and broke my arm.

About a week later, the *Bette Anne* sank in a midnight storm. She was refloated by the next morning, with the help of many other liveaboards on my dock. It was the nightmare we all know can happen. During that night I stood near the others, sometimes on a still-sunken dock, sometimes in four feet of water, mind and body numb with cold. It was near zero degrees. Inside we retrieved some floating wine bottles and toasted the diminishing water.

The instinct to reestablish one's home after a disaster must be the very core of the spark that is life. With my left arm, the next morning, I strung lines across my very wet cabin, and began drying out the thousands of pieces of paper in my writing folders.

Year five—well, anything would be better. Freak wave action had caused my boat to sink, bringing water into the cockpit faster than it was going out the scuppers. I fixed it, began replacing all the damaged insides of my home, and, near the end of year five, was able to afford a new roof. Although the thought of dryness had seemed like a far and distant heaven, I thought seriously about the consequences of fixing my roof. We all know writers must suffer. Would I write as well, not having to dodge the downpours? I decided to risk it, because, after all, my home, the good ship *Bette Anne*, deserved it. She had just survived the hurricane.

Stars and stillness stirred the sweetness of a gift—that soft September night and my place in it, still at sea on my floating home, after the hurricane. I had so little faith in my leaky craft. From the moment I had heard that the wind was rushing toward us, something sank inside of me, something with the stab of sorrow. This way of life would end. I was not ready for it to end. It was not time for it to end.

Hours after the storm, the air was still. A full moon lit the stillness like a great lantern, glowing deep in silent waters. All electric current had ceased, casting land and sea into a primeval peace, into an elemental light of ancient nights. I remembered the hours just gone, walking bent against the wind along the dock, gripped by sadness as I carried my cats and my dog to my jeep, to safety. I remembered also thinking how the wind was wild and wonderful, grandly conducting an intoxicating splendor.

And now it is year six. Soon the ice will be thick, the dock to land icy, the air thin. At night the stars pour down, a huge and splendid arc. Winter skies away from city lights expand my world. My ship is part of heaven and Earth, in universal space. The swans will sleep on the shifting floes, heads tucked into their wings, white mounds almost indistinguishable from the ice itself.

The resident dogs and cats will jump on the frozen waters, and all the wading creatures will find the few spots near shore where the wind's pressure on the waters has left an ice-free place, a locus for foraging food.

Will my lone loon survive, apart from the crowds of her fellow folk, if I cannot catch her and somehow find a way to remove that hook? It does not occur to her that she won't make it.

Like my loon, when things went wrong, I never thought to leave, so essential is the water to my life. It was the very cold of winter that held me. In the winter there is a grandeur to the water, far beyond the seas of summer life. A feeling of newness comes with the crisp mornings. The challenge of survival surrounds me in the ice-filled waters. The landscape, the seascape, are stark with hidden life.

And now Gavia, my loon, is here. My net is ready. Perhaps she will let me give her some nurturing, some assistance. After all, we are neighbors.

Hannah Merker

JUST PLAIN FOLK

By definition there is nothing ordinary about liveaboards, since less than one in ten thousand Americans is a liveaboard. On the other hand, away from their boat homes and dockside neighborhoods they are just plain folk like the other 9,999 of us. I have been fortunate to meet many liveaboards on my travels and occasionally to interview them about their fantasy lifestyle. Here's a sampling.

Meeting the Pinkertons

I met Kathy outside a Florida marina laundromat as she was struggling to keep Stole, an exuberant part malamute, part shepherd, part samoyed, and part wolf, under control. On several occasions I saw Kym, her teenaged daughter, slouched under the marina's pay telephone doing what any of her shore-based friends would be doing—talking on the phone. I decided to learn more about the Pinkertons—Al, Kathy, Kym, Stole, the mutt, and Tascha, the miniature schnauzer—and why they decided to become liveaboards.

The first thing you notice about the Pinkertons' home when you come calling at low tide is that it's a long jump from the pier to the front door. They live on a 33-foot Carver-Mariner cabin cruiser tied up at the Riviera Beach Municipal Marina. The marina has about 130 slips with about 20 to 30 percent occupied by liveaboards.

Al is in automobile sales, Kathy is a comptroller at a car dealership, Kym is in high school, and the dogs—well, they're just dogs.

MLF: Where did you live before becoming liveaboards?

Al: We had a house in Fort Myers with three bedrooms, two baths, and a pool. I owned 11 homes before making the decision to move aboard.

MLF: What made you decide to sell the house and buy the boat?

Al: It was my brother. He's been living on a 41-foot Morgan for the past 20 years, commuting between New Jersey and Florida. He said, "Al, when you get on a boat, you'll never get off."

Kathy: My initial reaction was: "No way! How can I live without a washer and dryer?" But here I am and doing just fine.

MLF: How did you pick the Riviera Beach Municipal Marina?

Al: That was easy. We went up and down the coast, and this was one of the only places that would accept liveaboards. No one wants liveaboards in this part of the country.

MLF: Did you have any boating experience before moving aboard?

Al: I've been around boats for 25 years, but I don't think any special experience is necessary.

MLF: What did you hate giving up most about your shoreside home?

Kathy: Nothing. We got rid of all our furniture without regrets.

Al: I'm never going ashore again to live in a home. This is where I want to be.

Kym: I miss the telephone. I give my friends the marina pay phone number and then sleep with the hatch open so that I can hear the telephone ring. Closet space is also a bit scarce.

MLF: Do you find yourselves with more or less chores on a boat? And has the pattern of who does them changed?

Kym: No, it seems that I still have to do everything around here.

Al: There's about the same number of things that need doing, but it seems you have to do them more often. A boat requires more TLC.

MLF: How do maintenance costs compare between boat and shoreside home?

Al: I think the costs are about the same. For example, the cost of hauling and painting is cheaper than painting a house, but you do it more often.

MLF: In what way have your lives changed?

Al: I'm free. I can cast off the dock lines at any time. I'm living alongside retired millionaires, doing exactly what they're doing, and I'm no millionaire.

Kathy: Al is Irish, and we call the boat *O'Funds*. That means we have zero money, but we're living like the rich.

MLF: How has life aboard affected family relationships?

Al: Interpersonal relations can be more difficult because of the confined space. You need to be more respectful of each other, and that's a good habit to get into no matter where you live.

MLF: Do friends and family think you're crazy?

Kathy: Oh, sure. My mother keeps saying, "How could you do this to Kym?" We have to keep assuring her that Kym loves this life as much as we do.

MLF: Are neighborhood relations at a marina different than on land?

Al: Marina life is much more friendly. Everyone is always looking for an excuse to have a party. No matter whether they own a $500 or $5 million boat, it's easy to walk up to a neighbor and talk to them and ask them to have a beer with you. Boat people are generally friendlier and easier to get to know.

MLF: Does living on a boat affect your work lives?

Kathy: Yes, when I'm late for work I tell my boss that the tide was too low to get off the boat.

Kym: And when I'm late for school, I tell them my mother fell in the water getting off the boat.

Kathy: Sometimes I come home from work and the boat is gone. That's when Al has come home early and decided to go fishing. So I sit by the pier and wait for my home to return. Sometimes the dinghy is there; we call it our apartment.

MLF: Does life aboard affect your hobbies?

Kym: Actually, I've gained new hobbies. I'm now into waterskiing, diving, and swimming. I love it.

Al: I like to fish, and this life is perfect for fishing. We're only four hours away from the Bahamas and great fishing.

MLF: Kym [a lithesome, blond woman], has boat life changed your social life?

Al: [interrupting] Are you kidding? This place is full of yachting transients, and they all make a beeline for Kym. At a marina you get to rub elbows with the beautiful rich people.

Kym: [smiles coyly]

MLF: Did you need any special training for this life, and did you have to become experts in anything?

Al: No. You learn to do a lot of little repair jobs for yourself, but I leave the big jobs to the experts.

MLF: What do you find most rewarding about living aboard?

Kathy: Life is more relaxing. Somehow the rocking motion has a calming effect, especially after a tense day at the office.

Kym: I like it. It's fun telling my friends at school that I live on a boat. People are envious of my life.

Al: I'm doing what I want to do. I'm not waiting for retirement. I'm free!

A Conversation with George Sass

I met George at a friend's wedding. It was a beautiful outdoor ceremony on a bluff overlooking the Severn River, not far from Chesapeake Bay. What made the scene even more unusual was that most of the male guests and the groom wore khakis and deck shoes with their sport coats. George was also wearing a bright-red bow tie. I decided that anyone who could pull off a bow tie with a deck shoe ensemble was worth getting to know.

George and his teenage son live aboard a 42-foot Grand Banks trawler in Annapolis. Four blocks from the dock he runs an ad agency that takes him to New York City several times a month. When not getting around in his frantic Madison Avenue life, George and his son cruise the bay, real slowly. George is about to get married to Stacey, a high school art teacher, who wants to share their liveaboard life.

MLF: How long have you been a liveaboard?

GS: My son, George Jr., and I searched for a long time for this wooden Grand Banks. We found her a little over three years ago, spent six months of hard weekend work restoring her, and have called her home ever since.

MLF: Have you always been a power boater?

GS: No, I'm a sailor at heart. I owned a 37-foot Dickerson ketch and still do a lot of crewing on sailboats, but nothing beats the trawler for cruising the bay and living aboard here in Annapolis.

MLF: What exactly drew you to a trawler and away from a sailboat?

GS: In my mind I see a trawler, with her steadying sail and relatively slow speed, as being closer to a sailboat than to a powerboat. It has more of a cruising home feel than a sporty, high-speed powerboat, and is more boat-like than a houseboat. I have as much room on her as I would have on a 50-foot sailboat, and my son and I can easily handle her. We probably couldn't manage a similar size or slightly larger sailboat by ourselves, especially in tight docking maneuvers.

MLF: Is there enough room for the two of you and your belongings?

GS: Oh, yes, plenty. We've adjusted well. At first we had to get rid of a lot of stuff that had accumulated in our house over the years. I remember making a series of trips to Goodwill, each time cutting deeper and deeper into what I thought I couldn't part with. It's painful to give away a good suit, even one you never wear. Well, finally, on the third trip, it too ended up on the Goodwill pile.

Now, three years later, I've paid more in storage fees than the price of buying all new belongings. I've also forgotten what's in storage. That's how much I miss the stuff.

There are plenty of people living in New York in apartments much smaller than our trawler, and they certainly don't have the view we have or the mobility.

MLF: Do you do much cruising?

GS: We're not much for staying tied up to the dock. Whenever we get the chance, we're out in the evening after work just to anchor in the peace and quiet around 2 miles from here. Then at 5:30 A.M. we'll pull up anchor and return for another workday. George Jr. enjoys cruising as much as I do. It's been a great father-son bonding experience.

I'm getting married in a week and my fiancée, Stacey, is looking forward to joining us in our liveaboard and cruising lifestyle.

MLF: Has Stacey ever lived on a boat, and does she know what she's in for?

GS: Stacey has been around boats for a long time. She's a high school art teacher, and during her summer vacations she used to do brightwork to earn extra income. That's how we met. I hired her to varnish the boat during the restoration. There's nothing like having an artist varnish your boat. We discovered our common love for boats, and soon varnishing sessions ended with a glass of wine and plans for our future. Her boating interests will complement our family bonding, and we're looking ahead to many years of family cruising.

MLF: Does she have any misgivings about living aboard a boat?

GS: She is all for it. She did a lot of boat sitting, so she is already an experienced liveaboard. Every once in a while she'll look out the window and out toward the bay and say, "George, can you believe this view? It's so wonderful, I'm almost feeling guilty."

There's no question that with three of us, space is at a premium. But we look at the positive side—it teaches us respect for each other's privacy, and it brings us closer together as a family and in shared experiences.

MLF: What are your future cruising plans?

GS: For the next five or so years we'll continue exploring the bay, slowly expanding our horizons toward Long Island Sound and New England. George Jr. will be in college during this time, and when he graduates he plans to join us on the *Big Adventure.* We want to do some extended offshore cruising. By then we'll be back on a sailboat, which will give us the freedom for quiet, long-range, self-reliant voyages. The three of us go to the annual boat shows, exploring the tent booths, buying new accessories for our trawler, and then we carefully inspect the offshore cruisers and dream about the *Big Adventure.*

We have no plans to circumnavigate or round the Horn. We just want the type of cruising that lets you say, "I don't know when I'll be back."

MLF: Have you noticed a difference in the company you keep now that you're a powerboater?

GS: Not at all. We still have the same friends we had when we were in a sailboat. We still go to rafting parties and raft up with the sailboats, only now everyone wants to come aboard our boat to party because there's more room.

I think the difference between sail- and powerboaters is exaggerated, especially in the case of slower boats like trawlers. I'm not talking about the over-powered rum-runners, with crews dressed in Ninja-black nylon jackets, constantly revving their engines or screaming across quiet waters. And I'm not referring to cabin cruisers and sportfishermen, cruising by at 20 knots leaving mountainous wakes. I'm talking about the common bond among boaters who go slow enough to enjoy the water. And that's what it's all about—enjoying the water.

However, unlike my sailing buddies who have to depend on the bay's fickle winds, I can schedule my cruises, go a little farther, and be back on time.

At first, we felt like traitors to the sail community. But that's over now. We are just enjoying the water, same as everyone.

MLF: Does living aboard affect your professional life as an advertising executive?

GS: Not in a negative sense. I occasionally use the boat to take out clients and, believe me, that's a lot easier on a trawler than on a sailboat. On a trawler you don't end up with a novice trying to sip a drink and at the same time keep the genoa sheet from strangling him.

It's much simpler to entertain on a trawler. The roominess and simple operation of the boat allow me to invite large groups out without much hassle.

MLF: Has living aboard interfered with your son's social life?

GS: About the only difference that I can observe is that he has to go to friends' houses for parties more often than they come to the boat. We're just not big enough for teenage parties. That may be a blessing in disguise. On the other hand, being a liveaboard makes George Jr. an interesting person with a special aura among his school friends.

MLF: What would you say is the most frustrating thing about living aboard?

GS: The most frustrating thing is finding qualified people to work on your boat, especially for complicated repair or maintenance jobs. I am taking maintenance courses and learning more and more about the boat so that I don't have to be so dependent on others. Boats are complicated, and if you don't keep on top of the maintenance, you may have a disaster on your hands.

MLF: What is the most rewarding thing about life aboard?

GS: Being in touch with nature, that's the highlight of this lifestyle. I'm now a much better person in my hectic Madison Avenue life because I can come home and feed the ducks that swim by my boat—my home!

Liveaboard Lifestyles

THE HERE AND NOW

After giving up a fast-paced life as a television soaps writer and shortly before giving up the helm as editor of the Living Aboard Journal, *Linda Grover reminisced about her liveaboard lifestyle.*

This will be our first full year of cruising, so we don't know as much about the life, its rewards or its tests, as many of you who are more experienced. However, it seems important today, as we're setting goals and making plans, that we keep in mind the reasons that we chose the lifestyle in the first place. It's so easy to become overburdened with duty and detail, to feel boxed in by expense and the awful necessities in life like dentists and the IRS. A boat home, if we let it, can lose its magic too.

Every time that threatens to happen in this household (boathold?), Tom drags out a note he saved that I had written to myself when we first set sail, way back in the spring. It never fails to help. Maybe some of you have similar thoughts that you'd like to share on keeping life simple and satisfying through every new year. Here's how mine goes:

12:21 P.M. aboard the *Almitra* out of Eau Gallie, Florida, on the ICW headed north at approximately 6 knots.

*Gently with
the Tides*

Clear skies, light winds, warm sunshine, good music, porpoises off the port bow, fishermen fishing and pelicans diving, the Captain in white terry cloth shorts (with a tan), food in the galley, a little cash in the bank, and adventure ahead. My kids all healthy and productive, my body sound, my mind at rest, the typewriter on the aft deck, a breeze delighting my skin, and what could be sweeter? "Let your home be not an anchor but a mast," says *The Prophet*, and I sing out my agreement with that. No wonder I could never find a home before; I'd tried only stationary ones.

Lest I forget, let this be a reminder, I have achieved contentment. Not complacency, or satiety, nor self-satisfaction, just that ordinary, elusive garden-variety thing called happiness—an absence of pain or worry about past and future along with a lively interest in and sense of keen awareness of the HERE AND NOW. Where have you been all my life, you lovely H.A.N.? Why has my gaze generally been directed either ahead or behind as I've employed, alternately, a painful squint or a blindfold to "face" things that were better forgotten or not possible to know. Guilt and Fear, so long misused by me, get thee behind me. Get lost. The sin is in not seeing and feeling and loving and living every hour as we pass through it bound we-haven't-the-remotest-notion-where. Walked last night across a high, endlessly long railroad trestle that was safe but scary, holding tight to Tom's hand, damaging his circulation perhaps but maintaining my cool. Learning slowly to feel at home and competent with the boat duties, remembering that "klutziness" and "stupidity" are largely self-willed. Imagine yourself doing it right, then do it! Cease escape in cheap reading, compulsive gluttony, and self-indulgent sloth—or neurotic ritual of any sort. "Someday" is today. Stop being about 40 percent there in any experience. Be here now. (Today, cruising up the ICW, that edict is hardly tough to follow.) Amen, and up on the Linda-deck (forward) for some sun before my turn at the helm. Wow.

Linda Grover

34

*Living aboard can sometimes have a competitive flavor. The CSTAR is
a biannual transatlantic singlehanded sailboat race started by Sir Francis
Chichester and Blondie Hasler back in the early sixties and continuing to
this day. Bill Gilmore, an ex commercial fisherman, wanted to give it a try
after having lived aboard boats and sailed them shorthanded for many
years. After all, this was only a 15- to 40-day sprint compared to those
nine-month 'round the world races.*

One of the greatest pleasures of cruising is the opportunity to meet unusual
and interesting people while momentarily tied up at a transient slip. These
encounters not only give you a chance to expand, vicariously, your own cruising experiences, but they also often add to your unforgettable life-list of
friends and acquaintants.

Liveaboard Lifestyles

One such memorable transient meeting took place at Beaufort Docks in
Beaufort, North Carolina. I was tied up two boats away from one of the sleek-
est and shiniest racing sloops I had ever seen.

Zafu, named after a Zen meditation cushion, was poised for a quick sprint
to England where her owner, Bill Gilmore, was planning to enter the
Carlsberg Singlehanded Transatlantic Race, CSTAR, formerly the OSTAR.
Having read many of the OSTAR accounts since the original Chichester versus Hasler match-up and feeling a little bit like an adult groupie, I jumped at
the chance to meet and talk to an honest-to-goodness singlehanded race com-
petitor.

Bill is a former party boat captain of a deepsea fishing business out of
Clearwater, Florida. He and his wife and children now live in New
Hampshire, but not too far from the ocean. For the past several seasons he
has taught sailing at the Hurricane Island Outward Bound school in Maine.
He and his wife are frequent cruisers aboard a Shannon 50. They have previ-
ously owned a Freedom 44 and a Clark Mills 56-foot, 3-masted schooner.

A few years ago Bill's wife gave him one of those beautifully illustrated
coffee-table books on singlehanded sailing. The idea slowly grew on him, and
before long he was deeply enmeshed in planning his CSTAR entry.

At first he wanted to enter his Shannon 50. But after thinking about the
competition he realized that a heavy cruising boat, in the largest 60-foot class,
would make a comfortable passage but also a very slow one. As long as he was
in the race he wanted to have a chance. He decided on a J-37 in the smaller
40-foot class. This boat suited his axiom for limited resources—go for a
smaller boat with the best equipment rather than a larger boat with less than

the best equipment. His careful planning and choice of equipment is clearly evident in *Zafu*. All of the considerable running rigging is well laid out and accessible from the cockpit. He has two roller-reefed headsails, a fully battened main, and an enormous drifter/reacher. The navigation station is brimming with the latest electronic gadgets, including a Satnav, radar, Weatherfax, and single-sideband transceiver. Bill admits to being a button-pushing junkie. The boat is equipped with water ballast tanks and large, clean storage spaces for extra sails and stores. One of the nice added touches is a stainless steel rail running all along the outer edge of the dodger providing a firm handhold within easy reach of the companionway.

When I met him, Bill had already completed his qualification run by taking a solo trip to the Yucatán. According to Bill, singlehanded sailing isn't without its special difficulties. Foremost among these is loneliness. He said that for the first three or four days he is really depressed. He doesn't eat anything more complicated than junk-food munchies and freeze-dried concoctions. He reads light, escapist literature, and most non-essential chores go undone. After this initial period, his energy and enthusiasm return. He can look forward all day to a can of chicken for dinner, and he starts reading weightier material that often requires several rereadings of a single paragraph before it's digested. Bill makes it a point of ridding the boat of anything that might remind him of his wife. He says that running into his wife's foul-weather boots can easily send him into a period of lonely depression. He is also reluctant to use his radio to call home because that also exacerbates his loneliness.

What about his race strategy? Bill figures that after about the first three hours of frenetic tuning and sail-changing activities in this two-plus-week race, he'll settle down to a pleasant transatlantic cruise. He doesn't think that singlehanding will be very difficult. His boat is overdesigned to compensate for poor seamanship, and he's had plenty of singlehanded experience even when sailing with wife and friends. Unless someone just happens to be in the right place to help, he feels that doing it himself is easier and faster than instructing someone.

One of the best things Bill has going for him on this long and arduous windward passage in the North Atlantic is his sense of humor. Several times during our conversation he had me chuckling over some anecdote, especially his experiences with the humorless U.S. Coast Guard. One of these stories concerned a boarding by a particularly serious Coast Guardsman. After finding no safety violations and probably being disappointed at finding no drugs, the officer asked Bill to lift up the cabin floorboards. The officer stared at the curving fiberglass hull around the bilges and asked, "What's in those tanks?" Bill looked him straight in the eye and with an equally straight face replied, "The ocean!" With that attitude, Bill is a winner no matter where he places in the CSTAR.

3

Decisions, Decisions, Decisions...

MOVING ABOARD is a big step for most. Cutting the ties with a land-based home is often a traumatic and fearful experience at first, and then one wonders how any other life is possible. For many the decision to move aboard is made after the children have left home or after the work-a-day responsibilities have been lessened or removed. Others, however, see the liveaboard experience as good for raising children and find the gently rocking boat a perfect end to a hard day at the office.

In general, boats are smaller than houses, and a common theme to the moving-aboard experience is how to part with all those possessions. Boats are also more complex and more difficult to have serviced by the "plumber," so those who move aboard soon learn the value of self-reliance.

Boat type doesn't seem to matter much in the decision to move aboard or in the angst one goes through before the transition is complete. In the following stories, liveaboards relate their unique circumstances in moving onto a houseboat, trawler, motorsailer, and sailboat.

In one case the move aboard is only a prelude to cutting ties completely with the land and going cruising.

The trials and tribulations and the joys and pleasures of living aboard are remarkably similar and offer a step-by-step guidebook to the dreamers. In many ways these accounts reinforce the age-old message: "Do it now."

HOUSEBOATS

Hannah Merker, a writer, bookseller, and editor, has spent more than 10 winters living and working aboard in Long Island Sound. Here she tells of her initial experiences in ridding herself of the whateverness of life and moving aboard a houseboat.

Gently with the Tides

Once upon a time, many years ago, I visited an island, a small rise of sand and palm trees, off the east coast of Panama. At high tide the island barely measured two acres. I had not known how small it was before I got there.

It was so contained I could feel its pulse, its aliveness, all the minute reaches of it as it expanded and shrank with the tide. I watched the island's life as the sun rose behind the 11 palms of the next island, as the shadows lengthened westward in the afternoons.

The island grew larger every day, a quantity not reckoned by any worldly span, only in the measurement of my mind. New vistas were always there, surprising me, startling a slumber cast by tropic heat, luring me around this smallness of surpassing size. One day, many years after leaving the island, I put a deposit on a houseboat, not a sudden decision, but one thought about for quite a while, always on the edge of my mind. Still, dreaming is one thing; acting out a fantasy, another. I went home that day searching for a yardstick.

I stood in the middle of the living room of my mini cottage with the wonderful view and drew a 10- by 20-foot rectangle on the bare floor. The hull of my new craft was 40 feet long and 13 feet in width; however, the cabin perched atop it, our intended living space, was what I saw before me outlined on the floor. The area looked pitifully small in that 16-by-30 room. I glanced around at all my furniture, my piano, my accumulated tangible life of nearly 50 years. I gathered my old boxer, my seven cats, myself, within the rectangle. How could we live in such a small space?

I looked out my long windows facing the sea. It was early September. Rough winds were battering the surf near the shore. It was quite chilly, almost cold. Was I really doing this? Would I want to be out there this night? Could my craft last through a Northeast winter in the water? My about-to-be home had always spent winters cradled ashore, protected, a plaything under the summer sun. "Grandma," as she was called then, had led a rather sheltered life.

Suddenly I saw my cottage as a castle of infinite size. Set high on a hillside, it was a cave of many rooms on descending levels, all windows facing the inlet waters that began across the street.

That night I decided I could part with nothing. I went to sleep.

In the clearness of the fall coastal morning, early, before the sun, yet later than the night, I scurried down the hillside with my old dog, helping him who once flew across fields and fences, a magnificent brindle blur. Now we slowly walked the low-tide sandbar, out to its distant sloping edge, collecting mussels for breakfast. The morning beach was calm, a fresh wind, crisp and light, leaning against us as we walked.

Later, at home, after mussels, I wrote a letter to a woman who had once said, "If you ever want to sell that wonderful old upright..."

I opened the back door of my truck and filled the inside with chairs and tables, beds and cabinets, pictures, pots—the whatevernesses of life. And every day thereafter I held a "garage sale" out of the truck, in front of my bookshop.

Decisions, Decisions, Decisions...

By late October the house was quite empty. There was a cot, some blankets, one pot, one frying pan, a few utensils, some clothes, some frivolous things, and 40 cartons of books. With these—and Barney and Zoe and Anna and Nicholas and Caro and Chrissy and Sarah and Earthy—I moved aboard my island.

Hannah Merker

MOVING ON...AND OFF

One of the realities of the liveaboard life is that sometimes it comes to an end and you return to the land. But you've been changed forever. The experience, according to Joanna Zwernemann, gave her a new sense of freedom, strength, and self-reliance.

The idea of people living on boats of their own free will had never entered my mind when, at the age of 18, I met the man with whom I was to share 43 feet of living space for two years of my life. Then I was weak. Now I am strong.

It was during my first SCUBA class; we were asked to stand up and give a capsule summary of our lives up to the point when we decided to become divers. The class was composed of seven physical therapists, two spoiled grade-school-age boys, me, and a bearded, earringed, rather outspoken young man whose summary consisted of only five words, "I live on my boat." I can remember at the time envisioning this poor soul cramped into a 16-foot Glastron bassboat like the one our family used to go fishing on. I felt sorry for him. He didn't have a car and once asked me for a ride home to his boat. I soon became best of friends with this magnificent man, whose vision of a self-reliant lifestyle, devoted to experience and thought, changed me from a naive kid with an unearned overabundance of confidence to an experienced sailor with a humble knowledge of my relationship to the forces of nature.

The boat was docked at a small marina on the Intracoastal Waterway. There were seven boats at Clem's, and all had families living aboard. My introduction and adaptation to living in the marina and on the boat were smooth, and utterly enjoyable. I was particularly impressed with the females who lived aboard. For unlike most women I'd come in contact with in the past, they had other things to worry about besides the length of their finger-nails, or what time the plumber was coming. In fact the liveaboards at Clem's would never think to call a plumber when something went wrong. The women (and the men) knew every inch of their living space, and knew how to repair things without calling in paid help. They had large tool boxes; some did beautiful carpentry, painted, sewed sails, worked on engines, and went out in gale-force winds to check lines. They were generous with advice and invited me to coffee at midnight for long talks about life in general. The people I met at Clem's, boat people, were the first real friends I'd ever had.

After a year at Clem's and many daysails with four of our best friends, after many long talks with all of the members of "Clem's Coffee and Yacht Club" about that voyage to the Bahamas we would all take together someday, it was finally time to do it. The Bahamacide division of Clem's Marina rose to the occasion and came through, quite literally, with flying colors. All of us quit our jobs, drained our bank accounts, and after grueling weeks of major modi-fications on the boat, our last task (a spur of the moment decision) was a homemade set of signal flags. It took five days of tedious sewing, three sewing machines, and the help of everyone in the marina to finish those flags. And if I had it to do all over again, I would not. If you want signal flags, buy them. You won't regret it.

We pulled out of the marina on New Year's Day with a beautiful 15-knot east wind pushing us toward our first destination, Key West, Florida. It would have taken plastic surgery to remove the smiles from our faces those first 24 hours, but things got hairy the next morning at about 2 A.M. The winds switched to the west as if to say, "Don't you even think about trying to go any farther." The seas rose to about 12 feet before any of us had a chance to try out our sea legs. Our smiles quickly turned to grimaces as the boat started to fall off 10-foot peaks with resounding shudders. There were six of us on board, and for the first three days and nights we beat to windward at 11 knots, making little or no headway. There was no moon, and the nightwatches, as we rushed into pitch-black darkness, trying to stay warm in between fits of throwing up, were some of the most miserable hours of my life. It was cold and scary, and more than once I was forced to ask myself, "Why?"

The trip was easier after the spell of bad weather tested our abilities. In fact, after those first days, 5-foot seas were a blessing. As things settled down, we managed to troubleshoot some small problems, such as where those gallons of water that kept dumping on our seasick heads throughout the night were coming from (through our heater chimney).

Although we did beat to windward for the entire 1,500 miles of the two-week trip, there were times when it was possible to answer the "whys." There were the schools of porpoise, sometimes numbering 50 or more, that traveled with us for miles on end. There were always reassuring hugs to be had, long talks on nightwatches, starry skies, shared last beers, and the pleasant boredom that brought out five cameras and wasted a lot of film. Then finally landfall in Key West.

It had been a harder trip on our friends than they had expected. All of us were 10 pounds lighter and beaten to the point of exhaustion. They left us and began recuperating at a Key West resort. I stayed on the boat. I was so damned proud of myself; with visions of Australia in my head, and a new figure to boot, I was convinced I could do anything.

The boat needed a few minor repairs. We had sprung a leak about a week into the trip and had been taking on about three gallons of water an hour. ("This is a bilge pump; it gives you big biceps. Have fun!") We docked at a wonderful marina in Key West called Safe Harbour. Most of the boats had liveaboards on them. They were great people and confirmed my hopes that boat people all over are special people. Key West inspires me. It is a cosmopolitan community full of writers, artists, con-artists, daily-grind dropouts, and people who find it harrowing to live away from the water. The island has ensnared me with its many personalities, and the spirit it exudes. The Bahamas seem farther and farther away as opportunities abound for me in this city.

I have moved off the boat after three months in Key West, and it is soon to move on without me. I live in a tiny house, far smaller than I would have considered possible before learning to live so compactly on the boat. My possessions have been pared down to a minimum. That is perhaps the greatest freedom I gained from my time aboard.

I have hung a kerosene lamp in my little bedroom. Its smell reminds me of quiet nights on the water. It's much different living in a house now. I will never lose my desire to live on a boat and am saving to buy one of my own. Here I do not have to pump the toilet—or the bilges. My electricity comes from I know not where, and the sewage is carried away to parts unknown. I no longer have to prime the stove or haul ice for the icebox. There is no sound of rigging slapping in the night to keep me awake. It is empty and common here. I feel disconnected, and I realize something many people who have never lived on the water may not: that the sense of anxiety many people feel without knowing where it comes from may stem from disconnection and uninvolvement in the most basic components of daily living.

On the boat I learned to be self-reliant and made a concerted effort to

Decisions, Decisions, Decisions…

41

understand how my surroundings worked to effect that self-reliance. That is what is missing from my life now. It is too easy. It never seemed that way before.

Joanna Zwernemann

TRADING A PICKET FENCE FOR A DOCK

I met Jackie Rosenberger on the west coast of Florida where she was happily raising a family on a sailboat. Not for one minute did she regret having abandoned her dream of the house with the white picket fence.

For Jackie, the idea of raising a family on board a boat was too far from the norm to even be considered. She grew up with traditional dreams of getting married, having children, and living in a house with a white picket fence. She has a husband and two lively children, Todd, age 10, and Julie, age 11, but as for the house and the picket fence, well, she traded them in for a dock and a 45-foot cutter-rigged sailboat.

Husband Dave, a former Coast Guardsman, is now an alternative education teacher. He is working on a master's degree and hopes to continue teaching and counseling. He very much enjoys the summer vacations offered by the teaching profession. Dave has always been around boats and the water and has nurtured the dream of someday living aboard. Jackie, on the other hand, has needed some convincing.

Their first boat was a 24-foot Flicka, which they used to cruise the Florida Keys and Dry Tortugas. From the time the kids were four or five years old, Dave talked of someday living on a boat. Jackie wasn't sold on sailing and especially not on full-time boat living on a 24-footer. Her response to Dave's dream was, "We have to have a bigger boat or no boat at all." As luck would have it, one day they rescued an errant dinghy belonging to a 45-foot Kadey-Krogen cruising sailboat. In repayment for returning the dinghy, they were given a tour of this spacious cruiser, and Jackie realized immediately that this could be a tempting alternative to the picket-fenced house. "Get me something roomy like this, and I'll consider living aboard," she said to Dave.

At about this time a combination of things led to their decision to move aboard. They had made a very good investment in their home and in the subsequent improvements that they had made to it. They became increasingly concerned with the deteriorating health of the nation's economy, general world stability, and their ability to recoup the gains made on their home. Lastly, Dave just wasn't having fun playing "Harry Homeowner." Although he loves boat maintenance, he hated house chores. The kids were still too young to object to a major upheaval in their lives, so they decided to "do it now."

After some searching they found a Kadey-Krogen for sale. The deal closed ahead of schedule and suddenly they were scrambling for a place to park *Tsunami* and live aboard. Since Dave taught at a Tampa school and Jackie worked at local doctor's office, they naturally looked to the Tampa Municipal Marina as a perfect location for their boat. Unfortunately, Tampa had had an unpleasant experience with a group of less than desirable liveaboards about 10 years earlier. As a result the dockmaster wasn't interested in liveaboards, and the city had a specific ordinance prohibiting liveaboards at the marina. Dave argued for an exception and even worked up a 12-point good-conduct plan for liveaboards that he intended to present to the mayor of Tampa to bolster their case. But it was to no avail; the mayor refused to meet with the Rosenbergers. It appeared to Jackie and Dave that the city was more interested in commercial shipping than in recreational boating.

Decisions, Decisions, Decisions…

Other "secret" liveaboards in the area did not come to the Rosenberger's aid because they wanted to keep a low profile and not jeopardize their own liveaboard status. With active kids playing along the docks, Jackie and Dave could hardly keep their liveaboard status a secret, so they began to look elsewhere. From a commuting standpoint, the St. Petersburg Municipal Marina was the next logical choice. There they found a perfect setting—plenty of friendly liveaboard neighbors, plenty of sport and social activities, and an atmosphere catering to the recreational boater.

Jackie says that there have been no earthshaking adjustments in moving from a house to a liveaboard lifestyle. Probably the biggest issue facing the family was over paring down their possessions. About a year before the big move they stopped buying toys for the kids because there wouldn't be room in the boat lockers. Todd still misses having a large permanent train set-up, but he manages with having to dismantle a little train set after each use. The loss of the train set is more than made up for by the outdoor life and the extensive junior youth sailing program at the local yacht club. Dave had problems parting with some family heirlooms, including crystal and china as well as antique furniture, but they have rented a storage locker until they decide the final disposition of these items. Once pared down to life's necessities, they found the boat spacious enough for a family of four.

The family has always been physically close, so the restrictive cabin is not viewed as a hardship, and with the benign Florida weather there's always the deck and the great outdoors. On the plus side, Jackie thinks that the confined space teaches the kids to be more courteous and respectful of people's private space.

One amusing aspect of boat living for the kids occurs whenever they have a sleep-over with friends. It seems that the parents of these friends take a special interest in personally checking out the kids' "home" and parents before allowing their child to sleep over. Of course, it goes without saying that the friends love it.

Jackie and Dave have no plans to circumnavigate or even to take off for any extended cruising. They're happy with their long summer vacations and more modest destinations. In the near future they hope to voyage to the Bahamas, Mexico, and up the East Coast of the U.S.

It appears that, for the Rosenbergers, replacing the white picket fence with a dock has brought a sense of freedom, closer family life, and more enjoyment of homeowner responsibilities.

Gently with the Tides

THE DECISION TO MOVE ABOARD

Probably the most elaborate and detailed letter I ever received on the subject of moving aboard came from Merilyn and John Piper. They were responding to several letters in which readers had asked for the nitty-gritty details of leaving a house for a boat. They both took turns narrating answers to the many questions with their own saga of moving aboard.

Liveaboard! God, what an exciting word. It always brings forth a pile of images in my mind. The millionaire on his gold-plated yacht, clipping coupons and smoking cigars. The cruising school teachers with a year's sabbatical and little money. The adventurous soldier of fortune who will work someplace only long enough to afford to move on to the next port of call. No schedules. No commitments. No worries.

The Dream

But what about me? Me, the middle-aged guy with a mortgage, a job, and obligations to my wife, society, and the banks? Why do I have to lug everything back to the car on Sunday afternoon and drive home in the hot summer afternoon to face the overgrown lawn? Why, indeed?

Well, to hell with society. As long as I don't break any laws, I really don't have to answer to "society" in spite of what my mother taught me about manners, the Puritan work ethic, and "society." The banks? Well, I'll have to cross that one eventually, but the big problem will be my wife. Now don't get me wrong. Mer is my best friend and has been since I first saw her and fell in love. But she was also raised by conservative middle-class parents who believed in home, family, property, and all of the "responsible" trappings of success, like a lawn to mow. To suggest living on board falls in the same category as suggesting that we join the circus as sideshow barkers—you know, not "proper."

I've been messing around boats since I was about 10, starting with a canoe at summer camp and working my way up through fishing boats, row boats, and a borrowed ski boat or two. I can still as a child remember the cardboard paddle boats with the rubber-band drives that I used to float in the puddles in

Oregon after it rained. Since it rains a lot in Oregon, I had many chances to dream. I never outgrew it.

Four years in the navy on a submarine exposed me to the wonders of the open ocean. Cruising at night, with the flying fish streaking by leaving a fluorescent wake, has to be seen. It cannot be described. Occasionally, one would land on the deck and be immediately scooped up for the frying pan. Or the joy of the porpoises playing in the bow wake. They would follow us for miles and suddenly disappear.

It taught me respect as well. The ocean can be awesome in a major storm. You realize just how insignificant you really are in the greater scheme of things, and yet it challenges you to learn the rules as defined by Mother Nature. If you're going to play in this game, you have to know the rules! I've stood many a topside deck watch underway, at anchor, or alongside. Warm summer nights or cold, wet, rainy ones. Ringing the ship's bell every four minutes in a fogbound harbor. You get the picture—I'm hooked on the water and have been since too many years ago.

Well, the first break came when we had to move to Virginia because of the job. You know the job—that terrible thing that takes away from our boating time but allows us to pay the slip fees. In any case, we came to Virginia where Mer's family lived. Why was this a break? Well, for two big reasons—one, I like her family as if they were my own, and two, her father owned a boat. Now I admit that I have always liked her father, but then again he had always owned a boat. It just shows what good taste he had.

It started as a casual flirtation—you know—"Let's go out for a spin with your dad, just to experience the feel of the water." Then it started getting serious. A three-day trip on the Chesapeake. A trip up the Patuxent River. It finally blossomed after four years into a full seduction: "Dad, can we borrow the boat for the weekend?" "Dad, I know it's on blocks for the winter, but do you mind if we go down and just sit on her for the weekend?"

Mer's dad, God bless him, knew that I was arranging a ménage à trois among his daughter, his boat, and his ne'er-do-well son-in-law. Although he never said so, I think he enjoyed the conspiracy and its eventual outcome as much as I did. One eventful day, we were able to report that Mer had successfully taken the boat out of the slip without help, maneuvered to the gas dock, filled up and returned to the slip without incident. With twinkling eyes, that was the day that he called her "Skipper" and presented us with our own set of keys to the boat!

The time had finally come. It was a cold, wet, and rainy Sunday in the fall. We had been aboard since Friday evening. We were huddled in the cockpit with water dripping from mysterious openings that only appear when it rains. We were breathing steam, and the bottom of the weather canvas was beaded up with moisture ready to dribble onto whatever or whoever was foolish enough to come in contact with it.

Decisions, Decisions, Decisions...

45

"Love of my life," I said, "how would you like to sell the house and move aboard a boat?"

With her father's twinkle, Mer looked me in the eye and said, "What took you so long to ask?"

To this day I am still wondering who was seducing whom.

The next two years were spent in that euphoric state of having made a decision to live aboard but not facing the reality of what we could afford or what was available. We went to the boat shows and looked at gold-platers with a critical eye and discarded them as "not quite us." But it was a valuable two years. We fell in love with any number of possible boats but eventually realized that most yachts do not have provision to stow the Christmas tree decorations, much less anything resembling a normal complement of clothing, tools, or spare parts.

We eventually came to the conclusion that a pre-owned (i.e., used—ergo, cheaper) trawler would be the answer to our needs. Note the old family-bred conservative approach here in spite of our wild decision to "join the circus." I had long since outgrown the need to go fast and was more than content to idle along enjoying the scenery. (I must admit that it is about the only thing that I have ever outgrown.)

Tragedy struck with the untimely death of Mer's father. The whole family pitched in to close down the old family farm and dispose of 50 years of accumulated belongings. Somehow, in this sad time, we realized the futility of collecting material things for someone else to dispose of after we were gone. The lesson was most valuable in the coming months.

We put the house on the market that spring, fully expecting to sell it within weeks. It was a good thing that we didn't. It took over a year to sell, but during that year we were constantly assuming that it would sell within the next few weeks. With that kind of pressure, it still took a full year to cull out everything but the few items that we really needed on the boat. We learned to be ruthless in what was thrown out, given to charity, permanently loaned to friends, or sold. The rule was, "If I haven't used this in six months—get rid of it."

Mer was really good at this while I kept putting off the final sorting out of my tools that I had been accumulating for 30 years. I can't say exactly why, but I have a collection of some 25 screwdrivers. Each of them is different and best qualified for a particular job. Now I admit that when I was on her father's boat, I could make do with one or two screwdrivers for just about anything—but you see, I knew that I had the truly proper one at home in case I needed it. Now I was faced with the reality that "at home" would be a boat, and I had to select my favorites.

It's about one year later, and I am still putting off these decisions. I keep discovering additional special jobs that will require just the right tool. Mer has not mentioned this weakness on my part, but I suspect that is because she has a stash of favorite kitchen goodies that she has not faced up to. Her unspoken respect of my frailties is a constant wonder to me, but most welcome.

The Buy

While all of this was going on, we were also looking for The Boat. We had talked to a number of sales representatives at the Annapolis boat shows, but they were interested only in new-boat sales. They looked in disdain at lowly peons who needed a pre-owned trawler. We answered advertisements in the brokerage section of the boating magazines. We talked to friends. We read the classifieds. We worried. Everything we could afford was too small, and everything we liked was too expensive.

We also needed a slip for The Boat, and we needed to find a storage place for the few family items that we had decided to keep, even though they wouldn't go on the boat. We wanted to stay at our present marina because we liked the people, the management, and the atmosphere. But our marina was built for the typical pleasure boats in the range of 16 to 30 feet. The marina was adding a new pier, however, so we put in a bid to rent the end of the pier where they could handle a bigger boat. We didn't have a boat, and we hadn't sold our home, but by golly we did have a slip! Since we were going to sell the house "in the next few weeks," we thought it was a good investment.

Decisions, Decisions, Decisions…

And then we found our broker! Now I have always felt that yacht brokers, used-car salesmen, real-estate developers, and snake-oil salesmen are all in the same category. We had been in touch with several since we had inquired about the brokerage ads in the boating journals, and most of them were ambitiously blind to our wishes. Sell at any cost and to hell with what the customer wanted! One of them even insisted that we wire an offer to Florida to "seal the deal" without even seeing the boat.

Since then I have found out the following: There is at least one (and possibly more) honest broker in Florida. Selection and prices are better in Fort Lauderdale than anywhere else on the East Coast. Asking prices are approximately 10 percent higher than the buyer expects to realize. Except for the custom one-off boat, if you find it anywhere else, you can also find it in Fort Lauderdale for significantly less.

Our broker, Camm, was a real pleasure to work with. He listened to what we wanted. He didn't push. He was sympathetic to our problem of selling the house. He was patient. He was also alert to our unspoken desires. He forwarded numerous listings that reflected what we had asked for. When we commented that this one or that one was not right, he listened and adjusted his evaluation of what we really wanted. As it turned out, I think that he knew long before we did just what we should have, and he steered us toward it. It finally fell into place. In just four days, it all happened! We had been negotiating with a potential buyer for the house for about eight weeks. We had gotten to that point of utter frustration when we decided to end the year's frustration and accept his less-than-hoped-for offer. On a Wednesday, we executed a sales contract on the house, and Mer produced two tickets to Fort Lauderdale for the following afternoon that she had reserved two weeks in advance. I don't know how she did it. It's like living with a wizard. You learn to accept it.

47

(That's why I could never have an affair—Mer would know about it before I did.)

Camm met us at the airport that evening and informed us as to our schedule of boat-looking for Friday. Four trawlers just exactly like what we had been asking for, two yacht types that might do, and one other trawler that was slightly larger than and different from what we had specified. He knew us better than we did. We had reviewed our budget and the proceeds from the house and knew the absolute maximum that we could afford. We held back a reserve and told Camm, "This is it. No more than this."

Well, on Friday he took us aboard the "other" trawler first. Like the first time I saw Mer, it was love at first sight. This may not make sense to some of you, but that boat talked to me from the moment I stepped on board. And I liked what she said. Yes, we went on to look at the other boats that had been set up for us, but they just weren't right. The trawlers that we had specifically asked to see didn't talk to me. If anything, they grumbled at being disturbed, while the yacht types just dozed with no interest or character.

On Saturday morning we went back for a second look at the "other" trawler. I had mentioned to Camm that I wanted to take some pictures of her. I'm not sure how it was arranged, but the two slips on either side of "our" boat were vacant, allowing a broadside shot from the next finger pier. Saturday afternoon we made an offer. That doesn't sound like much, but it was the result of a very careful analysis of what we could afford—taking into account the myriad other little things such as insurance, survey, delivery, repairs, documentation, fuel, provisioning, etc. After a couple of counter- offers on both sides, we had a deal! By God, we had a deal! We had done what we had set out to do—buy a liveaboard boat. That evening was one of those rare precious moments that only happen when a dream has come true but before you realize that even dreams have a few strings attached.

Sea trials had been arranged for the next Monday, so Mer and I spent Sunday walking the beach hand-in-hand, talking about all the little details each of us had overlooked or the features we had noticed. It seemed incredible, but we had just purchased a new home after being on board for less than three hours. And yet we knew—it was right.

Monday we took her out. In the past, on our 27-foot express, Mer and I had developed the habit of calling "Wake!" whenever another boat passed close aboard in order to warn the other to brace him- or herself for a roll. Now, from the flying bridge, we watched as several good-size boats passed close aboard leaving good-size wakes. No roll, no pitch. Just a smush as we pushed their wakes aside. Now here was a proper boat.

We headed up the inland waterway for a bit and turned out into the Atlantic. As we passed the sea buoy with nothing in front of us except blue water, I felt like the Ancient Mariner preparing to battle the elements. It's a feeling you can only get with nothing in view except a watery horizon. But this was not the great crossing; rather, it was a short trial run, so we came about and returned to reality and the shore. Naturally, we accepted the boat.

We returned home to close down the house, move out, and store what little we had retained of our possessions. Now that "the next few weeks" had come and gone, we were faced with the problem of a few hard-to-dispose-of items such as a snow blower and an electronic organ. We sent these off to an auction house with the instruction to sell at whatever we could get. It wasn't much.

I made it through final settlement feeling like a Vanderbilt or J. P. Morgan. Thousands of dollars passing through my hands as if I did this every day. Endorsing a check from the sale of the house with only a casual glance at all those numbers. Authorizing the wire transfer of funds from our mortgage bank to a Florida bank. I thought only major corporations did this. Power!

Decisions, Decisions, Decisions…

When it was all over, we bunked with friends. I suddenly realized that I had no fixed address and made sure that I always had five dollars in order not to be picked up for vagrancy. I don't know if they can really do that, but it seemed like a good idea.

Since I could not take several weeks off from the job (remember that I still had to work to support my family and ever-increasing creditors), we had arranged with Camm for a professional delivery crew to bring the boat up the inland waterway. But Mer, my fellow vagrant, no longer had a house to keep, so we decided to have her ride up in the boat with the delivery crew. That way she could learn the inner workings of the boat with professional guidance, take a much-needed vacation, and protect our interests all at the same time. It was a good decision.

Mer asked one of her close friends to ride with her. They packed up several boxes of items they would need on the trip, like dishes, boat hooks, and booze, and shipped them off to Camm. I really don't know if Camm gets that involved with all of his clients, but in our case, since we were dealing at long distance, Camm acted as our agent, broker, coordinator, and point of contact. I had authorized several things to be done to the boat as a result of the survey, such as changing engine zincs, recalibrating the depthsounder, adding a new filter, and bleaching out the teak deck just because I wanted a new-looking deck.

To handle all of these separate tasks, I had sent Camm a check to establish a slush fund from which he could pay the individual workers as they finished rather than sending us bills in the mail. This worked quite well. (Who would want to send a bill to an out-of-state vagrant with no fixed address?) It also established the precedent of having Camm pay our bills without our having to worry about them. All I had to do was worry about paying Camm!

The Trip Home (Merilyn)

I flew to Fort Lauderdale to pick up the boat. What a role I had to play, acting as if we could really afford all of this. At the time of final closing, the boat had been moved to the Bahia Mar marina as a central location for the several days of provisioning. Our yacht broker picked me up at the airport and escorted me to the Bahia Mar and through the security checkpoints to the pier where our new boat was secured. Admittedly, ours was the smallest boat in the entire marina, but this was heady living to be rubbing fenders with the real gold-platers.

That first evening, after everyone had left for the day, I suddenly found myself alone on the new boat. Every sound was new. Was that drip normal? Is that gushing supposed to be happening? How do I turn off the deck lights? With my imagination, the creaking lines, the dim light, and the ominous big gold-platers in the adjacent slips, I spent the night with visions of sinister plots, piracy, and drug runners.

With the next day, however, things returned to normal. Dean, the delivery captain, and Ken, the first mate, came aboard and took command over the final preparations. They announced, "Not to worry, we can fix anything," which was reassuring as well as prophetic. They could and they had to, on several occasions.

To digress to the ultimate decision to sell everything. We accomplished that by creating a three-ring notebook with a tab for every room and every closet. I'm serious. You'll go through everything, and if you don't write it down in its place you'll lose your mind. I called an appraiser and had her give me a verbal appraisal (that's cheaper than a written one) of those items we felt had some value. Next to each item she appraised I wrote the value. That gave me an idea of what to charge for the item when family and friends came in to have a look-see. For family items, I charged the family member one-quarter of the value. There were some family items I wasn't ready to be rid of yet, so they were tagged for the storage shed.

Since I had stopped working, I would spend my days going through a closet and set aside a shelf that would go with us. John would review the whole mess when he got home and generally would agree. This process took about three attempts before we had the "to go" shelf narrowed down to the things we (I) absolutely could *not* live without. Did this with clothes, games, books, records (They were all available for sale since a turntable on board a boat is kinda silly when you stop to think about it—but I did have some of our special songs taped for the cassette recorder), shoes, hats, the whole nine yards. I let John do his shop (which was a full-size garage stall filled with years of neat stuff), and he let me do my kitchen.

Once we had a pretty good idea of what we would be taking with us, we invited family and friends in to walk through the house and stake their claim on our furniture, books, pots and pans, etc. For those things that I could not let go because it would make the house look funny while showing it to prospective clients, I made a notation in the book that Karen wants this and has paid $x amount toward the final price. It made it all go real easy, and our friends were thrilled to have the stuff they wanted with an easy payment plan.

The stuff that didn't sell we had the local auction house take. I should have had a yard sale, but I was not emotionally up to handling that on top of everything else. We would have done better. I gave a lot of stuff to the Salvation Army and the local District Home—but be sure to itemize everything (you may think it is a pain, but for tax purposes it will pay off in the long run) and give it a dollar value: for instance, on a good office-type shirt I placed a value of $3.00 and worked from there. Hardbacked books were $1.00, and paperbacks were 50 cents. It was really a guess, but once I established the guesstimate I stuck with it for consistency.

It really is amazing how much stuff we accumulate during the years. And it is amazing how much stuff is still up in the storage shed that I haven't missed in almost three years. Guess it's time for a yard sale now!

The Boat

I could write reams about the boat. Here are just a few observations and some liveaboard tips.

You should strongly consider diesel for a liveaboard. It's safer, but diesel fuel can have its own problems—algae. If you are confident your dealer (or marina) has good fuel and your tank is in good shape, add diesel treatment at each fill-up according to directions. We bought a Florida boat that unfortunately had not really been cruised during the year before we found her, and algae had been allowed to build up. We should have had the tank drained and flushed in Florida and started the trip with fresh fuel. No matter where you buy your boat, I strongly recommend you have it totally fumigated prior to taking possession to rid it of roaches. Boats, particularly Florida boats, are a beautiful haven for those damn critters. I had never seen a roach until I moved on board. Have had it totally fumigated twice—once after we arrived home, and once this past spring when I spotted one. If you've got one, you've probably got lots. A small price to pay.

Just figured out that we haven't told you what type of boat we are on. She is a beautiful 51-foot Cheoy Lee trawler with a 15-foot beam and a 6-foot draft. She has three staterooms, each with its own head (and exhaust fan), pilothouse with appropriate electronics, galley (a must for me), large saloon w/wet bar and icemaker, enclosed afterdeck, stand-up engine room (a must for John), washer/dryer (with its exhaust), twin Ford Lehman diesels, 15kw generator for power while underway, two 600-gallon water tanks, and a 1,600-gallon fuel tank located under the amidships bed. Her bridge is complete with adequate equipment for cruising and maneuvering, a wet bar and icemaker. On deck are a hard Dyer sailing dinghy and an inflatable Avon with outboard, a contained life raft, and a steadying sail mast with boom for lowering the dinghy.

Her 6-foot draft at times causes us some difficulties. It limits us to where we can and can't take her. But, we bought her to live on and not to go running up and down the river. We try to take a two-week trip during John's vacation (remember, he still treks up the dock in that devil-created tie every morning) and a few anchor-outs if our tide permits. Because of her deep draft, she has gobs of storage. We have eight hanging lockers, a linen locker, and adequate drawer and additional locker space. We have four (with two slave units) reverse-cycle air conditioning units, and we can use them for heat until about mid-January when the river water gets below 41 degrees. We do not believe in kerosene heaters, so we have seven oil-filled electric radiators to keep us warm between January and March. It is quite adequate for Virginia winters (so far). The worst has been not getting the cabin above 58 degrees, but that is probably because we are also heating the enclosed cockpit, and that's only been a couple of days a winter.

We have insulated all of the lockers that open to the hull. We used good-quality rug underlayment with the vapor barrier, keeping the vapor barrier toward the locker door. Liquid Nails works wonders—but be sure the surface is dry. This also includes the overhead of any hanging locker that might be exposed to the walk-around deck. (I forgot one, and all of the clothes were damp and it took me quite a while to figure out what in the world was happening.) We also use the underlayment to tuck between the weatherboard and the handrail in the cockpit (afterdeck). We added firm insulation to the overhead in the cockpit and will be adding a headliner. That made a big difference last year in heat loss. We will be adding an additional weatherboard next year—we lose more heat through the weatherboard than we do through the roll-down curtains (which happen to be extremely good-quality plastic). It never stops—but then again neither do changes to a house-house.

To prevent mildew in the mattresses on the beds, we use Ensolite under the sheet. I usually have to order a sheet of Ensolite in the spring and the fall for our bed. Since the others don't get used more than once or twice, there has been no need to replace those. Ensolite can be purchased from sporting goods stores, but if your beds are regular size, you will probably want to order directly from the firm (North by Northeast in Pawtucket, Rhode Island, 800-556-7262).

Since we have good-size windows in the saloon/galley/pilothouse, we put heat-shrink on the outside so I can keep the windows clean inside. We both smoke, and if I don't wash windows on a weekly basis the cabin starts to smell a little stale. The first year we used the double-sided sticky, which was a pain to remove in the spring. Since then, we have added permanent, interlocking fastening systems on each window, and those can be obtained from the Energy Arsenal in Ivyland, Pennsylvania, 800-325-2826. This allows us to put the heat-shrink up, insert the spline, apply heat, and relax. Removal in spring is a snap. Yes, the heat-shrink does make a difference.

Damp Away dehumidifying crystals work well all year long and don't require any electricity. Most marina stores have them, but they are less expensive through Boat/U.S. Some mail-order catalogs have the dome style, which work equally well.

Plastic coat hangers or plastic coated ones are better than wooden. Wooden ones take up too much precious room in a hanging locker. Plastic drycleaning bags are good for your good clothes or clothes you don't wear that often.

We use a hanging laundry bag (with a spare so I can keep them clean along with the laundry). Fit a coat hanger at the top with a V-neck for putting the clothes inside. A zipper at the bottom allows you to unzip and let the clothes fall into either a tote or a laundry basket. I don't do laundry on board at the dock because it takes forever to fill the washer (plus I don't have direct hook-up to dock water since we have two separate tanks), and since the laundry up the street will do my clothes for eight cents a pound, I can't afford to fool with it on board.

Decisions, Decisions, Decisions…

You will find acrylic your best friend. Glasses, coasters, salt/pepper shakers, "dishes" for peanuts, etc. Plastic flatware with non-slip; silk flowers (there's even a spray that removes the dust!). Oh, your world will change for the better. You will surprise yourself at all you have to learn and how much you already know but haven't tapped yet.

So far the only disappointing thing both of us have found and we complain about (can't change it conveniently, so we don't complain much) is the lack of adequate lighting for reading, shaving, and going after zits. We would like to have less draft, but then we wouldn't have as much storage. Actually she is a perfect lady for us, and yes, she still talks to us.

Merilyn and John Piper

GONE CRUISING!

Sally Elizabeth Andrew and her friend are one of those lucky couples who heeded the message "Go now!" With combined backgrounds in anthropology and dockmastering, they cut their ties to the land, moved aboard, and headed out.

1990. The year we gave up our careers, steady "bankable" income, insurance benefits, friends, and television.

The year we left California and went cruising. The year we cut the ties that bound us to Monday to Friday, eight to five, "Cheers" each evening at seven on Channel 2, and "The Wonder Years" on Tuesday nights.

Thirtysomething and retired, well, sort of. Unemployed by choice. No children, ditto. With no fixed address. No fixed latitude. With one goal—to spend the next few years enjoying ourselves and each other. Sailing. Relishing our independence. Breaking from the temptation of conspicuous consumption and uncontrolled consumerism and the questionable ideal of upward mobility. Realizing our goal of independent mobility.

The announcement to our friends and co-workers of our impending departure was met with various responses. "That's great!" "You're crazy!" "How can you do this to me?" "Who will help us when you're gone?" Both our bosses understood and supported our decision. Neither asked "Why?" Our co-workers, however, felt somewhat let down and deserted. Who was going to be there to figure out why the computer was screwing up again?

Gently with the Tides

Not surprisingly, the hardest part of leaving Alameda, California, and the life we had come to love was saying good-bye to our friends, many of whom we should have spent more time with but were too busy with work and television. At our memorable bon voyage dock party, all we could do was quote Mr. Spock's Vulcan credo: "Live long and prosper—we'll send a postcard." We hid our sadness in leaving behind our friends' joy in seeing us finally make the transition.

Our cruise actually started seven years ago when we both decided on a commitment to future cruising. After we returned from a six-month sabbatical sailing in Mexico, we both went back to work determined to make enough money to finance our dream of cruising and a few years of independence. Since that time all our time has been directed toward making money, finding a larger boat, buying gear, and outfitting ourselves psychologically and emotionally and financially. All these aspects are equally important parts of a successful and happy cruise.

We're now able to live relatively cheaply, which makes me happy since most of our monthly budget is allocated to necessities such as food, fuel, charts, and occasional berthing. Our expenses average about $1,000 a month. But these expenses cannot be looked at in isolation. We are unemployed now, so no new money is coming into the coffers. We have put more than $70,000 into our Yamaha 33 during the last three years, most of which is money we will never see again because its only value is our use of the boat for the cruise. A lot of priceless time and effort have been put into planning, equipping, and customizing our boat so that we will be able to live aboard and cruise comfortably and safely.

Many of our friends have already gone cruising, some are still dreaming about it. Each of us has our own reason for wanting to go and our own expectations. But why have we, Foster and Sally, gone cruising? There's no single answer, no one reason. We didn't want to "get away from it all." Neither of us hated working and, in fact, Foster loved his job and the people he worked with so much that I had to practically break his arm to break him away. But we both wanted to sail to Alaska, and to points farther west and south. We wanted to live more simply.

The day-to-day realities of cruising change from journey to journey but are fundamental and predictable—weather and the concerns about wind, fog, tides; navigational headaches of finding secure anchorages and getting us there; provisioning with fuel, food, water, and books before running out; and keeping the engine and all other systems operating. These are quite different from our land-based priorities. For example, simple pleasures like cooking and eating, and reading and writing, assume a larger portion of our interest and energy when we are away from the city. And since a boat has a complex infrastructure, much time is devoted to keeping all systems—electrical, mechanical, rigging, plumbing—in tip-top shape.

It's a mistake to interpret our lifestyle as "playing," since there are very real dangers associated with cruising, as well as the obvious pleasures. The headaches associated with navigating from point A to point B are often survival oriented and, if not duly recognized, can affect our health and well-being and even endanger our lives. Little things mean a lot; miscalculating a tide may cost as little as a few hours of wasted time jogging into the current or as much as a hole in the bottom of our boat—our home. Our life now is about as real as it gets. Enough stressful things happen to make it real. We are not spending our time "playing."

Why have we chosen to be in limbo, neither working nor playing? We wanted to be independent for a while. We wanted to break away from the work-a-day world with its multitudinous headaches about minuscule problems. Granted, we could have stayed in California and kept working at becoming millionaires—and we both could have enjoyed working, but never forever. Both of us feel there is more to life than earning money just to accumulate goods and pay the bills. We wanted to break the cycle by accumulating enough money to afford freedom from work even if temporarily—the wealth to enjoy our health.

We're cruising because we get to do the things we like to do—sailing, hiking, being outdoors, being independent. The challenges and stresses of our quotidian life are now fairly basic unlike some of our friends'—we no longer have to deal with office politics, getting to work on time, putting up with bullshit simply to make ends meet. Our new priorities are: Do we have enough fuel? Is the weather going to get better or worse? Did I look at the chart carefully enough so I am not going to run us up on a rock?

But why now? Why not wait and buy a bigger boat and have more money to spend? A sailboat does not allow us to hang on to any possessions and toys. It's just big enough to be a home. A larger boat would have cost us several more years of painful employment, and we did not feel that the increase in size would be worth it. The costs associated with owning and operating a larger boat would have risen exponentially. We were anxious to make 1990 our year of departure, not the year 2000.

The world that we're off to see is rapidly disappearing. It's a world that in 20 years will be completely different, whether it's due to political changes, or ecological changes, or economic changes. The world is on a fast track. We want to see it now, before we're too old to enjoy it, before. . . .

Why sailing? Once our cruising-kitty goals were reached, we both realized that there were a lot of different options available—we could buy a mountain retreat, take a land cruise, do some extensive wilderness kayaking, take a luxury cruise on a liner around the world, or stick to Plan A and go sailing for a few years and several thousand miles. We opted for Plan A. It still felt like the right thing to do.

So are we contributing to society by going sailing? I've always felt that you can make a contribution by just getting out there and doing it. Letting other people see that you're doing it—and that dreams are possible—make it a contribution. We're not all Mother Teresas, dedicating our lives to helping mankind. Very few people are. Most of us spend our day-to-day lives working out our own little problems. The quality of life is what's important to us, and that's the choice we've made—to enjoy life to the fullest whether it's going sailing or returning to the big city and working.

Sally Elizabeth Andrew

Gently with the Tides

56

4
The Boat

WHEN IT COMES to boat styles, designs, specifications, and selection of on-board equipment, there are as many strong opinions as there are boaters. Periodically boating magazines will hold design contests for the perfect cruiser or racing/cruiser, and the results are usually an amalgam of wish lists and compromises. Those who live aboard their boats for any extended period of time share some of these same diversities of opinions, but in some respects they are surprisingly single-minded. For example, they may disagree on the best style or type of liveaboard boat, but most will agree on the overriding importance of storage space over cruising speed.

Slightly less than half of the liveaboards who currently own boats have chosen sailboats and motorsailers. Slightly more than one-third of the liveaboards have chosen powerboats, including cruisers, trawlers, and houseboats. About 20 percent of those interested in the liveaboard lifestyle are still in the planning and dreaming stages and have not yet made their final boat choice.

Obviously the choice of boat depends on a lot of factors, not the least of which is the deeply felt philosophical difference between sail and power. Another important factor is one's choice of cruising grounds. Whereas a motorsailer and sailboat are at home roaming the oceans, a trawler or house-boat is much more practical along the coast, in bays, lakes, waterways, and deltas.

The following are some responses to several years of surveys about living aboard.

Boat Size

Boat size seems to be a favorite statistic among liveaboards. Here the difference between sail and power is less distinct, with the exception of the much larger class of houseboats. Size is often a function of the crew's ability to handle the craft, especially in the close quarters of harbors, around docks, and crowded anchorages.

For liveaboards who usually operate their boats shorthanded, the average boat length is in the mid-30-foot range. Beams of 11 and 12 feet attest to the need for space and drafts of 4 to 5 feet or less reflect a desire for near-shore coastal cruising and gunkholing.

Age of Boats?

Another telling statistic is the age of liveaboard boats. The average liveaboard vessel was built in 1974 or 1975. And only nine percent of these boats are less than three years old. In a society accused of always exchanging their cars, tennis rackets, laundry soaps, and breakfast cereals for the latest, newest, and most improved, liveaboards seem content with the tried and true. The age of the boats also reflects a talent for the maintenance needed to keep them afloat, safe, and comfortable, and reinforces the need to be self-reliant.

Boat Materials

The overwhelming material of choice for boat hulls is fiberglass. More than 70 percent of the boats surveyed have hulls made of fiberglass, with 7 percent made of wood, another 7 percent made of steel, and the remaining split between aluminum and ferrocement.

Fewer than 1 percent of boats were reported to have a ferrocement hull. The small number of ferrocement boats is surprising in view of the backyard boatbuilding craze a few years ago that enticed so many dreamers to a life at sea.

Boat Features

One source of what constitutes a good liveaboard vessel is the response to "what is the most favorite and unfavorite feature of your boat." There is very little difference between the responses of sailboat and powerboat owners, with the obvious exception of sail performance and the performance of large motors.

Love-hate relationships are a frequent theme when favored and unfavored features are read together. For example, one owner loves his twin 350s power plant but complains of the lack of engine room space. Do you suppose if he had more room he would install triple 350s, and still complain? Another loves and hates the fact that his boat is made of wood. Similarly, another lists the teak trim as a favored feature and then complains about teak maintenance. One powerboater lists his motor as a favored feature when it works and his most unfavored feature when it balks.

By far the most popular feature was the layout of the vessel. Liveaboards have paid special attention to the design of their homes and have made the most of the limited space available. Among sailors, boat stability and sea-worthiness came in second as a favored feature. The most unpopular feature for both power- and sailboaters was some variant of the space problem. Lack of headroom, too little storage space, too few hanging lockers, and too small berths were the most frequent complaints.

Several liveaboards reported that they loved everything about their boats.

Choice of Boat Conveniences

There is an obvious conflict among liveaboards between getting away from it all and bringing it all on board. Many liveaboards have furnished their homes with all the modern conveniences, including freezers, microwaves, food processors, VCRs, and computers.

Powerboats with their greater power-plant capacity naturally lead in these onboard conveniences. Survey results indicate that, except for solar panels, wind generators, and computers, powerboats have more of everything. One sailing purist after checking off none of the conveniences wrote, "God. I feel deprived."

Navigation Equipment

Liveaboard homes are navigable vessels, as opposed to firmly rooted barge-like platforms, and often on the move. Therefore, navigation equipment and communications gear are important accessories. Almost all boats have VHF radios. The fewest boats have satellite navigation receivers. Sailboats appear better equipped for more adventurous offshore cruising with their higher percentage of sextants, RDF units, and Lorans. The need to communicate appears to be universal among liveaboards. There is an almost equal distribution of single-sideband transceivers between sail and power. Similarly, a significant number of boaters have ham licenses. In some instances both captain and mate have licenses.

There is no ideal boat design and no irreducible list of features and gadgets. The best one can do is listen to the experts—those who have made choices and *done it!*

LIVING ABOARD A GRAND BANKS

George Sass, an advertising executive, extols the virtues of the trawler design for its roominess and predictable, on-time passagemaking under power—a much sought-after feature for the busy boater with limited free time.

We're back. After a year of very pleasant and comfortable living in our restored house in historic Annapolis, Maryland, we've again moved aboard our Grand Banks 42, *Manitou.* For me, the decision to return to life afloat was easier than my original move aboard four years ago, because I knew what I was missing. I also understood that all the trivial inconveniences of living aboard were outweighed by the joy of living on the water. I had recently remarried, and my wife, Stacey, shared my love of boating and was looking forward to this alternative lifestyle.

Gently with the Tides

Years before my original move aboard, I had gone through life as a closet boater, wandering off to boatyards and marinas to walk the docks, looking at every boat and daydreaming about someday owning my own. In the evenings I would envy those who seemed so snug and cozy down below, envisioning that they were reading the great American novel if not writing it. During the day I felt drawn to the sanding, varnishing, and fitting out, imagining that everyone was getting ready for their 'round-the-world cruise. Eventually, I joined the ranks when I bought my first sailboat. I was hooked.

But I really came out of my closet when I bought a 1969 wooden Grand Banks 42 trawler to live aboard with my teenage son. It wasn't in the best of shape and there was a lot of work to do, but the price was right. Luckily, George Jr. had inherited my enthusiasm for boating and had already established himself as an able crewman on our Dickerson 37 ketch, and before that, on our 26-foot folkboat. Interestingly, I still think lovingly of that wonderfully seaworthy and simple pocket cruiser, and I probably had more fun-per-dollar on the folkboat than on any other boat. Do we ever learn that bigger is not always better?

The Switch from Sail to Power

After several years of cruising on my sailboats, I felt I needed the extra space and privacy that the Grand Banks offered if I was to live aboard successfully. Since I had every intention of cruising the Chesapeake Bay with my son, I also wanted a boat that the two of us could easily handle. I jumped ship from sail to power with some reservation. After years of cursing stinkpots that left me wallowing in their wake just as I was balancing a perfect wing 'n wing run, I suddenly felt like a traitor. When asked what kind of boat I had, I found myself almost apologizing and quickly qualifying my answer with, "I'm really a sailor, but I bought the Grand Banks to live on." Now, four years later, I haven't regretted the switch at all.

The most obvious benefit of switching to power is the amount of room we have. We have two separate staterooms with complete privacy. George Jr., who is now away most of the year at college, is comfortable and self-sufficient in the forward stateroom, having his own shower and head. Since he is an avid reader of every boating magazine and nautical book imaginable, we've added plenty of extra bookshelves and magazine racks for him. Little touches like brass oil lamps, teak-framed photographs of *Manitou*, and a great stereo system have made this his private sanctuary. Two glaring differences between this forward stateroom and most others on sailboats are the headroom and closet space. With 6 feet, 6 inches of headroom and a hanging locker you can practically walk in, you have the feeling you're in a room, not a cabin.

Our aft stateroom, even in its original configuration, is comfortable and spacious. Its head features a small, tiled bathtub, an abundance of storage space, and plenty of elbow room. Originally, it was furnished with two twin sea berths; we remodeled the stateroom after we were married to include a double berth. A small desk was added for a computer work station since our jobs require extensive writing. Again, there's a sense of being in a real room, because you stand up normally, you don't have to compensate for slanting floors, and you can see outside without having to stand on your toes. And, with the companionway opening to the afterdeck, one gets the feeling of having a porch or sun deck overlooking the water. This is not a bad way to wake up, or retire after a hard day's work.

The biggest difference between sailboat living and Grand Banks living is apparent in the main saloon. I loved my Dickerson 37, finishing the interior with beautifully varnished teak, custom upholstery, brass lamps and adding all kinds of nautical accessories. In fact, *Pentaquod* was photographed and featured in Ferenc Maté's *The World's Best Sailboats*. But there was always this undeniable feeling that I was "below" when cooking, eating, or relaxing. One literally and figuratively lost sight of what was going on outside. This is not a fault of the Dickerson (yes, I miss her), but it's a fact of life that being below on a typical sailboat is being down in an out-of-the-way, tunnel-like environment. Now some will say this is an advantage when sailing in the tropics because you get out of the glare and heat. Maybe this is so, but, personally, whenever I have the rare opportunity of sailing in the tropics, I like to see as much as I can.

The Grand Banks main saloon truly gives one the feeling of living on the water. The large windows offer nearly 360 degrees of vision even when sitting down, so you can easily look out at the ever-changing waterview. Cooking becomes a more pleasant chore, and dining is so much more enjoyable when you can take in the view. Now, when we visit friends on their sailboats, we have a difficult time adjusting to the lack of visibility. A friend of ours who also made the switch from sail to a Grand Banks says he feels like he's standing knee deep in water when he's back on a sailboat. If we ever switch back to sail, and we probably will at some point in our lives, we will definitely look for a pilothouse design that offers a good view.

Learning the Systems

While our Dickerson 37 was fairly well equipped, I was at first intimidated by the complexity of the systems on *Manitou:* two diesels, a diesel generator, two air conditioning systems, nine different water pumps, three batteries, plus an assortment of electronic accessories that had all seen better days. An aging intercom system that broadcast only static and engine noise, an autopilot that drove us in perfect circles, two depthmeters that never agreed, VHF radios that could barely communicate with each other, a radar that worked only when you hit it a certain way, a hailer that howled with feedback—all connected to miles and miles of wiring that had been cut, spliced, taped, and otherwise jury-rigged over the past 20 years by various owners. Discovering no less than a dozen extra wires hooked directly to the batteries, I felt as if I had awakened to an electrical nightmare. Having a background in electronics, I told myself not to panic and to just start somewhere. Four years later, almost everything works.

But the engines came first. Luckily, I had met the local Ford-Lehman service representative at a boat show, and he helped sort out all the engine problems, making some very wise modifications to bring these old but able engines up to date. They now have over 3,700 hours and are running stronger than ever. The cranky old Onan generator has never worked very well, even after replacing nearly every part. Gradually, I have been converting most of the 110-volt AC gear to 12 volts DC and plan eventually to replace the Onan with a 2,000-watt inverter to handle whatever AC needs I still have.

I continue to rewire parts of the boat and remove old wires that aren't connected to anything. Wires with splices have been replaced, and everything has been run to terminal strips for proper connections. All accessory equipment has been connected through an expanded DC panel with circuit breakers. I am still amazed that the previous owner didn't have an electrical fire or that the boat didn't disintegrate from rampant electrolysis.

One lesson I've learned from all this work is that when buying an aging boat with old electronics, you can count on replacing most of the equipment. The cost of new gear today is close to that of getting the old equipment repaired. And the biggest problem is finding technicians to work on old, obsolete gear. For a while I fought this modern tendency of junking old things and buying new ones, but I gave up in desperation. For example, I paid well over $200 for intercom repairs that were never satisfactory. Instead, I could have bought a new system with better performance for around $300.

Cruising Trawler Style

Do we miss sailing? Absolutely. But only parts of it. Let's face it, on how many days out of a 10-day cruise are the conditions right for a really good sail? A major part of the time the wind's either on the nose, "light and variable," or blowing so hard you've got your hands full changing the headsails, reefing, and simply holding on. Honestly, I think I've motored between Annapolis and New England as much as I've sailed. But we do miss sailing, so early last spring, after catching a severe case of cabin fever, we chartered a 33-foot sloop on the west coast of Florida for four days. We sailed 1½ days and had to motor the rest of the time. Now those few days of sailing were fabulous and worth the trip, but if we realistically consider how much we as sailors really motor, it's not such a big switch to cruising à la trawler style.

The Boat

Cruising by trawler has several advantages besides those relating to comfort. For one, we can plan our trips for more precise times of arrival and departure. Now this may sound contrary to the way of the cruising life, but for us, knowing we can be in port within a certain hour gives us much more freedom and a wider choice of destinations. Our cruising speed is a modest 8½ knots, not much faster than our Dickerson 37, but we now travel directly to our destination without concern for where the wind is coming from.

We've seen a lot more of the Chesapeake Bay in the past 4 years than in the previous 10 years of sailing. We've discovered that another advantage of cruising à la trawler is the freedom to do a variety of things while underway. Being a bit more relaxed while motoring than if under sail, the captain and crew can choose to catch up on some reading or get to those fix-it projects that are put off while in home port. We've arrived in port with a shortened maintenance list, ready to explore and enjoy the new sights. And, we've had hard-core sailors join us for a weekend and do nothing but cruise and snooze in total relaxation.

Now that we are experienced in both sail and power cruising, I find the differences between the two to be more imagined than real. After all, the common denominator, the reason for any boating, is to be out on the water. We enjoy gunkholing and watching beautiful sunsets as we fire up the barbecue and indulge in a cold thirst-quencher, whether we're on a friend's sloop or our Grand Banks. And to minimize these differences, we've even added a steadying sail. I guess one never gets over that feeling of hauling the halyard and raising sail.

Now, let's see, where are those brochures of the globe-circling pilothouse cutters we saw at the show?

George Sass

Our Nauticat

Motorsailers are a cross between sailboats and motorboats. Many will say that the cross doesn't work—you get the worst of both worlds. Henry Clew and his wife would argue with that sentiment. In fact they virtually sing their praises of the Nauticat 33.

We bought our Nauticat 33 after spending almost a year searching for the "perfect boat." To us, this meant a comfortable, liveaboard vessel seaworthy enough for some serious (although mostly coastal) voyaging. Our experience with our previous Ted Brewer–designed 32-foot cutter (an "EO-32" built in Taiwan) convinced us that we needed an inside steering position for really civilized cruising comfort in all kinds of weather. Also, since we planned some long passages on inland waterways, we wanted a boat that motored well. We were not, however, willing to give up sailing, as we still consider this a most enjoyable part of cruising life.

We started out looking at boats in the 36- to 40-foot range, assuming from our previous experience that we would need at least this much size for comfortable liveaboard space. What we found was that boats of this size with inside steering were scarce and expensive—as in more than $100,000 for a decent one. Also, we discovered that there are very few boats that truly offer the option of sailing comfortably from either the inside or outside position. Generally, if the inside position is really good and usable there is minimal visibility from the outside station. Then we came across a Nauticat 33 and were amazed at the amount of usable space this little boat had. She really has four separate cabins: a large aft cabin with good headroom, two berths, and lots of storage; a large pilothouse with a fantastic view even while sitting down; a main cabin with galley and convertible dinette; and an enclosed forepeak with twin berths. We were also impressed with the large fuel and water capacities—160 and 120 gallons respectively.

We took a brief trip to Finland to visit the Nauticat factory: Siltala Yachutsz, OY, located in Riihikoski (near Turku) on the Baltic Sea. The trip was thoroughly enjoyable—we saw hundreds of Nauticats—and we were very impressed with the professionalism of the factory. While there, we were able to make a few custom changes that make the boat more desirable from our point of view. We added a number of opening ports (they don't worry too much about hot weather in Finland), and we added a large hatch in the aft cabin that also serves to increase headroom. We also had them install dinghy davits on the stern, as there really isn't a good place to stow a dinghy aboard this boat without blocking visibility from the inside position.

Our new boat arrived at Elizabeth, New Jersey, and we picked her up there directly off the freighter. We motored to Mamaroneck, New York, where we had the masts stepped, then we sailed on up the coast to Newport, Rhode

Island, and Marblehead, Massachusetts, where the boat was hauled and stored for the winter—but not until early December! This is certainly a boat to extend the cruising season. On several occasions, we sailed—and even spent the night aboard—in below-freezing weather, and we certainly found the diesel-fired central heat much to our liking.

Over the winter we spent many weekends down at Marblehead installing equipment and generally commissioning the boat. One of the first items to go on was an Autohelm 5000 autopilot with a remote control at the outside steering position. This unit has proven invaluable in our cruising, as it keeps the boat on a steady course under virtually all conditions, and it relieves the helmsperson of much drudgery. In fact, it's almost as good as another crewmember, better in some respects—it doesn't eat and it keeps its mouth shut! The autopilot also allows the boat to be singlehanded very effectively, if necessary, as when the crew is asleep or seasick.

Other equipment installed on our Nauticat includes a VHF, satnav, speed/log, wind machine, and depthsounder. The latter three have repeaters outside in a pod on the pilothouse roof so as to be visible from the aft steering position. Finally, we also installed a rudder-angle indicator, a stereo/tape deck, an anchor windlass, and numerous 115-volt AC and 12-volt DC outlets throughout the boat.

It was a busy winter! The boat we chose was the standard long-keel ketch-rigged Nauticat 33 with bowsprit. We picked the long-keel version for its 4-foot draft, and we're glad we did. We've had great fun getting into shallow spots where many sailboats can't go. I also like the ruggedness and protection of the fully attached rudder and enclosed propeller. The other option offered by Siltala is the "fin keel" version, which has a 5-foot draft and presumably slightly better upwind performance, as it also comes with a $4^{1}/_{2}$-foot-taller mast and a bit more sail area.

Sails and Sailing Performance

As for sails, we chose the factory main, mizzen, and #1 genoa (120 percent) as well as a small storm jib that rigs to a removable inboard forestay. This arrangement works very well, as it eliminates the nuisance of having to pull the genoa around the forestay as is done on most cutters whenever you tack. We installed a roller-furling system on the headstay, and we use this for the genoa. It works so well, in fact, that we have never used the storm jib (except to test it). One reason for its success is that Hood sewed into the genoa luff a tapered piece of foam that causes the sail to roll very smoothly, making it quite usable at any stage of furling. This is the first roller reefing with which we've been completely satisfied. The line drive operates smoothly and effortlessly under most conditions.

Wherever we go, people are always curious about our boat. The first question they invariably ask is, "How does she sail?" My usual answer is,

"Better than she looks as though she would!" The truth is, the boat sails very respectably—for a cruising boat. Obviously she's no racer, and her upwind performance is less than spectacular. With the genoa flying we tack about 85 degrees but usually end up making good something over 90 degrees. Truthfully, we don't spend much time beating into the wind—I doubt that many cruising sailors do. When the apparent wind gets close to 45 degrees we generally turn on the engine. By dropping the genoa we can keep the remaining sails full as close as 30 degrees into the wind.

As for general sailing performance, the boat is quite satisfactory. It is reasonably easy to balance the helm under most conditions, and the boat has the steadiness and feel of a 40-footer. Initially fairly tender, she stiffens quickly as she heels. We can hold full sail, with the 120 percent genoa, on a close reach up to a 20-knot wind without putting the rail under or losing rudder control. The boat does tend to head up as she heels, so eventually you run out of rudder—it tells you it's time to shorten sail. In a freshening wind we often begin by dousing the mizzen, as this greatly relieves the weather helm. Next comes furling of the genoa followed by a reef in the main. Downwind, we'll drop the main altogether (in 30-knot winds) and let the genoa pull us along at $6^1/_2$ to 7 knots.

As for speed under sail, 5 knots is easily achieved in an 8- to 10-knot breeze and $6^1/_2$ knots seems to be about tops under good sailing conditions—the boat loves 15- to 20-knot winds. The Nauticat's speed under sail may be a knot slower than a racing boat of the same size, but it's not bad for a palatial cruiser.

Basically, I feel that whatever the boat may lack in sailing performance, it more than makes up for with its strong motoring ability. Most sailors don't admit it, but they do a heck of a lot of motoring—and most sailboats motor abominably! The Nauticat will power at 8 knots into a 30-knot wind. That's what I call impressive upwind performance!

The hull shape of the Nauticat 33 makes her a very efficient "traveler." We have motored into some very large seas without problems. The high, flared bow keeps the spray down and the rounded high stern makes the boat impossible to "poop" in the following sea. The propeller seems to be well placed, as it has never shown signs of cavitation even in the roughest seas.

Under power the boat is very maneuverable. She will even answer the helm in reverse! We have not found the extra windage of the pilothouse to be a problem—although many people ask about this. I'm sure it's a negative factor in upwind sailing, but under power, we're a heck of a lot sleeker than your average powerboat—and probably a good bit more maneuverable. The two of us can easily dock the boat. This, to us, is one of the big advantages of a "small" boat versus a bigger, heavier, less efficient model.

Accommodations

As I mentioned earlier, we chose the Nauticat largely because of its ample accommodations. We generally sleep in the spacious aft cabin, which we find very comfortable. Without the optional overhead hatch the headroom is just under 6 feet, so I definitely recommend this option for 6-footers. There is ample storage under the bunks as well as aft into the pointed stern. We also have a five-drawer compartment located beneath a night table between the two 6½-foot bunks and a small hanging locker with shelves inside. The NC-33 is also available with a large double bunk in the aft cabin as well as an additional head—an option worth considering.

In the pilothouse, we have a small table and cushioned seats for four to six people. The pilothouse is a source of constant joy to us, as there is a 360-degree panoramic view from this area—even while comfortably seated. The large sliding sunroof provides light, ventilation, and excellent visibility of the sails whether opened or closed. The chart table is enormous, and underneath there is enough storage for all our charts—and we have quite a few.

The main cabin is three steps down and has just 6-foot headroom, although there are places where a 6-footer can bump his head—you learn where they are quickly! We have the "Option B" dinette, which is comfortable for six people and converts to a large double bed—still leaving the passageway clear. The galley along the starboard side has a large, top-loading refrigerator (we requested this), double sink, and propane stove with oven. There is storage below, behind, and above the counter.

Forward to port is the head and across from it is a large hanging locker with shelves inside and a shelf on top (just big enough for a 9-inch color TV). The head is comfortable and includes a telephone booth–type shower stall and floor drain. Finally, the forward cabin consists of two 6½-foot V-berths with storage underneath as well as above along the sides. Generally, when we have guests, they adopt the forepeak. This gives us each privacy and leaves the dining table available for use at any time.

The Nauticat 33 is a unique boat. No other boat that we know of (except larger Nauticats) offers such excellent visibility from both inside and outside steering positions. We find ourselves using both positions almost equally (depending on weather) and, having experienced this versatility, we would find it hard to go back to an "ordinary" boat. The Nauticat 33 has a tremendous amount of space considering its compact exterior dimensions. And, to top it off, it's a quality act. The boat really looks and feels like a small yacht—rather than a plastic bathtub. The feedback from having built almost a thousand of these little ships over the past 15 years really helps. Of course, all this doesn't come cheap.

One reason the boat looks as good as it does is the lavish use of exterior teak. Keeping all the trim varnished is a lot of work (we know), but it does

The Boat

Gently with
the Tides

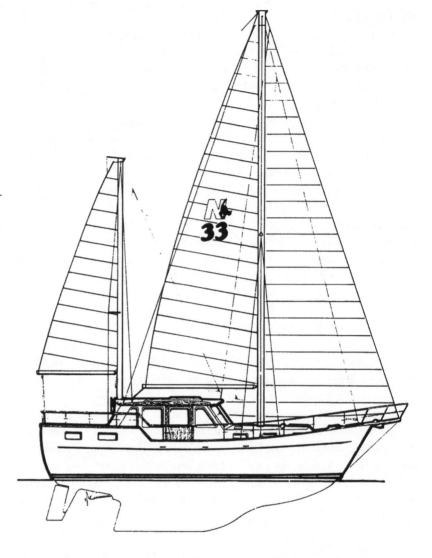

look great! An alternative is simply to let the teak weather naturally or to oil it occasionally (as we do with the decks). You can always spruce it up before you sell it! I don't believe any permanent harm is done to the teak by ignoring it and letting it turn silver-gray.

Cruising in a sailboat doesn't have to be cold and wet and cramped—or is that part of the mystique? How many people would select an automobile with no top for a cross-country trip? Yet, for some reason, the same logic is not applied to a cruising sailboat.

Henry Clew

THE FOLTIS 60

Constantine Foltis wanted to duplicate the amenities of a two-bedroom, two-bathroom apartment in a sturdy steel-hulled ketch with world cruising potential. He looked around at the available boats and decided to design his own.

Acquiring this boat is fulfilling the first part of a lifelong dream. This dream was to design a world-sailing cruiser—large and comfortable enough to live aboard graciously anywhere year-round—and have it built, then to cruise the world aboard it. I say this is the first part of the dream, because the boat is still under construction as of this writing.

After a lifetime of sailing in all kinds of sailboats and 30 years as a naval architect designing merchant ships for the U.S. Maritime Administration, I thought I would try my hand at designing my dream yacht. It started out as pure fantasy and merely a design exercise. Something like this could never work out, I said to myself, so it did not matter how big and expensive it would be. Paper is cheap.

Since it would be a home afloat, I designed the interior living spaces first, with most of the room and modern conveniences of a two-bedroom, two-bath apartment. I added an enclosed wheelhouse—it's cold out on the ocean, even in summer—and a walk-in engine room. After drawing a boat outline around all these features, I was rather surprised to find it was only 60 feet long. Oh well, it was only on paper, so it did not matter that the costs would be beyond my means. I continued to develop the design, using the commercial steel-hull design procedures I was familiar with, investigating various types of rigs that could be easily singlehanded in a vessel of this size, and checking out draft and overhead restrictions in some of the more well known inland waterways popular with cruisers.

It seemed that my fantasy had gotten out of control, and it began to take on a rather frightening reality. It was frightening because it was a first effort of this type, and I was not sure of the ultimate costs. We're still not sure.

To keep costs down, I decided to use commercial tugboat/fishing boat standards of workmanship, leaving off some finishing touches found on "gold-platers." I then continued in earnest to complete the design.

Shortly after construction started I met Helen, who was to be my wife. She was enthralled by my plans to live aboard and sail around the world. With her advice on the interior, we worked out the last of the details.

The Rig

The boat is rigged as a staysail ketch. There are five sails, all of moderate area. The four lower sails can be raised, trimmed, and stowed from the cockpit by a

The Boat

singlehanded sailor. The fifth sail, the main trysail, requires two persons but need only be set under light conditions. All sails except the roller-furling jib are self-tending. Three of the self-tending sails are also self-vanging. The lines for all five sails lead to either a powered capstan on the after cabin top or the anchor windlass, warping head forward, as well as to manual winches; therefore, all running rigging may be handled electrically if desired.

The masts are on tabernacles and can be raised and lowered by the crew for convenience in inland waterway cruising, a special option required by our travel plans. Hull draft of our boat is restricted by the limits of the European canal system, using a full shallow keel with narrow "wings" to help minimize leeway losses when closehauled. Other hulls could have deeper keels if shallow draft is not required. A deeper keel, either full-length or modified fin, would provide much better windward performance, allow the boat to carry more sail, and might decrease displacement by reducing ballast requirements. Conventional ketch, schooner, or cutter rigs can be fitted to other hulls with deeper keels, if desired.

Continuous speed under power is over 8 knots. Maximum speed under sail should exceed 10 knots. The 135 h.p. Perkins diesel provides efficient auxiliary propulsion with a 3:1 reduction gear and 31-inch diameter feathering three-bladed propeller, which is equally efficient in either forward or reverse. Use of such a large, efficient propeller is made practical by its feathering action when not rotating, which causes almost no drag when under sail.

The box keel structure is especially heavy and encloses the ballast, which is of lead pigs set in concrete. Most of the keel structure is below the canoe body and acts as additional ballast, but it has not been included in the ballast weight. Modern sand blasting and finishing techniques provide low maintenance. Deck and cabins are of steel and are welded to the hull, assuring a virtually leak-proof structure. All fittings are welded to the hull or bolted to welded studs or brackets, minimizing leak-prone deck penetrations. Hull, deck, and cabins are insulated with $2^{1}/_{2}$ inches of fireproof fiberglass insulation and lined with light-colored hardwoods for maximum comfort. Full climate control with central air conditioning and diesel-fired central heat provide comfortable all-weather living.

Steering is dual hydraulic, with a steering station inside an air-conditioned and heated wheelhouse for inclement weather and one in the cockpit for fair-weather sailing. Navigation gear is in the wheelhouse.

The Interior

The accommodations are divided, with the galley, dining, and lounge areas amidships and the staterooms at the ends, each with a head and shower. We will sleep in the great cabin aft. The forward area can be used as a suite or as two staterooms, depending on the way accordian-fold bulkheads and door are positioned. We expect to use this space as an office and work area when onboard alone. Headroom is 6 feet, 6 inches in most areas, including the wheelhouse.

The galley is fitted with all the conveniences of home: propane gimballed stove and oven, double sink, dishwasher, refrigerator, freezer, icemaker, microwave, and enough electric power to run these and most other common household appliances. Just aft of the galley area are a clothes washer, dryer, and trash compactor. There is pressurized hot and cold fresh water. Large stainless steel storage tanks, a reverse-osmosis water maker, and specially designed rain catchment gutters on the cabintops assure a plentiful supply of fresh water.

A diesel generator provides the power to run major 110-volt AC electric loads and to charge a large 12-volt DC battery bank. An inverter allows moderate 110-volt AC loads to run off battery power when the generator is not running and the boat is away from shore power. The boat's basic electric service is 12-volt DC, other than the household appliances listed. A wind generator and

The Boat

The Foltis 60.

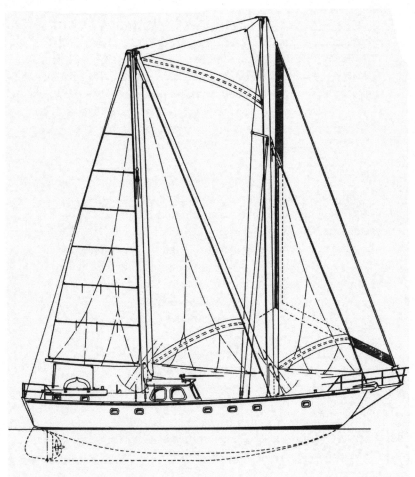

solar voltaic charger will supply a small 12-volt DC current to trickle-charge the battery bank. A walk-in, soundproof engine room houses the diesel propulsion engine and auxiliaries. Ample room around all equipment provides for convenient inspection and maintenance, plus a large workbench. The cockpit floor is a bolted watertight hatch that can be removed for major maintenance work, such as lifting the engine straight up and out.

The boat is still operable and liveable if all electrical systems fail. The sails may all be operated manually. Foot pumps for fresh and salt water are fitted in the galley and both head wash basins to provide non-pressurized water. The fail-safe outside solenoid shut-off valve on the propane storage tanks can be manually bypassed for cooking. Oil lamps provide emergency lighting. No external power is required for steering, but in case of hydraulic system failure, there is an emergency steering gear operable with a tiller on the aft cabintop.

With the help of the wind, rain, and occasional provisioning stops, we're all set to see the world on our Foltis 60 liveaboard home.

Constantine Foltis

BACK TO THE FUTURE: THE MODERN CHINESE JUNK RIG

*When I first started looking for a sailboat as a cruising and liveaboard
vessel, I diverted my attention from traditional sloops, schooners, and
ketches and focused on the Chinese junk rig. I knew from the start that
most of my sailing would be done shorthanded, and I wanted something
that was easily handled and comfortable.*

In his wonderfully illustrated book *Ships of China*, Valentin Sokoloff tells us that "A hand crafted sailing ship is a living thing with its own character and charm. A Chinese junk is even more so, and no wonder, as it was invented by an offspring of a nymph and a rainbow. His name was Fu Hsi, the first great ruler who, they say, was born in 2852 B.C. Then Lu Pan, founder of the art of carpentry, greatly improved the original design. Further generations of Chinese shipwrights gave Chinese junks their final seaworthy and practical shape."

When one has
Good wine,
A graceful junk
And a maiden's love,
Why envy the immortal Gods?

Li Po

The evolution of sailboat design in the West has taken place over a much shorter period of time and on a much different tack. Today the epitome of Western design is represented by America's Cup contenders and similar high-tech boats in the singlehanded CSTAR (transatlantic), the singlehanded BOC (around the world) Challenge, and the Whitbread 'round-the-world crewed race. Shades of these Bermuda-rigged competitors are seen in virtually every racing and cruising boat to come off the showroom floor. For the most part, the emphasis in these designs is speed and particularly performance to windward. There are obviously other aspects to sailing, especially to cruising. And that is where the Chinese junk-rigged boat comes in.

Several crusading Western sailors and boat designers, including Thomas Colvin, Angus Primrose, Blondie Hasler, Jock McLeod, and Alan Boswell, have long seen the distinct advantages of the Chinese balanced-lug rig as being far superior to the conventional rig, especially for shorthanded sailing and comfortable cruising. They have succeeded in marrying the basic junk design features with modern materials, replacing bamboo and grass mats with aluminum alloy and Dacron.

The resulting modern junk rig is designed for the family crew, single-hander, or shorthanded cruising sailors. The junk rig can be easily handled without requiring strength or endurance, and without leaving the safety of the cockpit. Sailing with this rig can be relaxed, enjoyable, and safe. It is a rig that is easily reefed, efficient for self-steering, and can do anything that modern rigs can do with much less strain on the crew or the boat. Foremost, it is a rig for a seamanlike passage: safe, quick, comfortable, and with the easiest ability to handle any sailing emergency likely to be encountered.

Elements of the Junk Sail

At first sight the rig's unusual appearance, as shown by the typical sail plan, may be confusing to the Western eye, but in effect it is extraordinarily simple, clever, and extremely easy to handle. The lug sails have full-length battens that lie across the width of the sail, from luff to leech, and divide the sail into panels. The top batten is the yard, which is a heavier spar than the other battens and takes the full weight of the sail. The bottom batten is the boom, which takes very little loading and therefore need be no stronger than the other battens. The head of the sail is secured to the yard, and the sail is raised from the cockpit by hauling on the halyard, which includes a purchase system between the yard and masthead. The sail is held to the mast by batten parrels that run loosely around the mast at each batten. The luff of the sail always lies on the same side of the mast and extends forward of the mast, making it a balanced lug sail. On one tack the sail lies against the mast and is held off the mast by the battens. On the other tack, the sail hangs away from the mast and is held by the rope parrels. A multiple topping lift system—lazyjacks—passes under the boom and lies on both sides of the sail, forming a cradle that holds the sail when it is reefed or furled.

Two additional parrel lines are led back to the cockpit to control the fore and aft position of the sail. The yard parrel is used to bring the yard snugly

The junk sail.

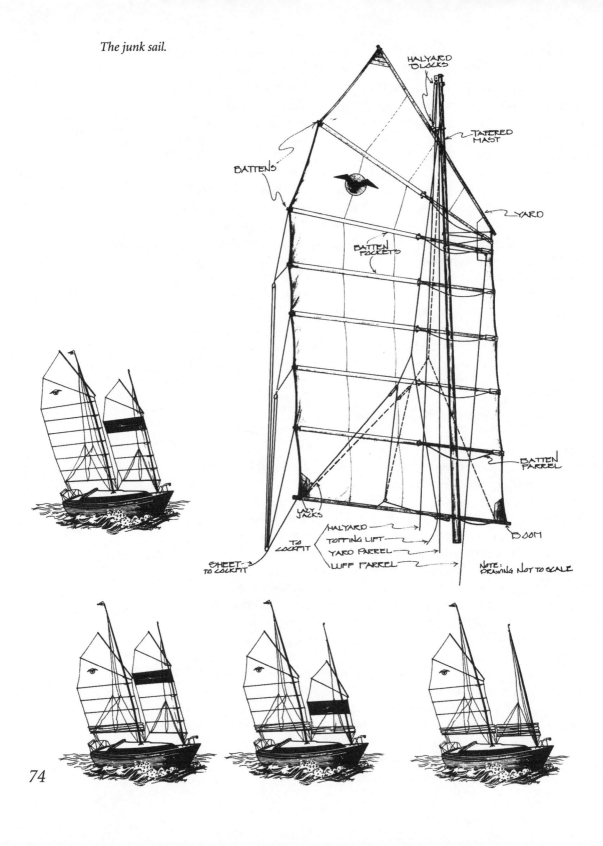

HALYARD BLOCKS

TAPERED MAST

BATTENS

YARD

BATTEN POCKETS

BATTEN PARREL

LAZY JACKS

BOOM

SHEET TO COCKPIT

TO COCKPIT

HALYARD
TOPPING LIFT
YARD PARREL
LUFF PARREL

NOTE: DRAWING NOT TO SCALE

74

against the mast. This is important only when the sail is reefed and would have a tendency to swing aft of the mast. Similarly, a luff parrel line is used to prevent the sail from swinging too far forward of the mast and to maintain tension on the luff. Both of these lines are used to shift the position of the sail and fine-tune the rig.

A single sheet system controls the after end of the boom and the five lower battens by a system of spans (sheetlets) and blocks. This gives control over the entire leech of the sail, not just the boom, and reduces the twist of the sail. The main part of the sheet system is one long length of line that runs through blocks and forms a purchase system so that loading on the tail end is light.

The portion of the balanced lug sail forward of the mast performs an important function contributing to the safety and comfort of this rig. When the wind and boat direction conspire to create an accidental jibe, the small portion of the sail in front of the mast actually dampens the motion of the sail and therefore slows down an otherwise violent motion. Both intentional and accidental jibing become much less hair-raising.

The lug-rig mast is stepped through the deck to the keel and is designed to stand unsupported. The loadings are taken at the partners where they pass through the deck and at the heel of the mast where they are stepped on the keel. The hull and deck are reinforced in these areas. However, the loadings on the hull are less than those imposed by conventional rigs, with taut shrouds and highly tensioned forestay and backstay, which combine to produce tremendous compression loading on the mast and stresses on the hull.

The combination of battens, parrels, and topping lifts makes the lug sail the fastest and easiest of all to handle and reef. To reef a lug sail, the halyard is eased from the safety of the cockpit and the sail comes down rapidly under its own weight between the lazyjacks, which collect the sail and hold it on top of the boom. The battens prevent the sail from billowing out, and their own weight, plus the sheet system, keeps them down. This makes it unnecessary to tie any reef points or to handle the sailcloth in any way. As soon as the halyard is eased and the sail starts to lower, the sheets get progressively slacker, the sail starts to spill the wind, and the boat begins to weathercock. Unlike other sails, the lug sail will not flog and damage itself. Being able to raise and lower sails like Venetian blinds provides an infinite combination of sail plans to balance the rig. The ability to vary sail area over a wide range of fore-and-aft sail combinations is especially helpful to the boat's tracking ability and the efficient use of automatic wind-vane steering.

Performance

How does the lug rig perform? It gives up some efficiency to windward but regains it in effortless tacking maneuvers and in superior running and reaching. And according to William F. Buckley, Jr., author of *Airborne*, "Gentlemen do not sail to windward." Off the wind the battens spread the sails for maximum surface area. This is especially important in light air when conventional sails have a tendency to collapse. However, apart from speed, the rig provides exceptional performance characteristics, including:

- **More Comfortable Upright Ride**—because the round-sectioned, free-standing mast is designed to be flexible so that it bends rather than the boat heeling. It acts as a giant shock absorber for the sudden forces of wind and sea. Sailing becomes less tiring and more enjoyable.
- **Less Hazardous Sail**—for the shorthanded sailor or the family crew because all sail handling can be done from the safety and the comfort of the cockpit. There is no acrobatic deck work and tacking is just a matter of ignoring the sheets and putting the tiller over.
- **More Stowage Space Below Decks**—because the sails are permanently rigged and there is no need for extra sails.
- **Peace and Quiet**—for the experienced sailor and the novice because the fully battened sails do not flog noisily and the control lines do not slap the deck like the Bermuda foresail sheets when tacking.
- **Less Wear and Tear**—because of less tension in the control lines, sails, and spars. Chafe and wear on lines and blocks is minimal and gear lasts longer.
- **Simple Construction and Maintenance**—is made possible with flat-cut sails, simple but reliable knots and splices in the rigging, and commonly used materials and engineering. Repairs are simple and materials are readily and cheaply available anywhere in the world.
- **Big Safety Factor**—because the failure of a single pin or shackle cannot bring down the mast. There is no highly stressed standing rigging. Heavy weather sailing is safer, more comfortable, and less of a strain on the hull and crew.
- **Many Sails in One**—because the Chinese junk rig can match every combination of foresail and mainsail with an infinite variety of settings. Compared with a Bermuda rig it is slightly less efficient to windward, but off the wind the fully battened sails are more efficient because they present more effective sail area and have no tendency to collapse in light airs.
- **Less Anxiety Over the "Man Overboard" Drill**—because the sails drop in seconds, by gravity alone, when the halyards are released. This can all be accomplished from the safety of the cockpit and the sails are automatically stowed with the booms in the topping lift systems.
- **Less Fear of Accidental Jibes**—because the balanced lug sail dampens the otherwise violent swings of the sail and boom during a controlled or accidental jibe.

- **Off-Wind Efficiency**—because full-length battens spread the sails for maximum effective sail area. Together with ease of tacking, the increased off-wind efficiency compensates for any loss in windward performance.

The key features of the Chinese junk rig are ease of handling, simplicity of use, and self-furling for the shorthanded crew. These features may not contribute to an America's Cup contender but they do add up to safe, relaxed, and efficient cruising with an emphasis on comfortable and safe passage-making. The junk rig may not be the answer for everyone, but it is an interesting alternative to the Bermuda-rigged cruiser.

The Boat

SOME THINGS WORK AND SOME THINGS DON'T

Ted and Ann Gordon, with dreams of summer vacations in New England waters and winter cruising in the Bahamas, caution that when buying a semicustom boat, like their Tayana 37, some things work and some things don't.

The Tayana 37 is a wonderful boat for cruising; it's a stable double-ender with full keel and 20,000 pounds displacement. This was the boat we wanted. We were taken with her pleasing lines and exquisite teak joinery work and finish. It was roomy—more room than we had ever had before. How could we ever fill it? And it was new; we could order just what we wanted—from cabin layout to winch placement on deck. After suffering the requisite months of anguish and indecision, we ordered hull #522, our first brand new boat.

The Tayana is built in Taiwan by the Ta Yang yards and is ordered in the U.S. through a local importer, who has the job of helping buyers specify the exact boat design that will be built and delivered. This is one of the joys of buying a new boat; within limits, and money permitting, you can get what you want. Some boats come in alternate configurations—select model A or B; but the Tayana comes like a blank slate. The alternatives are almost infinite. As soon as you've paid your deposit you specify *your* boat in great detail, but the gods and fate still play a big role in determining what's finally produced. There's always a slip or two between down payment and delivery. And we found out that what seemed so logical and right in design concept may not work out as planned. Therein lies this tale: how our boat evolved and how what we wanted changed when we saw it in the flesh, or at least in real fiberglass and teak.

Here's what we chose: a cutter as opposed to a ketch, on the basis of simpler sail handling. The cabin consisted of a double berth up forward rather than a V-berth because we thought it would be simpler to make the bed, an enclosed quarter berth aft to provide our guests with a modicum of privacy, a galley at the companionway, and an aft-facing nav station opposite the galley. The saloon table was fixed with a drop leaf surrounded by an L-shaped settee, and another settee opposite. We opted for propane to fuel a three-burner gimballed stove and cabin heater. The mast was to be deck-stepped to minimize any deck leakage and a 30-h.p. Yanmar diesel was selected for auxiliary power. One thing that we really wanted was placement of engine controls near the helm. The standard design had the controls on the cockpit bulkhead near the companionway and out of reach.

We wanted to be able to call for engine power quickly in tight situations. We wanted a mass—more than that, a crowd—of drawers behind the settee cushions for everything that had to be stored, from tools to silverware. Most of the electronic equipment was scheduled for installation in the U.S. during commissioning, but we planned where everything would go so that we were sure there would be enough room in the nav station panels. On deck, we thought through the winch sizing and placement, the layout of the running rigging, the deck material (fiberglass, if you please), and the companionway cover (teak would be fine). There was more, much more, in this process of selection and design. And it was fun.

Through luck, Ted had a trip in the Far East two weeks before hull #522 was scheduled to be shipped, and he stopped over at the yard in Kow Chung. It was a scene of great industry. People swarming all over the boat in an obvious frenzy to complete it before the shipment date. It sure looked like our design, but there were a few small differences. Like the mast: It was keel-stepped. Like the engine controls: They were in the standard place, far from the helm. And while he didn't have the dimensions with him, the spot for the cabin heater looked much too small, and the cutout for the stove seemed too narrow. Much discussion, in English and gesture, followed with their engineers. Nothing could be done about the mast; keel-stepped was stronger, anyway. The engine controls might be moved, but it was a big job and involved extending all of the engine wiring and mechanical connections. We settled for a parallel engine start switch near the helmsman's knee. Because he was sure that the heater space was too small, we redesigned the cabinet on which it was to mount. As for the stove cutout, we'd wait and see. (It turned out to be too small for the stove we had selected, so we switched later to a two-burner model.)

Don't get us wrong, the boat was magnificent. The helmsman's seat was a work of art. The stanchions were gleaming and braced against the bulwark like a brick fort, and the winches were placed and sized as planned. The layout looked terrific, and the boat had happy owners.

After 18 months, some of it in extended cruising (the Intracoastal Waterway, the Florida Keys, and the Bahamas), we really liked some of our choices. Other decisions were simply wrong. First of all, the next time we'll have the yard install most of the major equipment, like the stove, heater, and propane system, rather than installing these systems during commissioning. The factory can build-in what has to be built-in, and sizing mistakes won't survive this process. Sometimes they can get better prices, too.

We had our salesman perform the commissioning, and this, in retrospect, was a bad decision. We think that this was his first, or close to his first, post-delivery assembly. Simple things took too long. Tubing kinked where it shouldn't have, and quality suffered.

The assembly job is inevitably complicated by the fact that the factory is halfway around the world. Things that the factory supplied fit together very well, but the trouble came in the installation of the new equipment. We became so dismayed by the process that we took the boat before it was finally commissioned, gave it a sea trial, had a surveyor look it over, and finished it ourselves. It became *Candide,* after Voltaire's character who was always searching for the best of all possible worlds. That crowd of drawers didn't work out so well, either. We found that drawers are neat, all right, but nothing taller than the drawer itself can fit. So on one unforgettable Saturday I attacked the drawers, made large cutouts and plywood covers, and converted the space behind the port settee into a major storage hold, the "cave," which can now take a pot for boiling lobsters. The double bed in the forward compartment is probably just as hard to make as a V-berth would have been, and when heeling there is sometimes a lee edge that can dump the resting person. On deck we would have chosen to have even less teak, if possible.

In the class of "I wish we had done it at the start rather than later" are the electric windlass (we started with a manual one), the all-chain rode (we started with a chain-rope combination), and the air conditioner, which we found a near necessity in the Southern summer, fuel- and water-tank gauges to replace the original unreadable dipsticks, and a 100-amp generator to replace the inadequate factory standard 30-amp device.

We bought and installed an integrated set of instruments: knotmeter, depthmeter, and wind speed and direction indicator. The main instrument is mounted at the nav station and is repeated via digital cable at the helm. The setup is ideal except for one fault. When one instrument goes out, they can all go out. Sending the main unit back to the factory (twice) blinded us completely.

The wiring to the nav station instruments turned out to be too puny, so it was replaced. The compressor unit for the 12-volt refrigerator was badly placed behind one of the settees, but moving it to the deep lazarette has apparently solved the matter. Access to the lazarette is constrained, we wish there were more room to climb down. In making the mods to the boat, we learned another lesson that others before us have learned as well: When a yard is to make mods, always get a firm price before the work starts. Many things

*Gently with
the Tides*

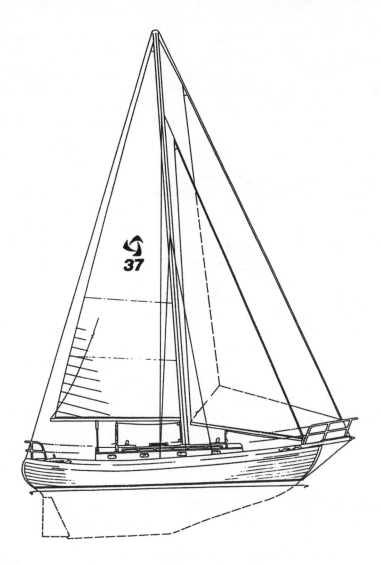

worked out well. The overall layout is better than most, even though the next time privacy for our quarterberth guests won't be a high priority. The prism we mounted in the deck over the shower lights up the whole head area. The opening ports and hatches are a delight, although we've given up on cleaning the bronze. The enclosed shower is what we had hoped it would be. The no-leak stuffing box doesn't leak. The Yanmar just runs and runs (where's some wood to knock on?). The stainless water and fuel tanks are adequately sized and well placed amidships. The arched helmsman's seat gives visibility that otherwise would be absent. The quarter-wave ham radio antennas work like a charm. The roller-furling jib has never let us down, and it turns out that, as we thought, the staysail is small enough not to require furling gear of its own. For the main, though, we added lazyjacks. The dingy davits are working out well; it's a lot better to hoist the inflatable than to tow it. The list is longer, but you have the idea.

We're off *Candide* now but will be back on board in a month or so. When we go on board it will be like going to our second home. There's a lot of us in the boat—thought, love, and money. And, all things considered, it's been worth the effort.

Ted and Ann Gordon

THE UNUSUAL

Ninety-nine out of a hundred boats weekending on the Chesapeake or San Francisco bays or in transit on the Intracoastal Waterway are look-alikes based on a handful of basic boat designs. Occasionally one sees something unusual like the Chinese junk schooner described above or the following two liveaboard character boats.

The Boat

The Classic Tjalk

Looking like she sailed straight out of a Rembrandt or Vermeer painting, the antique Dutch sailing ship *Encore* arrived in Baltimore's inner harbor to kick off the second season of the Holland Boat Company, a young Euro-American firm hoping to popularize this type of vessel here in the U.S.

The lavishly appointed and lovingly restored former sailing cargo ship (called a tjalk) was built in northern Holland at the turn of the century, and is one of the finest of her type still in existence. She was once part of the vibrant fleet of family-owned and -operated sailing ships that transported cargo and passengers across the North Sea and along the inland waterways of Western Europe. Put out of business by much larger engine-powered craft, these beautifully curved, hand-built classics languished for generations, floating with forgotten majesty in the backwater canals of the Netherlands.

In the early 1960s, things began to happen. There was a general realization among the Dutch people that these old tjalks were national treasures, surviving legacies of that prosperous proud era when the strength of the Dutch Merchant Marine transformed a small country into a premier world power. The Society for the Preservation of Round and Flat Bottom Yachts was formed. And a traditional lemsteraak yacht was presented as an official gift of the Dutch people to their queen, Beatrice.

This renewed interest had an electrifying result on the sluggish trade in these forgotten ships. No longer could a restorable tjalk be sailed away for a song out of a farmer's backyard canal. A true market emerged. The sight of beautifully restored sailing ships gliding gracefully past century-old windmills into picturesque harbors is persuasive advertising. Unrestored ships became

*Gently with
the Tides*

harder to locate, and the prices went up, especially for premium yachts and those large enough to charter 10 or more. The strength of the German mark and the great number of German tourists in Holland placed a great share of the remaining quality boats in German hands, while many French people, even those with no previous boating experience, purchased tjalks for use as chic, floating Parisian apartments and vacation homes in the southern provinces.

In 1985 a 65-foot tjalk was transformed into a nightclub in Paris and became an immediate success. This gave the founders of the Holland Boat Company the idea to further the growing popularity of this classic vessel. They sailed the 85-foot *Morning Star* in celebration of the Statue of Liberty centennial and followed that up with their first U.S. sale of a 33-foot tjalk in Newport, Rhode Island.

The people of the Holland Boat Company hope that what makes these vessels so popular in Europe, a combination of authentic collectability and real practical value, will also spark American interest. The tjalk is a beautiful and rare object that can sail in $3\frac{1}{2}$ feet of water, go 8 knots under power, and has enough interior space to actually live on. The importers say that it is only a matter of time before these beautiful, antique vessels become a permanent fixture on the American boating scene.

Lillie

After realizing that I wouldn't be sailing away for several years, I began looking for a better liveaboard. Most people live aboard very large sail- or powerboats "while getting ready to leave" on extended cruises that never materialize—or on barge-type vessels that aren't intended to ever be moved.

I wanted maximum comfort, but I also wanted to cruise extensively in the protected waters of Puget Sound. I was willing to give up sail since it seemed as though, dollar for dollar, I could get more cubic feet in a powerboat. For six months I looked at everything, even a derelict tugboat.

The Boat

I finally decided to build my own, modifying a basic barge hull form in order to get acceptable motoring performance. Many years ago in California, a scow schooner evolved that pretty well proved the concept. From that point I tapped into a long-standing interest in Chinese junks. I've been a modest student of Chinese sailing craft for a long time; once I built a Great Pelican (another San Francisco design) and rigged her as a junk, complete with bam-

Lillie.

83

boo battens. I'm really an old-style, unrepentant romantic and really liked the idea of that great aft cabin with dramatic windows as a sleeping area.

Things really began to fall into shape almost by themselves from that point on. The Chinese shapes all evolved around the use of a few wide planks in geometrically simple shapes, rather than Western forms using many smaller pieces in lighter, more complex shapes. The Chinese way lent itself perfectly to plywood and epoxy methods.

We laid up flat panels, right on the shop floor, using two layers of $^3/_4$-inch plywood. These side panels were put in place on temporary molds where the two major interior bulkheads would be, and then the front and rear transoms were attached. There was no need for other forms, nor for lofting. The thick topside panels took their own fair curve. Chine logs were installed and partial floor timbers put in place. On these the bottom was fastened, again two layers of $^3/_4$-inch plywood. The whole hull got two layers of cloth and epoxy with extra tape at the corners. Now with the hull turned over and leveled, the two interior bulkheads were positioned, the floor timbers were built, and the sole installed. Again, no lofting and no calculations!

We have a relatively mild winter climate in the Pacific Northwest, and I made a decision to ventilate rather than insulate between the ceiling and the outside skin. The entire boat has free air circulation, and dampness and condensation have never been a problem.

Steering from the front takes a bit of getting used to but has its advantages. One can almost always put the bow of a boat where one wants it to go, and I have more than once approached a windward dock straight on and simply stepped off with bow and stern lines in hand.

Lillie has an easy, seakindly motion, and her underbody design gives good directional stability. Her hull form is so efficient that as little as 10 h.p. moves her along at 6 knots.

She has turned out to be an unusual houseboat based on a hull form derived from ancient Chinese river craft. Her design ancestors were burdensome, shoal-draft vessels of between 30 and 80 feet in length, often poled or towed against the current under billowing downwind rigs when conditions permitted. Literally hundreds of variations on this basic style evolved over the years. *Lillie* is the newest member of an ancient line of liveaboard boats.

Brooke Elgie

5

The Ship's Complement

MANY SINGLEHANDERS and shorthanded cruising couples consider their autopilots and windvanes a part of the crew. They even give them personal names and often talk to them on long passages. Fortunately (or unfortunately) these helpful robots don't talk back except for the occasional squeal or growl signalling the need for oil or replacement of a warn gear. Other crewmembers, from the animal kingdom, provide companionship, amusement, and sometimes watchkeeping duties, but at the expense of a good deal of attention.

About 75 percent of liveaboard boat crews consist of couples, with the remaining 25 percent either permanently or temporarily single. Children of all ages can be found on about 12 percent of liveaboard boats. Most of the captains are male, although there is an increasing trend toward females taking on the responsibilities of the captain or some form of shared captaincy. Regardless of whether the woman is captain or not, there is a growing awareness that women should understand more of the complex technical and mechanical operations of a boat both for the safety of the crew and for enjoyment of the boating experience.

Raising children on a boat has its own unique pluses and minuses. Special safety features have to be thought of for wandering infants and youngsters. Ways of dealing with formal education while cruising have to be considered. Extended cruising at younger ages may deprive children of social peer relationships. On the other hand, many liveaboard parents are glad that they can shield their children from the peer influences of bad habits. They also feel that a liveaboard child can learn an invaluable lesson from the cultural contacts made during a cruising experience. Geography, navigation, meteorology, and nature topics are also excellent materials for a child's education that he or she easily can pick up in the course of daily boat living.

Thoughtfulness, private space, communication of differences, shared experiences, shared responsibility, and authority... are some of the themes often mentioned in connection with the ship's complement and the liveaboard lifestyle.

In most instances the captain is a male and the mate a female. And therein lie a multitude of differences and sometimes conflicts.

MALE/FEMALE RELATIONS

Why (some) women balk at boating is an age-old topic worthy of endless discussion. At the risk of taking a sexist stand, Roland and Janice Smith, the founders of the Homaflote Association and the first editors of the Living Aboard Journal, *made the following observations—long before the height of the feminist revolution.*

We are impressed by the number of couples on their second marriage, the first having broken up in part because of differences in their outlook on boating. We have seen this repeatedly on our cruises and also as boat dealers, and working at boat shows. We have some thoughts on why women, some, anyway, balk at boating... and what they and their husbands can do about it.

1. Both parties must be in accord regarding: the kind of boating contemplated, i.e., living at a dock, leisure cruising, bluewater passages, etc., and the size and type of boat they need and can afford and which they both can enjoy.

Related to this is the often unrecognized difference in viewpoint each brings to boating. The husband may be seeking relief from distractions ashore, a means to be a father-figure to his children, teaching them boating skills. His wife may be fearful of this change from the known to the unknown—a situation in which she may appear clumsy, a situation that is not a relief from the house but a duplication of household chores and frustrations.

To her, boating may not mean getting away from problems but rather shouldering a whole set of new ones: lack of labor-saving galley equipment, damaging exposure to her complexion or hair, hands becoming dry, cut, maybe blistered and fingernails broken, lack of privacy, the substitution of relatively crude facilities for the comforts at home. To her, boating may represent physical discomforts, possible injury to herself, her children, and/or her mate.

2. Sailing rail-down in intense racing competition may appeal to her husband more than it does to her. Boating should be fun...coastwise cruising in quiet waters, at moderate speed, is far more interesting to some women than trying to see how fast you can get there.

3. Men may learn by trial and error, or from boating courses; some wives get little instruction except from their husbands—often only piecemeal orders while engaged in general boating (where the consequences of error are likely to be greater). And then, errors following orders given without adequate explanation and often in unfamiliar terms are accompanied by shouts, criticism, and recriminations.

4. Some men who are Dr. Jekyll ashore become Mr. Hyde on a boat. Men may be more competitive than women; a boat becomes a weapon, a means to victory over some rival—possibly over the crew who cannot be dominated at home. Racing offers such an outlet, with victory improving the skipper's self-image while whipping wife and children in the struggle. One wife has said quite seriously, "I could kill him!" Then there are the spit-and-polish-Bristol-fashion tyrants. Since women tend to sense such dangers, they may well balk at the dock.

5. More men than women tend to take command of a boat, just as they first drove automobiles, as much by default by women as from male insistence. Whatever the cause, it's usually the man at the wheel, the woman with the lines. The master-crew relationship is worsened when the master doesn't know exactly what he wants done or how best to do it. Mistakes are hard to admit; anxiety breeds tension, fear, and frustration—sometimes boat damage too. The result is unhappiness.

6. Boats demand attention, often more than enough to prevent or limit time devoted to home projects. Related is the financial strain caused by the constant need for some new marine gadget, adding to the cost of dockage and maintenance, all for his "other woman." All this is hard for a wife to take in the face of the need for the children's dental care, music lessons—even some new clothes for herself. And there is also the sometime rub of too much togetherness, especially on a small boat and over extended time.

The Ship's Complement

Roland and Janice Smith   *87*

What to Do?

Agreement must be reached on the kind of boat, the kind of boating, and how the boat is to be operated. One family we know agrees: In a tight spot, his decision is followed without comment; otherwise, decisions are reached in family conference.

Get the right boat of adequate size, and within the family's ability to buy and maintain. Buy a boat that can easily be made comfortable.

Both husband and wife must be prepared to operate the boat. Both should take the basic boat-handling courses available through power squadrons and the Coast Guard. The confident wife is one who understands boat handling well enough to anticipate the next move and be mentally and physically ready to act if and when it may be necessary. When the husband knows what he is about, and the wife knows what she is about, they can cooperate to the satisfaction of both.

Once a woman's fears have been allayed and knowledge has replaced uncertainty, and when the basic comforts have been provided, she may come to see that boating may have some advantages for her. She can escape unwanted community organization pressures; she can find relaxation and health for herself and her whole family in the simpler life aboard; she may discover that a natural appearance is more desirable than the result of hours spent in beauty salons; she can have her husband and her family to herself, free of being the family chauffeur and free of days and nights as a "boat widow"; and she is in a perfect position to control his obsession with his "other woman." In such a situation, neither he nor she will have any thoughts of what love might be the second time around.

Beverly Bakes also reminded us of onboard conflicts when she sent in the following account.

Not too long ago I was speaking with a man who had just enrolled in Yale University's graduate program. His pursuit is to become a playwright. While we were chatting about his aspirations, I happened to mention that my husband and I live on board our sailboat. He decided immediately that it would be a great topic for a play. After brief contemplation, he added that in order for the play to work there would have to be conflict.

Conflict? What could he mean by "conflict?" Gerry and I get along just fine …don't we? Of course, we do have our "Odd Couple" tendencies—Gerry being very fastidious (an extremely valuable trait on board a 32-foot boat) and myself being…well, what is a nice word for the opposite of fastidious? I guess neatness, or lack of the same, is a definite source of conflict.

Unfortunately, people who aren't neat usually are not organized either. Speaking from experience, I can say that an unorganized sailor in the galley can be another definite source of conflict. Sailor against circumstance, or vice versa. It takes awhile before you realize that all the ingredients you so carefully noted in your cookbook and removed from the food locker are now directly on top of the locker that contains the pots and pans you'll need in order to cook the dish. And then there was the question of what fit on the bulkhead over the stove better, the spice rack or the depthsounder. The depthsounder won, and my spaghetti sauce now comes out of a jar because the spices are located in the locker with the pots and pans! I won't even bother to go into the difficulties I encountered in trying to prepare a coffee cake in my nifty folding oven that fits over the top of my equally nifty two-burner stove, but I will tell you that the depthsounder may never be the same. Yes, organization can be the main ingredient in any recipe on board a sailboat.

Of course, the same principle applies to any of your everyday, taken-for-granted chores. Take, for instance, showering in marina facilities. Now there's a real breeding ground for conflict. One of the first dilemmas you encounter is: Do you put on the clothes you want to wear for the day, get to the showers, take them off, and put them back on; or, do you add a second set of everything to the towels, shower paraphernalia, hair dryer, etcetera that you are already carrying? And, could it be that my toothpaste and toothbrush have developed a dislike for one another? Strangely enough, one or the other is always in the bag that's still on the boat. And let's not forget how hard it is to remain on speaking terms with the person who so deftly removed your shampoo before you left the boat because he ran out. What's more, do you have any idea how many calories are burned with a quick dash back to the boat because you remembered your suit but forgot your blouse? Add a rainstorm to all of this, and it positively boggles the mind.

This brings us to yet another set of conflicts presented by what we live-aboards term "straight jobs." That means being employed by companies that expect things like wearing suits and having a telephone—and they don't mean the one at the end of the dock. If you want to see conflict, just watch two grown people fight over one tiny hanging locker. I've got news for you. We both lost. We've got bulkhead to bulkhead clothes. What's more, our neat little boat has a fireplace that has given us the privilege of smelling as though we've been picnicking all winter long.

My personal conflict with our boat is that we have separate bunks. Cold nights can be lonely, and I may not be neat but I love to snuggle—although I'm not certain that's the correct term for two people in one bunk! "Cramming" might be closer. No pun intended. When I insist on snuggling, we have a choice. It's snuggle or sleep. But then, the line becomes hazy when you snuggle and parts of you sleep.

I guess there is plenty of conflict in our "household" for any of you budding Neil Simons. But you know something? I think the greatest conflict we've encountered in our new life occurs when it's a beautiful morning and we have to walk away from our boat for eight hours and pretend we'd rather not be sailing.

Beverly Bakes

The Ship's Complement

89

SHE'S IN COMMAND

*There has been a strong upsurge in boat-handling courses specifically
aimed at women. These courses offer an opportunity for women
to be taught by women and to share in the camaraderie
of all-women captains and crews. I have been tracking this
trend to keep informed and to stay modern.*

Some time ago a friend sent me a news clipping with the headline WOMAN
RESCUED AFTER FOUR DAYS ON CALOOSAHATCHEE. The article went
on to say that the husband of a retired liveaboard couple had fallen off their
anchored boat and died after an apparent heart attack. The wife was unable to
flag down passing boats and remained helplessly anchored for four days and
nights not knowing how to operate the boat or how to summon assistance.
When help finally arrived, after her husband's badly decomposed body had
been found farther downstream, she was listed in fair condition, suffering
from dehydration.

The newspaper clipping was accompanied with a personal note to fellow
liveaboards reminding them of the importance of the crew, man or woman,
knowing how to operate the boat in an emergency and how to use distress
flags, flares, and the VHF radio.

This tragic story reminded me of a much less dramatic but equally significant incident many years ago when I first learned to sail. I was crewing for a
couple on an Annapolis-to-Bermuda-to-Maine cruise. Barbara and I were on
the tail end of the 4 A.M. to 8 A.M. watch, and we heard George, the captain,
stirring in his bunk and getting ready for his shift.

The sails were down, and we were motoring in an uncharacteristically calm
ocean. Minutes before our long monotonous shift was to end, a fluke wind
came up, heeled the boat over, unravelled the loosely flaked mainsail, and
managed to tangle the halyard around the spreaders. I was a complete novice,
not knowing a sheet from a halyard, with no idea of how to correct the problem. Barbara, on the other hand, an accomplished sailor and co-owner of this
lively 40-foot racing sloop, stood there helplessly moaning, "George is going
to kill me!"

As I said, this was a less dramatic incident than the opening story. George
did not kill Barbara and we went on to have a wonderful sail to Bermuda and
back to Maine. But what strikes me now, almost 12 years later and with a lot
of voyages under my belt, is the painful similarity between these two women.
In both cases they represented the all too familiar, and less than equal part-
nership with their male counterparts in managing their floating homes. I am
not suggesting that we do away with the supreme role of boat captain as master of the vessel, and I do understand that with most couples the male is the
traditional captain, but the mate has the responsibility to be sufficiently

knowledgeable and confident to take charge or at the very least not be yelled at by the captain. In addition to the responsibility of being there in times of need or emergency, she also owes it to herself to gain the satisfaction of knowing enough about the boat and its operation to enjoy the boating experience fully.

In the past few years several women's groups have sprung up to enhance the boating experience by teaching women boatmanship and providing a support network of similarly minded women. One of the advantages of these organizations is the opportunity to learn and practice boating skills within a supportive environment apart from family or other close relationships. All one has to do is remember the horrors of learning how to drive a car from a family member to underscore the importance of this benefit.

Five unique organizations, helping women learn to sail and enjoy the experience, have come to my attention—Womanship, Women for Sail, The Phoenicians, Women at the Helm, and Sailing Women. Some of these groups may have dropped out for lack of business, others may have sprung up in their place. Regardless of which groups are active at the moment, they all share a common theme—helping women to enjoy sailing and boat handling in an environment dominated by men.

"And Nobody Yells"

That's the motto of Womanship, an Annapolis, Maryland, organization that has been offering sail- and powerboat courses since 1985. Suzanne Pogell, founder and president of Womanship says, "As I look back over the years, I find that learning to sail has meant different things to each of us...the thrill of actually making a boat slide through the water; personal accomplishment; fun, relaxation, and recreation; the confidence and security that comes from knowing what to do and when to do it; camaraderie; a new challenge; self-reliance; doing something for oneself; fitness; and becoming the best one can be. My own discovery of sailing, just a few short years ago, led me to create Womanship as a way of sharing the remarkable opportunity with other women."

One of Suzanne's students described 30 years of sailing experience in terms of sandwiches—because that's what she'd made, not decisions. Her husband had handled those, as husbands and boyfriends usually do on boats. So when her husband died she went to Womanship to learn to sail. Not just learn to sail, she already knew more about that than she'd realized, but to manage a boat by herself, to take command of her vessel, to be captain as well as cook.

Womanship was the first organization to use boats and hands-on training courses taught by women to help other women comfortably learn for themselves. Womanship now offers week-long cruise courses taught by licensed women captains in Chesapeake Bay, Florida's West Coast, the San Juan Islands, Cape Cod, Long Island Sound, and the Virgin Islands. For more

The Ship's Complement

91

information contact Womanship, 410 Severn Avenue, The Boat House, Annapolis, Maryland 21403 or call (301) 267-6661.

The Phoenicians

Their brochure says that the symbol for water of the ancient Phoenician maritime culture has become the letter "W" in the English language. It has also become the logo of the International Yachting Association for Women. This organization was established with the belief that there are many women around the world interested in boating who would like to join an organization committed to their interests.

Casey Whitten, founder of this group, realized that most yachting organizations were established for men only. She felt the growing need for an international yachting organization for women that provided an opportunity for women to grow in boating knowledge and skills through education and training, providing a pool of knowledgeable, well-trained women to crew or captain boats and filling the need for a professional organization through which serious women boaters can achieve recognition and respect for their achievements.

Membership in The Phoenicians means being kept informed through a newsletter, educational opportunities, and most important, being part of a worldwide network of friends and supporters. (Casey recently left the organization, and to my knowledge no one has taken over the helm. A pity.)

Women for Sail

No, it's not the cry of a white slave trader on the high seas. It is a sail training program aimed at giving women the confidence and experience of handling a boat by themselves in a supportive, non-threatening atmosphere. Each student crewmember gets to learn it all with no yelling, no arbitrary cutting the trip short, and no banishment to an observer's role.

Jill London, the founder and president of Women for Sail, says that typically, most women accept a subordinate role on board even their own boats. They settle for the galley chores and deck swabbing while the men man the helm and plot the course. She goes on to say, "In fact, Women for Sail students do learn galley chores and deck swabbing as necessary and honorable chores. But they also learn engine maintenance, the philosophy of boat and sail design, course plotting, proper anchoring techniques, docking skills, marlinespike seamanship, Loran navigation, and other essentials of sailing."

An important and fundamental lesson, according to Jill, is the danger of assuming that nothing will ever happen that the captain can't handle. The person you count on to be at the helm may not be there all the time. If he gets hurt, gets ill, or falls overboard, whoever else is aboard is suddenly in charge. That's not the time to reach for *Chapman's.*

The staff of Women for Sail are licensed women captains. They work at a profession they love and get a kick out of introducing others to what they themselves enjoy. Their most delightful moments come when the women they teach go from nearly hating to say the word "sailboat" to enjoying the sport so much that, as one of them said to her husband of nearly 30 years, "Honey, if we ever get divorced, I want the boat."

Women for Sail courses are offered in the Gulf of Mexico and Chesapeake Bay. For more information contact Women for Sail, 3467 South Wakefield St., Arlington, Virginia 22206 or call (800) 346-6404.

Women at the Helm

Rochella Cooper founded Women at the Helm after successful careers as educator, artist, and entrepreneur. She was looking for a new career when she realized that her hobby could be a career. "I took my first sailing lesson on a Sunfish in 1972 with the intention of teaching my three young sons. Little did I realize that during the ensuing years I could explore and discover uncharted waters, literally and figuratively. I cruised the blue waters of Florida, the Virgin Islands, and Yugoslavian Dalmatian Islands. I learned new skills, a new language, and gained confidence in my growing ability to communicate with assertiveness. For me the appeal of sailing is the sound of the water, the wind in the rigging, and the restorative alpha waves. It is also about learning leadership, teamwork, interpersonal relationships, and confidence building."

The courses are under the direction of experienced women instructors drawn from women with local racing experience, long distance cruising experience, and experience in marine-related industries. With her background as a Montessori instructor, Rochella schools her instructors in the Montessori techniques of encouraging students to begin talking with one another about what they are doing from the moment they step aboard. She explains that, "hands-on experiential learning helps internalize unfamiliar concepts and procedures."

The courses offered by Women at the Helm are given along the Texas Gulf Coast, Galveston Bay, and Clear Lake. For more information contact Women at the Helm, Watergate Yachting Center, 1500 FM 2094, Suite 3472, Kemah, Texas 77565 or call (713) 334-4101.

Sailing Women

This is the newest sail training program targeted at women. It was founded by Helen Johnston and three of her cousins as a nationwide network of sailing clubs for women. The organization is headquartered in Newport, Rhode Island. The aim of this program is to teach women recreational daysailing in a noncompetitive environment. Women instructors will be used along with one, two, or three students in a J/22 daysailer. Classes have been planned for

Manhattan, Boston, Newport, Rhode Island, and Portland, Maine. Classes will also be formed in Southern California cities.

One of the unique features of this program will be a membership organization based around a Sailing Women VISA card, which will permit card holders to take courses or charter boats in various parts of the country. This will allow members to sail and make professional and social contacts when visiting other cities. An annual fee of $75 will include dues in the organization and the VISA card. The organization also hopes to publish a newsletter for the membership.

For more information contact Sailing Women, Box 550, Newport, Rhode Island 02840 or call (401) 846-0410.

Gently with the Tides

You may wonder why a male has gotten on the bandwagon of women's boating courses. Like many boaters, when I go sailing I want to share the enjoyment, sense of responsibility, and workload of keeping the vessel shipshape and on a safe course. With both captain and crew sharing in the navigation, maintenance, and boat handling, everyone can enjoy the total experience. I'll be glad to make a sandwich or two if she'll help me find the next landfall.

I also know that a large part of the positive boating experience for me comes from being in charge of a small universe, understanding how it all works, and feeling confident in what I know. It's only natural to want to share these good feelings. Having a knowledgeable mate alongside is the key to more enjoyment for both the captain and crew and the peace of mind that in times of crisis the mate can comfortably and competently take charge and be in command.

For more reading on this subject, with an emphasis on the role of women captains and mates, check out:

My Ship Is So Small by Ann Davison
Once Is Enough by Miles Smeeton
Cruising in Seraffyn by Lin and Larry Pardey
*Northern Light: One Couple's Epic Voyage from the Arctic
    to the Antarctic* by Rolf Bejlke and Deborah Shapiro
First Crossing by Malcom and Carol McConnell
The Handbook for Non-Macho Sailors by Katy Burke
Atlantic Circle by Kathryn Lasky Knight
Alone Around the World by Naomi James
Neptune's Apprentice by Marie De Santis

RAISING BABY JANE

When I finally got around to buying my own cruising sailboat, I went looking for one that had been used as a liveaboard boat in the hope that all

94

the bugs had been ironed out. I found Jill and Adrian Alpine who had
sailed from England with an infant daughter. She was now four years old,
and Jane assured me that all the "bugs" were out. Jill and Adrian took
great delight in describing the raising of baby Jane.

It is December 1987 and we're land-bound, for the moment, here in Hobart, Tasmania. The snow has just settled on Mt. Wellington, and the wintry scene takes me back to another snowfall eight years ago and half a world away. Back then the snow lay thick on our 32-foot yacht, *Hiri Moale,* tied up at a marina in the south of England. Jill and I were eagerly expecting the birth of our daughter, Jane.

Jane was six days old when she started her liveaboard life. She was nearly five years old when she left the boat, a continent away and a seasoned sailor with thousands of sea miles behind her.

Was it hard work raising a child aboard a boat? Did the child suffer? Would we do it again? These were just a few of the questions asked by friends and family, especially those unaccustomed to a boat and unable to comprehend anything different from their land life.

On reflection, we would answer with a resounding, "Yes!" It was hard work in some areas, such as the constant washing and drying of nappies (British for diapers). It was easier in other respects because Jane was nearly always an arms length away and well contained in the cozy cave-like confinement of the boat's cabin. Was it dangerous? No more so than on land and in many respects much less dangerous than taking your child on the highway. For us the advantages far outweighed the disadvantages. One very pleasant advantage to a family cruising foreign lands is the way in which a child can help establish relationships among adults. In the Latin countries and in the West Indies, children open many doors that are closed to adults traveling on their own.

One of the hassles with newborns is their constant need for nappies in huge quantities. We used toweling nappies on Jane with a plastic nappy cover. These were available in the U.K., as were the disposable type. However, our funds were limited, and we didn't think it would be such a hardship, at the time, to wash a few nappies. Little did we know. Washing and drying the nappies became one of our most annoying chores. When we started sailing the boat, our lifelines were always festooned with drying nappies. On occasion, I'm sure we flew a greater area of nappies than sails. We could just hear those retired Royal Navy officer types living on the waterfront wondering what the world was coming to.

Jane was on bottle feedings by the time we left England to tour the continent. Heating bottles was not more of a chore than it would have been on shore. We had a propane stove that worked out quite well. It wasn't long before the formula gave way to milk and solids. We used the unrefrigerated

The Ship's Complement

(U.H.T.) milk containers. As a matter of fact, our bilges were often loaded with 180 liters of this stuff for Jane and about 40 liters of wine to sooth the adults on board.

Disaster struck in France when we couldn't find nappy liners. Jill searched the department stores from the northern end of the canals all the way to the Mediterranean. In fact, the quest for nappy liners became such a cause among our cruising companions that while in Majorca, a Swiss-German friend of ours stuck the name "Nappy-Liner" in large vinyl letters on our hull. The name was so appropriate for our situation, that we left it on until we sold the boat five years later.

Perhaps we were fortunate in that Jane never posed any "unsocial behavior" problems. She rarely cried, she went to sleep when she was put down, and she ate the same things we did and never required special baby food. She was either the perfect child, or my memory is rapidly failing me.

When she first moved onto the boat, Jane slept in a Moses basket in the main saloon, which we were able to keep at a constant 70 degrees Fahrenheit with our Tailor diesel heater. As summer approached and we cruised to warmer climates in the Mediterranean, we moved her up into the forecastle, still in her Moses basket but with the added protection of a lee cloth. Later, in Spain, we bought an oblong "lobster pot" play pen that we placed in the saloon during the daytime and in the forecastle at night.

In her early years she was well contained below deck. We fitted the top on the stove with pot holders so that inquisitive little hands couldn't tip over pots and pans. There were no electric outlets on the boat, so little fingers were perfectly safe. At this stage we felt that she was much safer on the boat than she would have been on land.

We were in Gibraltar for the winter of 1980 prior to our big crossing of the Atlantic. The boat was in a marina while I worked to restore the cruising kitty. Jane had the opportunity to learn how to walk on a relatively stable surface for a change.

She was now living on milk, yogurt, and fruit. The fruit was often given to her by vendors much like candies are given to small children. To the Spaniards and the Gibraltarians, children are very important and the object of much affection. Before we left Gibraltar, Jill took Jane to the doctor for a checkup. Like all mothers, especially with their firstborn, she was very eager to confirm that we were doing all the right things. She was particularly interested in knowing whether Jane should be eating more than just milk, yogurt, and fruit. As far as the doctor was concerned, the diet was just fine and he wished that many of his other patients were doing as well as Jane. We were very happy to hear his assurances, especially since we were about to embark on a long voyage.

Once Jane was able to walk, she was no longer restricted to the boat's interior. Often while on deck and under sail we would realize that Jane was no longer tucked-up in her berth when her bald head followed by a toothless smile slowly rose up the companionway. From that time on she was made to wear a safety harness whenever she came topside. The harness was light but very strong, and we clipped it to a U-bolt in the cockpit before she was allowed out of the companionway. The length of the harness lead was adjusted to restrict her to the cockpit.

At this point we wondered about netting the entire boat to give Jane more freedom. I had been keeping a watch on other boats with children on board and especially those with netting tied to the lifelines. It appeared that all the boats that were in need of netting always left the bow un-netted so as not to foul the anchor and the mooring lines. If a child were allowed to run free on deck, it wouldn't be long before they found the hole, possibly with disastrous results. We decided not to net and to rely on the harness instead. Jane soon learned that she was not allowed topside without it. She also quickly learned how to put the harness on by herself, a task that many adults struggle with.

During our cruising life we were rarely in marinas and preferred to anchor-off. The passage between an anchored boat and shore is the most dangerous for a child. When Jane got older we had a life jacket for her. When she was a baby, we were concerned that the jacket would turn a small infant face down to drown. We never had any problems, but we never solved the question of a life jacket for an infant.

We did have one very harrowing experience in one of those situations very close to shore when you let your guard down. We were in Madeira returning to the boat from a dinner party on shore. We had no flashlight with us and I was holding Jane under my arm. I'm not sure exactly what happened, but the next thing I knew both Jane and I were in the water. I was winded by the fall off the pier and Jane, only 20 months old, had slipped out of my arm and into the gap between the pontoons supporting the pier. It was by chance that my hand came in contact with her foot as I frantically searched for her in the ink-black waters. I grabbed her foot and handed her up to Jill who was still on the pier. We believe that the plastic nappy liners gave her sufficient buoyancy to keep her from sinking out of reach. This was one time we were thankful for those nappies.

This was also the one time Jane did not have her life jacket on while off the boat. We didn't think the jacket was needed when we were tied to the pier. However, we made a solemn pledge to always, always have a life jacket on Jane whenever going to and from the boat.

Amusing Jane was Jill's department. We were very fortunate because when Jane was a baby she slept a lot or was content to play with simple toys. By the time Jane had grown to an age where she wanted to be amused and needed friends, we were cruising in short hops around the West Indian Islands, Venezuela, Haiti, and the Bahamas, so no trip was long enough to cause boredom.

Seasickness never seemed to affect Jane. As far as I can recall she felt "funny" on only about three occasions when we were bashing into a seaway and she was bouncing around in the forecastle trying to read her children's books. It made me sick just to watch her. Perhaps she was sick at times and unable to communicate her condition, but she didn't show any of the normal physical signs.

The older Jane became the more she appreciated the many and varied places we visited on our cruises. She matured rapidly and showed a sense of responsibility well in advance of her years. One of the features of cruising is that friends are made quickly during short layovers. Jane has learned this lesson well, and she has extended this to her relationships on land. She is very open and actively welcomes friendships.

So what are the disadvantages of having a child on board? When they get older there are problems with acquiring formal schooling. Fortunately, Australia is well geared-up for correspondence courses. We have been land cruising down-under and Jane has been "attending" correspondence school. The program has proven to be first-rate and very comprehensive. Now that we're in one place for a couple of years, Jane will be attending regular school. We'll be able to see how well the correspondence courses prepared her.

A regular school environment will also expose Jane to lots of new friends. This is one area where the cruising life is somewhat limiting for children. It isn't so much a problem of quantity as it is a rapid turnover of friends. We briefly meet other cruising friends and then head off in different directions. Inevitably, we meet again and again on our respective cruises, but the turnover is still high. This has been a particular problem for us because we like to anchor-out in more remote places and away from the popular spots jammed full of charter boats.

Our advice for all those with children, of any age, who are wondering whether or not to go cruising—in a word, go! Undoubtedly, you will have different experiences and form different opinions about children on board. But one thing is for sure, you will have the unique experience of actually seeing and participating in your child's (or children's) growth. In these hectic times, this is the biggest plus of all.

Adrian and Gill Alpine

LIVING ABOARD: A TEEN'S VIEW
P.J. Lantz wrote us a letter several years ago about her life aboard. The mailbag is full of such descriptions but rarely from a teenager—they have better things to do than write letters. P.J. was 13 and had some interesting reflections on her unusual lifestyle.

Just another manic Monday. That's the way it was the day the boat went into the water on March 31. We had already been living aboard for several weeks, but it still took time to get resettled.

Living on the boat is really fun once you get used to it. My friends love it, especially my close friend Brandi. We usually rent a house in the winter, which we call "the house." But we also call the boat "the house." Sometimes I can really confuse Brandi! My friends at school think it's pretty great to know a kid that lives on a boat. Some of the boys start to tease me if we're reading a story about the water, and the one giving all the answers is me. But living and cruising on the boat does have its advantages: You get to understand science, history, and geography a little better than you might normally. At least I think you might. But if the boys could only get out on the water they might see things the way I do, and stop teasing me so much (especially Donni and Casey).

The Ship's Complement

I'm 13, and my family and I live on our very nice, homey Allmand 35. We've been living on boats since I was seven or eight. It's really fun, but it can be work. Even though I may grumble about cleaning, vacuuming, and making my bunk, I really love it. There's one thing I really don't like, but still have to do, and that's clean my room. That can ruin my day. I have so much junk, and I hate to part with some of it, but I must. We customized my room so it would be more comfortable, with a built-in radio/tape shelf (which all of my tapes are falling out of), a hand-held VHF holder, shelves that almost completely circle the bunk, and best of all, a built-in heater. My room is not usually the cleanest place on the boat. This may be due to the fact that I brought on board a large rabbit, a small cat, a small reindeer, and a very small bear (all stuffed, of course). Or maybe it's because I don't like to clean very often.

I hate not having all my clothes on the boat at the times that I want them. I also have to be careful of what kind of clothes I bring with me; I can't have anything that needs a lot of ironing (boys don't have to worry about that very much). My mom and I share much of our clothing, and that helps to cut down on the space that each of us needs. We also put cedar closet linings in all our hanging lockers to take care of the condensation problems.

Cooking is a lot of fun on the boat, too. We have a microwave, which makes things easier. I get to cook just like you would in your kitchen at home. The only difference is the size of the stove and the refrigerator. And, above all, you have to clean up right after you get done.

The real fun comes after the bridge is open for the season and we get to head out for the weekends. To see all the places that have been hidden from view all winter can be exhilarating. It's also kind of fun to see if you can get to shore as fast with the aft line as you used to be able to. One of my favorite things is to get in our dinghy and go to a nearby town for an ice cream cone. My friend Brandi comes with me, and then we really go through a lot of gas. We're constantly going to get something from town.

Then, in July, the fun of the season really starts. Vacation! We almost always go to the North Channel or someplace up there. That's really great. The people are usually pretty friendly, and once in a while you meet somebody that you stick with for the rest of your vacation. The scenery is just gorgeous, and I could just about spend the whole day just going around and seeing all the little coves and bays. And another great thing about living on a boat is if you don't like your neighbors, you can just get up and leave. Sometimes it can get pretty loud out there if someone starts having a party.

At the end of the season it's back to school and getting ready to take down the mast and getting ready for the eventual haul out. When the colder weather sets in it starts to get a little harder. We're always joking about building an addition in which we could place our boots and snowsuits (we never use them really). However, we have gotten caught in snowstorms a couple of times. It gets really interesting getting on and off the boat then. One time we had snow in the cockpit, and my mother started joking about making a snowman. We could have had a small one if we had wanted to. In colder weather it's always nice to sit in a nice snug anchorage and watch the geese go overhead. It even gets nice to just curl up with a good book and read for the whole weekend. We're always on the boat for my birthday, and I really like to pick a harbor and have a relatively quiet day or so. Sometimes we go to watch the sunset over the peninsula. Once in a while they get almost as good as Canadian sunsets.

After we've hauled out and have gotten squared away for the winter, we like to take a little rest to plan the next year's agenda. Maybe we even do a little adventuring to wherever we might be going the following year. Then its back to work on the boat, and the countdown to the launch time set for the next year. And that's the end of a perfect year of living on board and cruising on the Great Lakes.

P.J. Lantz

DO YOU WANT A LIVEABOARD PET?

Janet has written a wonderful book called, How to Live Aboard a Boat, *published by William Morrow Co. In an excerpt, she offered this advice to the readers of the* Living Aboard Journal *who might be planning to bring on a crewmember from the animal kingdom.*

If you love pets and have them in your home, you'll continue to want the companionship and help of a pet when you live on a boat. Or will you? Before you run down to the pet shop, think about the pros and cons of having a dog or cat on a boat.

On the plus side, an animal is usually a faithful friend, entertainment for the whole family, a conversation-starter with strangers, and a very practical accessory. One singlehander found that his dog woke him in plenty of time to take stock of approaching freighters and change course if necessary. Dogs and cats have wakened sleeping families in time to save them from fire. Big dogs have thwarted break-ins, even small dogs can warn you of unwelcome boarders, and cats are the most effective mousetraps on the market.

There are problems, both for you and for the pet. Some marinas won't accept liveaboards with pets. You have to walk the dog in all weather, which may mean walking well inland from the dock to find a suitable place, or rowing the dog ashore. (However, we once anchored near a boat with a German shepherd that had been trained to jump overboard, swim to the island, do his duty, then swim back.)

You're living in close quarters, so a pet means less room and more odors—sometimes smells may be so repelling that your guests are aghast. Pets make extra cleaning problems when they track sand and salt water aboard, spill food, shed hair, or do gymnastics in the litter box. Some foreign countries require that pets be quarantined, causing delays and expense. It costs money to feed a pet, get medical care, and pay for whatever grooming is necessary. The pet can't go everywhere with you, which means leaving it alone aboard or, for long trips, ashore, paying for kennel care. A cat with a yen to sharpen its claws, or a teething puppy, can gnaw through a fortune in custom upholstery or nylon line in $2^1/_2$ seconds.

Pets have a mind of their own, and we've seen many liveaboards whose schedules had to be changed because a dog or cat (usually a cat) wandered off. Some of these pet owners finally gave up and went on their way. Some looked for weeks, advertised, offered rewards, and never did find the pet. One searched the bush on a Bahamian island for days and finally found his cat caught in a hole, nearly starved.

There are problems for the pet, too. The list of hurt, missing, and injured liveaboard pets is a long and sad one. We once found a ship's cat nearly dead of dehydration because she had been licking her salt-covered fur, but could not find fresh water. We've been there, or have heard firsthand, about a dozen pets that have fallen overboard. One was eaten by a shark, many were never seen again, one had to be destroyed. One adorable pup was missing and assumed stolen. Few breeds of dogs are sure-footed enough to be safe on the open sea, and even cats can fall overboard. One was asleep in a sail on deck when suddenly the sail was raised, slinging the cat a boat length ahead. Fortunately the owner was able to fish it out as the boat sailed past. One couple got up one morning to find their kitten clinging to the outboard rudder, mewing pathetically. It had fallen over during the night and couldn't climb back aboard. One of the most diabolical discomforts suffered by boating pets occurs because most can't use a marine head (we have seen cats, however, that could). Underway, well-trained animals suffer for hours because the part of deck they had been taught to use is awash, or because the owners ran out of the brand litter, or newspaper, or carpeting the animal had been taught to use.

Only you can decide whether the service and friendship of a pet will be worth the problems to both the pet and you.

Janet Groene

A Ship's Cat Grows Up

About 30 percent of liveaboard boats have a dog or cat or both in the crew manifest. Donna Schlosser tells about her kitten, Tecuya, and her introduction to life aboard.

The 8-inch-long ball of fur scrambled over the 8-inch-high cabinet ledge beneath the sink. A tip-top dance over a 4-inch-wide plank carried the 10-week-old kitten across a clutter of bottles and cans harboring cleaning liquids. One more careful step put the pint-size feline inside her litter box, which rested on a platform outside the boat cabin but inside the weather-free shelter of the cockpit storage area.

As our new ship's cat, Tecuya, gained weight, length, and agility, she soon chose to poise herself on the kitchen cabinet ledge and leap onto the litter platform without the aid of the plank bridge. Human ingenuity and feline adaptability had solved the problem of where to place a litter box on board a 33-foot sailboat.

Although the litter problem yielded a quick solution, we didn't have initial success in finding a stable area for her food and water bowls. Whether at sea or at dock, we stepped in mushy cat food on a regular basis. The merits of indoor-outdoor carpeting's ability to absorb large spills from the water bowl earned our hearty praise often.

Tecuya took pleasure in sinking her claws into the carpet and lifting it from the floor as food and water bowls developed a precarious angle of inclination. With a snap of her paw, she dispatched the baggage to the floor once more with a resounding thump. Eyes grown wide, our fascinated feline watched the water spill from her bowl and the food tumble around her feet.

We asked ourselves how to end her game usually about 2 A.M. as our miniature lioness played the carpet trick in the glow of the full moon shining through the cabin windows.

Man's genius eventually triumphed. My husband rigged metal tubing under the bowl's edges. At each end of the tubes, he formed hooks that slipped into brackets mounted on the engine compartment wall. Then we watched as the juvenile delinquent approached, firmly stuck claws into carpet but failed to budge the rug because of the solid weight of the mounted bowls.

Success in circumventing two challenges of living with a cat on board did not shed light on a third dilemma. We had failed to devise a strategy that could deep-six Tecuya's paralyzing fear of engine noise when we slipped dock lines and took to the sea.

Bewildered, I watched our neighbors glide from their slip. One cat sprawled in the softness of the mainsail stacked on the boom while the other feline stood on the bow as a combination figurehead and scout. Tecuya, to my chagrin, instead headed directly for the forepeak closet at the first sound of an engine. There, she wedged herself into the linens and remained while we cruised.

Unfortunately, the lair provided little security for the spooked cat's nerves. Whether from fear or seasickness, on each sail she lost control of bodily functions while ensconced on freshly laundered sheets and towels. Extra visits to the laundromat after weekend boating excursions turned Sunday evenings into gloomy affairs.

Six months passed before a light shined in our addled brains. Insight came on a visit to the pet shop where we noticed animal carriers of several dimensions. We purchased a large carrier, and with renewed hope looked forward to a weekend sail.

Tecuya howled when we tucked her inside the box with its three walls punched in a Swiss cheese pattern of holes and its door of metal lattice forming a fourth side. Our neighbors in the boat next door popped their heads through the hatch thinking the cat had fallen overboard.

Despite the commotion, we persisted. The box occupied a position in the cockpit as close to the centerline as possible, in the shade and facing prevailing breezes. Toys and a favorite towel accompanied the reluctant one into the box. Food and water did not, for she steadfastly refused all sustenance when en route.

After a few excursions, we knew we had met with success. At the first indications of passagemaking, Tecuya willingly ambled toward the cage rather than bolt for the forepeak. The ship's cat has now logged more than six years of sea voyages in the security of her cat carrier.

Has our liveaboard cat led a limited existence because of the boat's small quarters? We doubt it. A boat can provide ample challenge for a cat's curiosity. Numerous storage places do not reveal themselves until a cushion is lifted or a drawer is removed. Tecuya finds her way into any usually inaccessible area as soon as an opportunity presents itself.

We learned to make sure of the cat's location before closing accesses we had opened. Still, she survived 10 hours in a storage closet with no ill effects.

When we arrived home and opened the door to hang our clothes, she rolled from the interior and landed at our feet. We froze and then laughed as she opened her eyes, stretched, and strolled to the water bowl for a drink.

A boat offers an endless number of levels where a cat can display agility. A whirling dervish can begin with a jump from a bimini to a boom to the cabin-top to the cockpit seat to the interior. Inside, the mad race continues with a leap from the chart table to a bookshelf to the sofa to the bed. Each spot just mentioned has a different height.

The finishing act occurs when the rampaging cat attacks the carpet we wrapped around the support pole of the saloon table. While she claws the modified scratching post and stretches her back to its fullest, our furniture, covered in nubby fabric, escapes destruction.

A stray tree frog, traveling shellfish, unlucky lizard, or off-course insect offers the ship's cat a rousing onboard chase until we manage to rescue the unhappy visitor. The jungle cat stalks herons, pelicans, and seagulls perched on board or nearby, but always loses her prey to the air the instant before a pounce. Fish jumping across the water often lure her to precariously balanced positions as she leans over the water for a better look.

We chose to raise our cat as a complete liveaboard for several reasons. She does not roam the docks nor fellow boater's craft. In return, we have no complaints from neighbors, and we have no flea problem. Slipping the dock lines does not first entail a search for the ship's cat in home port or visiting port.

Tecuya's territorial stance would seem an outgrowth of her exclusive onboard existence. We warn friends and acquaintances that she might nip a finger or toe until she learns the owner's smell. On the plus side, she has proven an ice breaker when we come into new ports. "What is her name?" and "How does she like the boat?" are two standard questions. Her habit of howling at anyone attempting to board would certainly encourage intruders to find a less obvious vessel to pillage.

We live in Florida for perennially warm cruising grounds and choose not to air-condition our boat. Can a furred creature find happiness when temperatures hit 92 degrees plus? Absolutely. A belly laid against the boat's fiberglass floor will feel 10 degrees cooler by virtue of the surrounding water. A tent over the cabin gives shade, acts as a wind tunnel, and serves as an enticing lounge.

Although Tecuya has an onboard existence, our veterinarian keeps her shots current. Travel outside the United States requires evidence of inoculations when entering foreign ports of call. Should owner and cat become unexpectedly separated, at least the animal enters the landed world armed against disease.

Tecuya has survived three surprise overboard dunkings, two as a kitten and one as an adult. Each time, she instinctively grabbed the netted pole we extended and clung firmly as we brought her within arms' reach for rescue. After a freshwater rinse to counteract the saltwater dunking of her skin, the subdued cat lay low for just a day or two before recovering her usual aplomb.

People and animals have traditionally compromised their habits to live together. Tecuya perches atop a bimini to observe a seascape rather than sprawling in a second story window or backyard tree to view a landscape. We lose space to a litter box and live with a scratching post in our saloon. Such small prices, though, bring the three of us each other's company and a seagoing life overflowing with daily adventure.

Donna Schlosser

*The Ship's
Complement*

6

Marinas, Anchorages, and Liveaboard Rights

SOME LIVEABOARDS choose to be in a perpetual state of motion and come ashore only for short periods of time and sometimes only in remote places. Others are permanently docked at marinas or spend a good deal of time anchored or moored in popular harbors. But regardless of one's length of stay, marinas and anchorages are an important fact of life, if not a necessity.

Unfortunately, in many areas, shoreside neighbors have enacted policies and regulations that make it difficult, if not impossible, to be a liveaboard. There seems to be a growing movement nationwide to limit or prohibit living on boats for extended periods. In some places "extended" means anything over 72 hours—a typical three-day holiday weekend. Restrictions come in the form of marina policies, community ordinances, or state laws. At the root of these restrictions is a complex set of motives and perceptions, including the fact that liveaboards typically spend less money for boating supplies and marina services; they may not pay a fair share of local taxes; they represent a prohibited residential use of public trust resources; they pollute the water; their presence clutters up the vistas of their shore-based neighbors; in small communities cruising liveaboards unfairly compete for scarce jobs by accepting lower wages; and worst of all they're viewed as simply different, living an alternative lifestyle, and are therefore undesirable.

In an ongoing survey of the San Francisco Bay area, the *Living Aboard Journal* reported that of the 60 or so marinas in the area representing more than 20,000 slips, only 600 slips were "officially" available for liveaboards, and there is a lengthy waiting period for most of these slips. Anchoring privileges in the bay for extended periods of time are severely limited. The unofficial liveaboards are often called disparaging names like "sneakaboards" and "hideaboards," and those at moorings are referred to as low-life "anchor-outs." The basis for the San Francisco Bay restrictions stems from California State rulings that the bay is a public trust resource that can accommodate commercial, industrial, and recreational uses but not residential use.

Similar restrictions against liveaboards exist in San Diego Harbor, the Intracoastal Waterway through Florida, the Florida Keys, Hawaii, the Mississippi River, and many other prime boating areas. An informal survey at the Annapolis power- and sailboat shows indicated that there is growing resistance to liveaboards on Chesapeake Bay. Several of the planned marinas in the bay will not, or have not yet decided to, allow liveaboards.

The accusations surrounding environmental, economic, or residential abuses and the enmity over alternative lifestyles are not new to liveaboards. In 1984 Dan Spurr, writing for *Cruising World* magazine, interviewed several boating associations, including the editor of the *Living Aboard Journal*, and came up with the following observations:

- Kicking out undesirable, squatter elements—shady characters in shabby boats—is a frequent argument for local liveaboard restrictions. Boating groups agree that a few "bad eggs" have hurt the image of liveaboards.

- Empirical data on the environmental damage done by vessel pollution is tenuous, but states increasingly believe that sewage pumped from vessels is hazardous and can contaminate shellfish beds in protected harbors. Liveaboards are quick to point out that boat sewage is negligible compared with untreated municipal wastes, urban and rural storm runoff, and agricultural runoff.

- Liveaboard opponents claim that people on boats do not pay the full share of taxes needed to pay for the upkeep of facilities, litter pick-up, public schools, fire and police protection, and other community services. Boaters reject this argument and point to marina slip rents being similar to apartment rents where the building owner pays the taxes.

- Liveaboards threaten city types with an unfamiliar lifestyle. "Gypsies, beatniks, and freeloaders," snort the city dwellers. "Jealousy," reply the liveaboards. "Maybe we're resented because we're free from the trappings that are strangling some of them."

- Landowners claim that neighboring waters are for all to enjoy and that liveaboards deny others the opportunity to enjoy the waters fully. Liveaboards feel that making a boat a home is just as much their right as it is for another person to choose living on land.

For a long time no one cared what domestic activities took place in coastal waters. Now it has become trendy and fashionable to develop the waterfront and living aboard may not be what the community had in mind for this newly discovered and much-prized resource.

Many boaters combine recreation with their residency as they cruise and dally along this country's wonderful shoreline and inland waterways. Many choose to live on the water as a relaxing counterpoint to their hectic urban work life. Others take long boat voyages to discover new places and to experience and enjoy America. And still others dream of someday participating in this lifestyle. It would be unfortunate to have these people labeled as undesirables, or to see overly narrow definitions of public trust resource use or exaggerated claims of water pollution deny boaters the privilege and pleasure to live aboard.

There are more than 5,000 marine facilities in the U.S. that advertise slips or moorings for rent or sale. However, only a small number, less than 10 percent, have been reported in surveys to accept liveaboards.

RESTRICTIONS IN SAN FRANCISCO BAY
The San Francisco Bay area, with a highly developed shoreline, a shrinking natural environment, and a burgeoning population, represents a perfect example of the clash between the personal rights of live-aboards and the government's eagerness to protect the common good. With my attorney friend, Kit Armstrong, we asked a lot of questions of local liveaboards, marina owners, and the government.

If you're contemplating living aboard in the San Francisco Bay area, be warned that there is a serious shortage of liveaboard slips. Also, prepare to be part of a long-standing controversy over your privilege to reside as a liveaboard on the bay waters. You may even find yourself called a low-life "anchor-out" or a "sneakaboard."

San Francisco Bay, the second largest estuary in the U.S. after Chesapeake Bay, is actually a series of bays fed by the Sacramento and San Joaquin rivers. The collection of bays commonly called San Francisco Bay includes three main bays—San Francisco, San Pablo, and Suisun—and five lesser bays called Richardson, San Rafael, San Leandro, Honker, and Grizzly. The entrance to this vast estuary eluded many of the 16th-century West Coast explorers, including Sir Francis Drake. A Spanish explorer, Juan Manuel de Ayala, is credited with the first exploration of the estuary in 1575.

The bay is surrounded by nine counties with a combined population of about five million. The bay and adjoining Sacramento–San Joaquin River Delta offer residents and visitors an unmatched variety of boating experiences. A network of quiet waterways in the delta, broad reaches in the protected bays, and ready access to the Pacific Ocean make this an attractive area for both sail- and motorboating and living aboard.

We spent a few unusually warm and sunny days in "the City by the Bay," scouting marinas and the liveaboard situation. Our limited survey of marina operators and government officials yielded some surprising results.

There are about 65 marinas within a 40-mile arc drawn from the Golden Gate Bridge. This arc encompasses the entire estuary and the western entrance to the delta. Available data indicates that 20,000 slips is probably a good round estimate for the total number of berths in the bay area. Our survey of 37 of the 65 marinas included about 13,000 slips, including about 600 official liveaboard berths. But that's not the whole story.

The three simple questions in our survey—How many slips do you have? How many of these slips are for liveaboards? How long is the waiting period for the liveaboard slips?—drew a variety of answers and non-answers. Some marina operators indicated that they have no liveaboards at present and will not allow any in the future. One marina operator has a few liveaboards (less than 10 percent), but when they leave, no new ones will be permitted. Some have a very limited number (less that 10 percent), usually for security purposes. Many claimed to have 10 percent of their slips reserved for liveaboards according to their permits from the Bay Conservation and Development Commission (BCDC). A few marinas were very secretive about these facts and refused to discuss them over the telephone. Only one marina indicated more than 10 percent of its slips were occupied by liveaboards. In all cases except one, the liveaboard slips are fully rented and the waiting period estimated to be several months to years.

Attitudes toward liveaboards varied among marina operators. One of the major port authorities on the bay flatly refuses to allocate any of the hundreds of slips under their jurisdiction to liveaboards. Staff there admitted to having several "unofficial" liveaboards, but none of these were legally tied up to the port's slips. This policy has been established by the previous port director, who had an unfortunate experience with the floating slums that arose in Honolulu during the overcrowded, housing-short conditions of World War II.

The present port director is himself a liveaboard sailor, and although the official policy has not changed, there are now a limited number of "unofficial" liveaboard privileges granted to well-screened persons and well-inspected vessels.

On the other hand, an ordinance of the City of Martinez, near the delta, limited liveaboards to 5 percent. The harbormaster would be happy to increase it to 10 percent. He feels that the added security of having live-aboards at the marina is worth any inconvenience. He even insists that live-aboards install telephones on their boats so that they can call him in case of an emergency at the marina.

The liveaboard controversy around the bay takes in three distinct groups: non-navigable "houseboats" that are firmly moored to piers; navigable vessels that are tied up at marina slips; and assorted navigable vessels and non-navigable assemblages of flotsam and jetsam anchored out in a very limited portion of the bay. Local government agencies have characterized all three groups as constituting a residential use of the bay under California law. Such use is in direct conflict with established public trust uses, which do not include residential use.

Houseboats

"Houseboat" is a misnomer for the floating homes encountered in our survey of the Alameda, Richmond, Berkeley, and Sausalito waterfronts. These units are actually elaborate frame houses built on floating platforms and tied to piers and pilings. In no way do they conform to any normal definition of a boat, and they are certainly not navigable. Many of these homes are architecturally quite attractive and imaginatively designed, with striking angular shapes and extensive use of windows and stained glass. The prices for these structures are in the hundreds of thousands of dollars. Marin County has the largest concentration of these "houseboats" and has strict building-code requirements for them, including sewer hook-up. The BCDC permits these structures, most of which were there before the agency's creation, but does not allow new houseboat marinas. BCDC does allow for a limited number of new houseboats at existing marinas.

Marina Liveaboards

The situation for marina liveaboards is a little more confusing. The state legislation that established BCDC also defined the uses to which the bay could be put in concert with the public trust uses of the state's tidelands. These uses include recreational boating but not residential use. The legislation gave BCDC the authority to issue permits governing bay water usage under these definitions in an effort to halt further filling of the bay. These permits eventually extended to marina liveaboard slips.

BCDC became involved with the liveaboard issue in 1978 when the Berkeley Marina requested permits for its liveaboards. (Another movement started in Berkeley!) Although residential use of the bay technically was not permitted, BCDC decided that a limited number of liveaboards was beneficial for the bay in providing security for recreational use of the bay. After conducting an admittedly incomplete survey of marinas, BCDC determined that liveaboards used 2 to 6 percent of the slips. They therefore established what appeared to be a reasonable 10 percent quota for each marina to cover demand for liveaboard space.

Unfortunately, since the time of the survey many of the marinas have chosen to set more restrictive quotas on liveaboard slips ranging from 0 to 5 percent. Our survey results suggest that the 10 percent quota, plus the often more restrictive policies of private and public marinas, result in a demand that far exceeds the current supply of liveaboard slips. In other words, the 10 percent estimate may no longer be a reasonable quota if only demand is considered.

BCDC has established its limits in order to enforce California law protecting designated uses of the bay. The stated reason why so many marina operators and communities more strictly limit liveaboards include not wanting to get involved in domestic squabbles that invariably arise in a residential community, provide public services such as parking and school busing, incur additional government regulations, or monitor and enforce liveaboard regulations. One marina operator thinks that allowing liveaboards under BCDC rules would eventually lead to having to provide wheelchair ramps at the piers.

Our survey numbers indicate that only 5 percent of the slips in the bay are officially allocated for liveaboard use. Taking into account the "unofficial" liveaboards, the "sneakaboards," the "floating offices," and the reluctance of some operators to talk with us, we'd estimate that the actual number of official and unofficial liveaboard slips is closer to 7 or 8 percent of the total number of slips, or about 1,500.

Anchor-Outs

The controversy over liveaboards is most noticeable in Richardson Bay outside of Sausalito in Marin County. Here a small group of 100 to 150 persons are anchored near shore in everything from expensive yachts to what can only be described as piles of junk. The counterculture and somewhat anarchic lifestyle of these anchor-outs, together with government evidence that their sewage affects the water quality in the shallow bay, has spawned a highly polarized and adversarial debate over anchoring rights in Richardson Bay.

Even though this group represents a small, isolated number of individuals, it undoubtedly contributed to negative reactions to liveaboards throughout the region. Apart from any question of their being unsightly or navigation hazards, the BCDC considers them just another form of residential use of the bay and therefore illegal.

Evidence of how seriously the liveaboard controversy is taken is the marina operator we encountered who refused to talk about liveaboards, would not permit us to take pictures, and threatened us with bodily harm if he learned that we had talked to the BCDC about his marina! The unfortunate thing about this controversy is that as long as it persists, liveaboards who want to stay put for longer than a month will have a difficult time finding slips or anchorages in San Francisco Bay.

Michael Frankel and Kit Armstrong

NATIONAL MARINA CONFERENCE

Marinas are big business, and like other businesses their owners have banded together in an association to promote, educate, and research their unique niche in the marketplace. I attended one of their conferences to get an inside view of the marina business from the owner-operator's perspective.

It was four degrees in Boston at the site of the 5th National Conference on Marina Operations and Management—an atmosphere conducive to keeping conferees indoors and attentive.

The conference was sponsored by the International Marina Institute, a non-profit professional organization for the marina industry, dedicated to the dissemination of information services, training, and research to its members. The conference brought together more than 250 marina owners and operators, developers, consultants, designers, educators, manufacturers, financiers, regulators, and lawyers, all of whom are involved in the marina business in one way or another. The aim of the conference was to expand the professionalism of the marina business through an exchange of experiences and information resources.

The topics covered over the three-day meeting included: marina and boatyard operations and practices, personnel and customer relations, public and customer management, and liability and risk management. There was even a session on the experiences of women-owned marinas entitled, "I want to see the manager, where is HE!" The presentations by owners and managers from across the country highlighted the complex and multidisciplinary aspects of marina operations in an increasingly "bottom line" business environment. One speaker advised the audience that if their marina was more than 80 percent occupied, then it was time to raise the rent. Another described a wet versus dry boat-storage rate schedule designed to encourage winter haulouts to dry storage so that the marina would have a better chance to suggest maintenance and enhancement services.

Other operators stressed customer services designed to bring in business prospects. For example, it was suggested that technical seminars be offered during slow winter months to bring in experts from the paint and electronic industry as a way to offer a useful service while at the same time generating business opportunities. Outdoor public functions in the summer months were suggested as a way to celebrate holidays, create good will, and generate business. Several owners stressed the benefit of attractive landscaping with picnic areas and other amenities for boatowners and their guests.

Considerable time was devoted to personnel selection, career advancement, and job training. One manager at a resort marina told of his policy to hire only women dock handlers because in his experience they were neater, more courteous, friendlier, more attentive to their duties, and gentler to the boats being maneuvered and tied up. He also made a point of paying more per hour to the trash-collecting and bathroom-cleaning personnel because, unlike dock handlers, they didn't receive tips. He recounted an amusing experience with trying to hire foreign summer students from Ireland. He said they were terrific, no-nonsense workers for about three weeks, and then they became Americanized.

The lawyers at the conference did their best to frighten marina owners with the worst possible scenarios of liabilities associated with marina operations. They pointed out that a boatyard may be designated as a hazardous waste "Superfund" site because of empty, discarded bottom-paint cans or old batteries on the premises. They had plenty of not-so-funny anecdotes about "vicarious" liabilities from accidents caused by seasonal teenage workers— would you believe drag racing Travelifts across the marina parking lot?

I was invited to participate as a co-panelist in a workshop entitled "Managing Liveaboards." My fellow panelist, a marina owner from Olympia, Washington, was very much opposed to liveaboards because they presented her with additional demands and refused to pay for weekly services normally offered to weekend guests. One of the examples mentioned was the burden of having to sort large piles of mail for individual slip renters. It seemed to me that this particular problem could have been solved with the help of the U.S. Post Office. She and other marina operators also brought up the problems of unleashed pets wandering on (and messing up) the docks, cats crawling on other people's boats, the accumulation of "stuff" on the docks, derelict-looking vessels, higher volumes of trash to be hauled, extra parking spaces needed by liveaboards, and several other complaints.

There was a spirited discussion over the pros and cons of allowing liveaboards. The benefits noted were: additional marina security, availability of experienced residents in case of emergencies or simply as helpful hands, a sense of community during the otherwise desolate weekdays or winter season, and an opportunity to charge for legitimate services associated with the higher or unique demands of liveaboards.

During the many presentations by marina operators and especially at the liveaboard workshop, I kept notes on the types of marina amenities that would enhance the liveaboard lifestyle, such as telephone service, cable TV, mail and package delivery, shoreside storage facilities, cold food and freezer lockers, car parking, message center, FAX services, etc. Many of these items can be electronically metered or costed in such a manner as to create a fair exchange between the service offered and the cost of providing it. This would go a long way toward reducing unnecessary tensions between marina operators and those wishing to live aboard.

There are social and technological trends afoot that are attracting people to the liveaboard lifestyle in increasing numbers; for example, earlier and more active retirements, disaffection with urban life, boat designs with luxury accoutrements, and technical innovations making it easier for shorthanded couples to operate larger and more complex boats. More and more people will realize their liveaboard fantasies, and conferences such as this will continue to benefit both the marina owners and operators and their liveaboard customers.

DOCKOMINIUMS

The concept of selling a 40- by 15-foot plot of water between pilings and a finger dock sounds ridiculous to people accustomed to buying solid, unmoving land. It may even sound bizarre to those who have grown accustomed to condos. But the deal-makers have come up with something new for boaters—the "dockominium."

Will Rogers once said, "Buy land; they're not making any more of it!" Now some shrewd developers are looking under the Brooklyn Bridge and wondering if the same advice holds for the water.

Whenever you mix developers, investors, and lawyers in the same brew, you can expect some new and innovative scheme to turn a profit. Well, buying a 40- by 15-foot patch of water between pilings and calling it a dockominium certainly qualifies as a bold new scheme to make money for some, save some for others, and leave some wondering. The notion of buying slip space isn't new. Back in the early 1970s, it first appeared in the San Juan Islands off the Seattle coast. Apparently there was a severe shortage of slips in this prime cruising area, and the sale of slips (with all the cash up front) was the only way to fund the creation of new marina space for a burgeoning boating market.

Since then the concept has flourished on the East Coast. There are now several hundred dockominium (or some form of slip ownership) marinas spread over many states. Typically, a slip can cost anywhere from $1,000 to $3,000 per foot, plus maintenance fees. In the late 1980s, *Motor Boating & Sailing* reported slip costs as high as $4,000 per foot and noted that some investors had purchased slips for $100,000 and sold them less than two years later for $400,000. Purchase arrangements usually involve a 10- to 20-percent down payment and a 10- to 20-year period to pay off the bank mortgage. There is a secondary market in slips resulting from boatowners moving up to larger boats and investors who buy and sell slips for a profit. But as with other forms of real estate, there are often soft periods and these examples are by no means the rule.

What Led to the Dockominium Concept?

Those who are in the know, namely developers, investors, and lawyers, argue that the following forces created the dockominium concept:

- Owners of marinas typically make a very small return on their investment and are therefore unable to raise the money to adequately maintain, modernize, or expand their facilities. The International Marina Institute reports that the average return on investment is a low two percent, a number well below the threshold for justifying a bank investment.
- There continues to be a growing imbalance between the number of boats manufactured and the number of slips available to house those boats. The National Marine Manufacturers Association estimates that there are 40 boats built each year for every new slip created (note that not all boats require slips). And the low return on investment of marinas makes it difficult to raise money for the construction of new marinas to fill the gap.

It is sometimes difficult to separate the chicken from the egg, but it might be argued that the lure of quick profits is strong inducement to convert traditional rental-slip marinas into condominiums and therefore another factor in the growth of dockominium conversions. Others might argue that the profits are simply an outcome of the low return on investment and the shortage of slips. However, there is no argument that marinas are not very capital intensive businesses. Dock structures have a useful life of about 12 years. This creates a continuing need for capital while at the same time promising a low return on the capital needed. Marina operators have historically been poor businessmen running "Mom & Pop" operations, neglecting maintenance and modernization for new generations of boats, and living off the continuing depreciation of the facilities. There are strong pressures to eliminate marinas in favor of "higher use" residential and commercial waterfront development with phenomenally higher returns on investment. And there are increasingly complex regulatory requirements associated with zoning restrictions and environmental protection which make it costly, if not impossible, to maintain a marina, let alone construct a new one.

From the Marina Developer's Point of View

Developers point out that a marina conversion, properly done, represents a cure to what ails the system.

- The dockominium offers a reasonable return on marina investments.
- The moneys raised from the sale of slips afford the opportunity to make substantial improvements to a facility and assure the upkeep of the property and the environmental protection of the area.
- The dockominium permanently commits the property to a water use.
- Investment purchases of dockominiums assure the continued availability of rental slips.

According to developers, these favorable outcomes are the result of being able to generate more money more quickly when a property is sold in pieces than when sold as a block. And because the conversion of the property results in many owners, the likelihood that the facility will stay a marina permanently is virtually assured. A frequent scenario for the creation of a dockominium is as follows: A small family-run marina is approached by a big outfit with plenty of cash. The developer doesn't want to buy the marina outright; he just wants to convert the existing slips to long-term (99-year) leases, create more of them, and generally improve the property. If he bought the marina outright, then he'd have to "work" for a living. If he wanted to work for a living, he wouldn't be a developer. The marina owner, usually saddled with huge debts and a slow return, agrees. The property gets the money it needs for new slips, much needed improvements, promotion, and the gauntlet of regulatory processes to get the permits for expansion. The owner remains as caretaker if he wants; the developer gets his return up front since the buyers finance and the banks pay off; and the lessees don't have to worry about a slip, for the moment.

From the Boatowner's Point of View

For those with plenty of cash or the ability to get the cash from a bank, the dockominium deal sounds great. It assures them of a slip and locks them into a fixed rate for the slip (maintenance fees and variable mortgages aside). It assures them of the necessary funding to maintain the marina. And should they want to sell the slip, there is a good chance that a profit can be made on the initial investment.

But there are risks. What do you buy when you buy a piece of water? Do you buy the water surface? The muddy bottom underneath? The air between the pilings and the dock? It depends. There are several ways to "buy." You could acquire a fee-simple interest in a property that entitles you to use a specific part of the common area including a slip. This is similar to a condominium. Because of the question of who owns the bottom, you might acquire a 99-year lease to the use of a slip and common area. You may buy a share of a corporation and be given the right to a specific slip owned by the corporation. You may buy a membership in a private club that entitles you to a specific slip owned by the club.

The type of ownership depends on state laws based on apartment ownership and uniform common interest ownership. In many states, the term "condominium" refers to an interest in, over, or under land, including spaces that may be filled with air and water. Therefore, a buyer would acquire complete ownership of the dock space adjoining the slip and the exclusive right to use the slip space, and an undivided interest in common areas of the docks and properties above the waterline.

The risks of slip ownership, regardless of the type of ownership, stem from the fact that the state owns the bottom land as a public trust resource. It grants the marina operator a permit to operate the marina and allow the construction of docks out into the water. Unfortunately, the permit period is generally less than the long-term lease or condominium period. This means that there are no guarantees of future permits.

The Army Corps of Engineers is charged with the responsibility of maintaining navigable waters. If, in its judgment, the dockage or breakwater extending into the water is impeding navigation, it can demand the removal of the dockage or prohibit expansion and modification. The corps also can deny maintenance and dredging permits in the event that a marina's docks need replacing or the marina becomes silted up. And at the local level, states have little experience in taxing dockominiums and may radically alter property-tax rules, changing the value of the investment.

For those unable to afford the steep initial price of a dockominium, those not interested in committing such large funds to one place, or those not willing to take the investment risk, this may not be such a good deal. And the rental slips that are available as a result of someone else's investment will undoubtedly be more expensive due to the profits expected by the developer and investor. Furthermore, slips available for rent generally will be larger than required by the boatowner and therefore cost more than at a typical rental marina.

So, as in most things, there is a good side and a bad side to the dockominium concept. It will help marinas survive by resisting the pressure to convert to apartment condominiums and trendy waterfront shops, but in the process, slip spaces (for rent or purchase) will become more expensive and tend to drive the middle-class boater off the water.

Remember the old saying, "A boat is a hole in the water that you pour money into?" Well, now you can add, "And the water around the hole can cost more than the boat."

THE KING OWNS THE BOTTOM OF THE SEA
Liveaboard restrictions, anchoring rights, and new concepts of slip ownership have focused new attention on the age-old question of who really owns the water.

"…And the waters above are held by the sovereign in trust for the public to use in navigation and commerce." This concept predates the Magna Carta. Hundreds of years of common law have evolved around this concept. Many of the notions of public rights and ownership involved in the recent development of dockominiums also are applicable to the growing trend restricting liveaboard anchoring privileges and liveaboard slips at marinas. On board their boats, masters of their fates and captains of their souls are also subject to the responsibilities imposed by the law.

There are several classifications of waters, submerged lands, and the overlapping jurisdictions over their uses. A number of these terms are relevant to understanding the rights of boaters in the largely unfamiliar arena of navigable waters and public trust resources. (See "Terms and Definitions" below.)

The two circumstances facing boaters who choose to live aboard their vessels are the liveaboard rights on a vessel tied to a dock at a public or private marina facility, and the liveaboard rights on a vessel anchored or moored in navigable waters. The following discussion refers only to navigable boats and not to floating house structures that do not, in any way, resemble navigable boats.

Marina Restrictions

A marina facility can be a private enterprise or a public facility. In either case, the owners, whether private citizens, a corporation, or a municipality, can adopt rules and regulations that determine the nature and character of the facility and thereby impose restrictions, such as the length of time one can "live" aboard a vessel. These restrictions can be based on specific zoning rules or limitations of public services needed to support a liveaboard community, for example, parking spaces, trash collection, access to schools, fire protection, water pollution control, etc. However, restrictions cannot be based on unreasonable or prejudicial opinions such as race, color, lifestyle, place of origin, age, etc.

A marina's docks and slips generally protrude into navigable waters that are under federal jurisdiction for purposes of navigation, commerce, and travel. The docks and slips are also located over submerged lands that are held by the state in public trust. The property rights of marina owners over state submerged lands and within federal navigable waters derive from riparian (or littoral) rights associated with the ownership of the associated shore or uplands. Under riparian rights, owners are allowed to erect piers and wharfs into public trust resources—waters and submerged lands—so that trade, travel, and recreation can be accommodated on these waters.

In the case of dockominiums, the "owner" of a slip is actually owner of a portion of the riparian rights and a portion of the wharfs, associated common shorelands, and facilities included in the dockominium arrangement. The association of owners is then at liberty to impose restrictive covenants similar to those of a homeowners association attempting to protect the character of the neighborhood.

Terms and Definitions

Admiralty—as in "admiralty court" or "admiralty law"—refers to federal rules and jurisdiction over the high seas, territorial and internal navigable waters, and maritime activities.

Navigable Water—Waters navigable in character, over which interstate and foreign trade and travel may be conducted, are public waters within federal admiralty jurisdiction. All waters that cross state boundaries and those that ultimately connect to the high seas are considered federal navigable waters.

High Seas—those parts of the sea beyond terrestrial or internal waters.

Territorial Sea—3 mile seaward limit of each coastal state. (In Florida and Texas the territorial limit in the Gulf of Mexico is three leagues or 9 miles.)

Internal Waters—navigable waters inland of the demarcation of the High Seas Line, which are under federal inland navigation rules. Seaward of the demarcation line International Rules of the Road apply.

Contiguous Zone—a portion of the high seas and submerged lands out to a 200-mile limit, over which the federal government exerts economic controls for fishing, mineral, and other natural resources.

County or Community Waters—waters and submerged lands that lie within the incorporated limits of a political jurisdiction. Enforcement over these waters may be delegated by the state to county or local authorities.

Submerged Lands—refers to the lands under waters, including navigable waters, under the federal Submerged Lands Act of 1954. The federal government retains rights over these lands with respect to navigation, commerce, national defense, and international affairs. However, ownership rights or the rights of management, administration, leasing, use, and development are assigned to the states along with the common law trust obligation to use the lands in a manner consistent with public interests.

Riparian—pertaining to a riverbank or lake shoreline.

Littoral—pertaining to a seashore.

Public Trust Resources—natural resources such as water bodies held by the sovereign (state or federal government) in trust for the public's use in navigation, commerce, and fishing. Public trust easements have been held to include the right to fish, hunt, bathe, swim, to use for boating and general recreation purposes, and to use the bottom of the navigable waters for anchoring and standing.

Generally, the boater is at the mercy of marina regulations, which may or may not restrict living aboard. There are no constitutional rights or federal regulations that guarantee the right to live aboard at public or private marinas.

Anchoring Rights

The freedom to travel on navigable waters that are held in public trust is guaranteed under federal admiralty jurisdiction. States may enact laws regulating harbors, pilotage, and other safety and management regulations for their territorial waters, but these laws cannot conflict with federal laws. However, freedom to navigate does not automatically include the right to use state- and local-government-owned submerged lands. Navigability of waters does not deprive a local government of jurisdiction over territory within its limits, which may include submerged lands adjacent to its shoreline.

Anchoring is an act of navigation protected in all internal navigable waters, territorial waters, contiguous waters, and the high seas. This act of navigation is covered by admiralty jurisdiction over the Rules of the Road for both inland waters and the high seas. These rules specifically define an anchored vessel and the day and night signals used to identify anchored vessels. Therefore, the act of anchoring is guaranteed under federal admiralty jurisdiction on navigable waters. However, nothing in the Rules of the Road or other federal regulations of navigable waters specifies a maximum length of time a vessel may remain anchored at any given spot, assuming the vessel is not interfering with navigation along the waterway. The act of anchoring (or mooring) also requires a physical connection with the submerged land. The submerged land along navigable waterways is owned, or held in public trust, by state or local governments. As a consequence, the state or local government has a say in how this submerged land can be used. Several state and local governments have prohibited residential use of submerged lands but have not interfered with use of the overlying waters for navigation, commerce, travel, or recreation.

The problem for liveaboards arises from the uncertain standards used to distinguish between the boater's intent to "anchor" temporarily or to "reside" permanently. In some instances the distinction between anchoring during waterway travel and anchoring as a resident hinges on the length of time the boat will be anchored, in other instances on the definition of the boatowner's "principal" residence. Having a shore-based address makes anchoring less like an act of residency. However, this leaves open the question of how to define a principal address—is it where mail is received, where one votes, where taxes are paid, where one stays the longest period over a year's time?...

It is important to understand how these laws of multiple jurisdictions apply to living aboard. However, the underlying issue is usually one of lifestyle and not a specific law. Lifestyle differences often evoke prejudice toward and questioning of the character of liveaboards. At the root of many liveaboard restrictions or the lack of amicable compromise between live-aboards and their land-based neighbors is a difference in lifestyles, not issues of taxation and pollution.

Why Is the Liveaboard Becoming an Endangered Species?

Fifty years ago there were liveaboards, maybe fewer or maybe the same number in relation to the land population, but no documented evidence of liveaboard restrictions. What happened? Why is there a problem today? According to Herbert Markow, author of *Small Boat Law*, "It begins at any busy metropolitan street corner as frustrated people try to weave through sidewalk crowds to catch departing buses, or try to beat flashing 'walk' signs at intersections that do not allow time to hustle from one curb to the other, or try to drive with ill-timed traffic lights on choked streets. Others crawl the high-speed expressways at rush hour. From this so-called rat race the population seeks escape for a day, a weekend, or sometimes for life. If all these escapists were distributed evenly over the seven seas there would be no problem."

Unfortunately, liveaboards are not evenly distributed. Although many seek solitude, many more congregate around communal facilities, urban amenities, and fewer and fewer pristine surroundings. It is the sharing of these facilities, amenities, and natural resources that creates the problem. Land-based residents have established public services, land-use restrictions, and a system of community taxation that addresses their needs and obligations. The boating liveaboard anchored off a community's shores or tied up at a local marina may not be paying a full share of the true cost of those services and resources. For example, in Los Angeles, boatowners pay a property tax of 1.5 percent of the boat's depreciating value compared to a real-estate tax rate of 1.25 percent, generally on rising property values. On the other hand, in Annapolis the real-estate tax rate is 1.4 percent, and there is no property tax on boats.

In an economic sense the phrase "free society" is a contradiction in terms. Unless you're a singlehander on a raft, living off your wits in the middle of the ocean, living isn't free. Living in a "society" has its real and social costs. And for boaters one of the most painful costs is liveaboard restrictions imposed by a system that these boaters are usually trying to escape.

What Can Be Done to Limit Liveaboard Restrictions?

Boaters may feel outraged at any loss of the "freedom of the seas," not unlike the cowboy's loss of the "open range." But as populations continue to grow and society, by necessity, becomes more complex, such freedoms are naturally eroded. To the extent that boaters look to the courts for relief from liveaboard restrictions, they should understand that the trend of the law has been to support expanded state and local regulations imposing community values over the rights of individuals. The frontier mentality has given way to more governmental authority in the name of order, balance, social cohesion....The larger, denser, and more congested the community, the more precise the rules and the more difficult it is to argue that government is unfair. It is the tyranny of the majority.

Liveaboards are a small vulnerable group in a much larger land-based society. It's the boaters' responsibility to learn about the concerns of the community and possible legislative initiatives before it's too late to alter peoples' mind, and conflicts arise. In many instances it may already be too late to avoid tensions between those seeking freedoms and those seeking order, control, and structure. Then the solutions to reducing tensions lie in grass-roots politics more so than in a search for some inalienable constitutional right.

Each boating community is unique, as are the local issues facing liveaboards. However, the most important common denominator is the need to avoid the image and perception of liveaboards as freeloaders, squatters, or some other form of deviant, anarchic, or immoral characters. To avoid the there-goes-the-neighborhood syndrome, a few steps should be considered to survive within the system:

- Understand the local rules and regulations pertaining to living aboard a vessel while at anchor, moored, or tied to a dock. If there are no such rules, then it is important to exhibit good citizenship behavior to avoid any restrictive legislation. It is also important to be alert for any signs of public complaints and opposition to liveaboards and to deal with complaints as soon as they surface. This will help avoid creating a polarized community that ceases to be rational.
- Meet with other liveaboards in the area, either formally or informally, to share information and to promote exemplary liveaboard conduct.
- If complaints surface or if legislation is proposed against liveaboards, strengthen ties with other liveaboards in the area to share in the resolution of conflicts and to present a united front.
- Isolate the nature of the complaints or the specific points in the legislation. Prepare responses to refute or deal with the specific complaints.
- Investigate the legal basis for the proposed legislation to determine if any conflicts exist with overriding laws, such as those for interstate commerce, civil rights, etc. Seek legal assistance in those instances where laws may be in conflict.
- Present a united and well-informed front at local hearings.
- Isolate individual decision-makers and arrange small group or one-on-one meetings to make separate presentations regarding the issues prior to or following public meetings.
- Publicize the issues and, especially, the points in favor of liveaboards.

Acquaint the community with your presence, the issues, and your desire to be a good neighbor. Stress the positive aspects of being part of the community.

- Consider the possibility of offering to pay a surcharge to offset the community costs of servicing liveaboards.
- If all else fails, move on to "bluer waters."

Living in a society, whether on a boat or on land, is not getting any simpler. As we continue to crowd together on shrinking waterfronts along intracoastal waterways, estuaries, rivers, lakes, and sea coasts, conflicts will arise. And although many of the issues will be lacking in substance, the conflicts between landowners and boaters will be very real. Specific complaints will focus on pollution loads from a few vessels, the lack of property-tax payments to support local police, fire, and schools, or a strain on available shoreside parking spaces. But often the real issue will be the unique liveaboard lifestyle, which may be viewed as a threat to the character of a community. Only patient grass-roots campaigns can eliminate such prejudices. The law is only of limited help in this conflict.

Liveaboard Rights

THE OTHER SIDE OF THE DOCK

It's only natural to expect some dockmasters to be liveaboards. Like the proprietor who lives over the shop, there are liveaboards who live and work at their marinas. The following are two amusing accounts from "the other side of the dock." The first is from Dojelo Russell, who with her husband had a brief encounter running a marina on Chesapeake Bay.

Until recently, we were just an ordinary boating couple who took a lot for granted: a well-maintained marina; clean and comfortable facilities; and security for our boat and gear. In some places, we had those things. In others, we didn't, so we'd empty the shore locker and move on. Only when something went wrong did we give much thought to what the marina operators actually did, or how they did it. I'm sure we never wondered why they did what they did.

How quickly a flow of events captured our attention! We were happily settled in a small marina in the "northern neck" of Virginia. With its 25 covered slips and 15 outside slips, it was typical of many of the owner-operated facilities that dot the Chesapeake Bay shoreline. Suddenly, our marina was sold. The buyer was a developer who wanted the acres of lovely bay-front land that surrounded it. He had to buy the marina as part of the package, but he immediately put the marina itself back on the market.

123

Next, we watched in dismay as the former owners, who had built the marina and always managed it themselves, got ready to move away from their home on the property. Our care, security, and maintenance were going with them! We were recently retired and had become spring-through-fall live-aboards—the only ones in the marina. So it made some sense that on the day the former owners moved away we were asked if we would manage the marina for the new owner until he found a buyer for it. Why not? We were going to be there anyway. We had been in this particular marina long enough to care about it and worry about possible deterioration before re-sale.

We had boated on the Chesapeake for more than 20 years. From our experiences there, and from cruising the Intracoastal Waterway, we thought we knew a lot about marinas. A few times we had even kept an eye on this one while the former owners slipped away for an errand or brief vacation. My husband has been a state agency administrator, and I had been a professor in a large urban university, so our professional backgrounds surely qualified us to do something so simple. Between us, after all, we had two master's degrees and one doctorate! Even the tiny salary would be useful since it would be "earned" income and thus eligible for the IRA account. The deal was made. That first afternoon alone at the marina was exciting. We had a bunch of keys to try out as we entered "owner only" areas. We had a little cash box, full of change and small bills, which we carried around until we found a place to hide it. We could even open the soft drink machine! We could turn the gas pump on and off and already knew how to pump gas. Now we could learn to work the credit card machine. As we walked through the marina that first night to check all "our" boats, we were awed by our new importance in the nautical scheme of things.

As always, the sun did come up the next morning. We encountered the reality of the learning that occurs when you start to walk in someone else's moccasins, though, in our case, it was in deck shoes! First, we realized that our domain was dirty. Neglected during the last pre-closure weeks, public areas were not up to their normal standards. Someone had to clean up the place—*us!* Next, we counted sodas. Not only were there not enough for the next weekend, we didn't know where to get more and couldn't find where the machine was hiding its change. On to the gas pumps; there had to be more in the tanks by the weekend. People began coming by: people who wanted a slip, people who were curious, people who wanted to sell us things. We began to see the outlines of our little "summer job."

True to our backgrounds, we quickly started to get things "organized." We created new boathouse rosters and updated data. We revised the rules and regulations for boaters. We devised little forms on which to report our financial activities. But lots of things refused to become organized. The ice machine would break down according to its own internal schedule. The drink machine would refuse to deliver a soda only when we were busiest or at the other end of the property. If the gas supply got a bit low, all boatowners would decide to fill their tanks. People promised to come fix things but didn't show up. "Russell's Law," previously modeled on Murphy's profound observation that everything always takes longer than you think it will, was amended to read: "And boats honk for fuel at precisely the moment the meal moves from the stove to the table."

Looking back now, we can see more humor than we did then. The bathhouse, for example. I'd cleaned bathrooms; who hasn't? In our pre-retirement days we had good domestic help at home, so on many boating weekends I had mused on the irony of a hobby that had me sitting on the floor in the head, scrubbing away at the fixtures, and reminding myself that this was "recreation."

But public bathrooms? It was a chore to be approached grimly, with rubber gloves and powerful cleansers. The bathhouse was one of the places that refused to be organized. There were just too many doors, and they kept getting in my way. It was an exciting day when I learned I could make them stay open by detaching a little coiled gizmo from the door frame. The first attempt at hosing down the floors created a small pond full of hair and small dead bugs, with a scum-like layer of talcum atop. And the floors all seemed built to contain, not drain. My social conversation began to center around problems like how to get mold off bathmats.

Relationships with fellow boaters changed in unpredictable ways, as we ceased to be "peers." In some ways, we moved "up," in others, "down." Some of the changes were delightful. People we had known only slightly came by with helpful ideas, gadgets to make life easier, and gratitude for our "holding the fort" during the change of ownership. Some others, however, would stretch rules, complain about minor items, try to use us as a 24-hour message center, or honk repeatedly and rudely for gas even though they knew it took time for us to get to the gas dock. In our clean bathrooms, some boaters would carefully wipe off sinks and leave the area spotless. Others would leave a shambles after showering and even throw trash on the floor instead of in the basket, presuming, I suppose, that I was there to clean it up: a condescension that was a little hard to accept after the authority of a university classroom! We learned a lot about ourselves as well as our fellow boaters.

The marina was sold to new owners in four months, but, oh, how much we had learned in those four months of being in charge! There were dull moments—far too few—and exciting ones, like one of the unexpected bay "nor'easters" that flooded the basin, jeopardized several boats, and kept us in frantic, terrified motion until the water began to recede. Day by busy day we developed more appreciation for those men and women all around the bay who add so much to our boating pleasure. We don't claim to know much about big marinas with hired managers and uniformed dockhands, but we have learned some things about the operation of small marinas: the skills required, the personal costs to the operators, and a bit about the economics.

First, marina operators, male or female, have to fill multiple roles that demand special skills. Somehow, they have to combine the authority of a sheriff with the knowledge of a sea captain while they perform tasks ranging from menial to highly skilled. It's not an easy mix.

They are security guards, in the fullest sense. Not only must they protect our boats from theft or vandalism, they have to watch our lines and water-lines to be sure we remain secured and afloat. Our former owner patrolled the boathouses at least twice each day and often added a water patrol by skiff, noting any minor deviation from normal. He—and we—saved several boats from sinking—just part of the "service."

When a variety of people interact within a small space, there has to be an authority figure. Somebody has to set rules and enforce them, or there can be neither safety nor comfort. In our pre-manager days, we used to join in the griping and game-playing that went on about marina rules. Suddenly we were the enforcers, and even our years of administrative experience didn't make it easy.

Marina operators are expected to know answers to all the questions. What's the best way to get to a particular anchorage or another marina? Does my engine sound funny? Who's a good mechanic for diesels? With new boaters, teaching becomes even more important than answering questions. Often, new boatowners don't know how to dock properly, tie off their lines, read the meaning of buoys, or apply the Rules of the Road. Sometimes the questions and actions are funny, and a sense of humor helps. Other times they can have you running down the dock with a line and a prayer.

Good marina operators are also the central link in the marina grapevine: who caught how many fish, where they're biting, who's in the hospital and how's he doing, what the new nearby restaurant's like, who was by to see you while you were out and their message. Such exchanges help make a marina a little community, as ours was. For us, at least, having this community was one of the real joys of boating.

Second, the personal costs are high. In four months, we were away from the marina together only for a few errands and one cruise that had been scheduled before we agreed to take care of the marina. We felt like one of us had to be there all the time to watch the boats and be available if needed. It's a 24-hour, 12-month job. Our years of flexible hours with weekends and holidays "off" had not prepared us for such extensive confinement, and we still wonder how people can tolerate it for many years.

Worry became a constant in our lives. An overdue boater was a problem because if something was really wrong, something had to be done. An approaching storm keeps your ear to the weather channel, in between trying to secure loose gear and respond to phone calls from anxious boatowners. Concern about liability becomes a part of life, since a marina abounds with opportunity for oversights and accidents. Empty slips cause another kind of worry, we're sure, as do boaters who miss or delay dock rent payments while costs go on.

For all this, the economic returns seem very small. *Why* do they do it? We were amazed at how thin the profit margin was on gas, drinks, ice, and marine supplies. We had assumed that dock rents, plus these incidental profits, produced a good income. But as we weighed the income against seven-day weeks, frequent stress, and the amount of capital invested, it seemed quite small. Even at today's interest rates, the investment in our particular marina would earn more tucked away in worry-free certificates of deposit.

Certainly, motivation is different for different people, but we've come to believe that for most marina owners, it's as simple as a love for boats and the bay—the same dynamics that bring us boatowners to the marina. Like us, they've chosen to put substantial resources into a world they love. While our investment serves only us and our friends, theirs serves many more, including us. We cannot imagine the bay without its many small family-owned boating facilities. Would we "run" a marina again? No. But are we glad we did? Yes, very glad. We have never again taken for granted this true "service" occupation, and we have remembered to say "thank you" a lot more than we used to.

When our former owners left the marina, we boaters had a lovely party to say "thank you" to them. We had balloons, gifts, and speeches and signs that expressed our appreciation for the many years they had added so much to our enjoyment of boating. But now I wonder why we waited so long to say those things. That's the message!

Have you hugged your marina owner lately?

Dojelo Russell

Liveaboard Rights

A DAY IN MY LIFE AS HARBORMASTER
The second "other side of the dock" story comes from Sally Elizabeth Andrew, a liveaboard with her harbormaster friend in San Francisco Bay.

There are tough days on every job, but yesterday was just too much. I used to think that harbormastering was the best job in the world. But now . . . well, let me start at the beginning.

Yesterday was Friday, the end of the week for most people but the start of a busy weekend at the marina. Still, I celebrated the end of the week like many other boatowners by going out for an evening sail. There was a beautiful sunset, and with the full moon rising over the hills, we flew the spinnaker for a run down the estuary and back to our slip. At nine o'clock we met some friends at the local hot spot for fajitas, margueritas, and Coronas. It was a pleasant evening.

On the way back down to the boat after dinner, my pleasant reverie was broken. I heard some thrashing in the water about halfway up one of the docks. Upon investigation, I discovered a naked drunken woman trying to keep herself and her duffle bag afloat. She was crying and having difficulty breathing in between sobs, so I quickly dragged her and the bag from the water and wrapped her in my jacket. Her boyfriend had literally thrown her off the boat after an argument. I presume her belongings followed shortly thereafter. I talked to them both for a few moments and after they both cooled down, left them alone to kiss and make up. Because my friend Elizabeth was staying aboard my boat that evening, I was anxious to keep the mood that had been created at dinner. We had just settled into a cuddle in the V-berth when the phone rang. Why I ever put a phone on board I'll never know! I tried ignoring the first hundred rings, but when it persisted, I figured it must be something serious.

"Hello?" I said, half expecting to hear that a hurricane had somehow generated offshore and was heading our way.

"There's a loud noise coming from somewhere in the marina," said a man's voice. "My wife and I can't sleep."

I inquired as to the nature of the noise and where they thought it was coming from but I couldn't figure what on earth they were describing. The suggestion that they close their hatches met without success. "It's too hot," said the caller.

"Thank you, I'll check into it." Click.

I had every intention of just ignoring the complaint and going back to more enjoyable activities, but duty wouldn't allow it. Besides, the mood had once again been broken. "I'll be right back," I assured Elizabeth, and went topside to investigate.

It took awhile, but I finally found the source of the noise, an unmanned truck with a very noisy generator on a construction site about a half mile away from the marina. Unfortunately, the noise was not very loud close to the source but was particularly piercing directly downwind in the slip of the two unhappy berthers. I let them know where the sound was coming from and that there was nothing I could do about it. They thanked me, and I returned to my boat and my now sleeping friend.

I too was soon fast asleep and was dreaming of tropical isles and sandy beaches when there was a pounding on the hull. Oh shit, what now? I leaned out of the companionway. "Yeah?"

It was the security guard. "Hello. You are the harbormaster? I think there's a boat taking on water."

"How much water?"

"Quite a bit I reckon. It's my first night on the job, and I don't really know too much about boats."

"How low in the water is it sitting?"

"Oh, pretty low. . . ."

"How far?"

"All the way I reckon. It's down!"

I got dressed again and accompanied the guard to where the boat, a 52-foot poweryacht had indeed "taken on some water." The only part of the boat that was above the water was the flying bridge! Surprisingly, the dock had not gone down with the boat. Instead, the dock lines had sawed nice neat lines up through the hull! On the way up to the office to call the owners, I reflected on why these things always happen in the middle of the night, never in the middle of the day!

With the owner informed and on his way, I called the Coast Guard and notified them of the fuel seeping out of the sunken boat's tanks. They informed me that we had to get a private contractor to set up the booms and do the environmental cleanup. Trying to protect the environment at three o'clock in the morning is not easy. Good thing this wasn't the Exxon *Valdez!*

When the distraught owners finally arrived, they surmised that their mechanic had not replaced the broken water strainer on the engine intake and that it had come apart. Apparently, the boat had been slowly taking on water all evening. When the water reached the open ports in the hull, it went down quickly.

By the time I got back to my boat it was dawn. Adrenalin still running, I decided to take a long, hot shower and take Elizabeth to breakfast at Albert's Restaurant. After a few cups of coffee, I was ready to take on the day. It was Saturday morning, and the weekend usually brought people into the office for friendly chats and the trading of tales.

In fact, someone was already standing at the office door when I arrived. Apparently, a boat had come adrift in the night and was fetching up against his boat down the aisleway. Would I please come and remove the transient vessel?

That task completed, I went back to the office and played the messages off the answering machine. The third message was a death threat from one of the berthers. And he sounded, well, deadly serious. This guy often came down for a weekend of sailing and left his dog tied to a cleat or roaming the docks for the entire day while he was out on the water. I had received several complaints from his neighbors and other concerned animal lovers and had recently notified him that he had to abstain from this practice if he wished to continue berthing in the marina. He apparently didn't like ultimatums, so this was his "counteroffer."

The police had no sooner left with the incriminating tape as evidence, when a boy came running into the office to ask me to help him retrieve his mother's bicycle from the water before his parents returned. After a trip to the maintenance yard to locate a grappling hook, I spent 30 wasted minutes trying to extricate the bike. Just as I was about to give up, the youngster remembered that the bike had fallen the other way. I had been looking on the wrong side of the finger!

At eleven o'clock, I received a call from the owner of a neighboring business. "You better stop polluting my waterfront!" he said. I thought he was referring to the ongoing cleanup around the sunken motorboat, but before I could respond, he said, "Brown sewage is floating everywhere and I know it's from your marina. Your berthers must be pumping their holding tanks into the water!"

I too had noticed the recent phenomenon—brown slime clinging to everything from shore rocks to boat bootstripes. Earlier in the week I had called the Coast Guard to inquire as to the nature of the stuff and was told that the profuse and recent rain had caused an abnormally high production of brown algae in the estuary. That, yes, it did look disgustingly like raw sewage, but, no, it was not harmful. I explained all to this to the concerned business owner.

"I'm sorry, it is not my marina, it is not sewage, and it will not be disappearing for a while." I stated matter-of-factly.

"Don't lie to me, I know it's raw sewage!"

"Call the Coast Guard if you don't believe me. Have the water tested, but please don't make such silly accusations without facts to back them up." I hung up the phone.

My God, what a day! I am used to complaints about deserted dogs, wild cats, phantom poopers, and other such calamities. I've heard complaints about people doing their laundry in the shower stalls or even showering with their pets. These occurrences are mundane. Sometimes, they're even funny. Like the time a berther came in to tell me about some weird stuff all over his deck. After a walk down to his boat to look at his deck, I had to inform the gentleman that the "weird stuff" was heron shit. But today was not funny. Today was taking its toll on me.

The next person to come into the harbor office was a guy who wanted to complain about his boat turning orange. "Orange?" I asked. Apparently his boat turned orange because the guy in the slip next to him had been refinishing his mahogany cabintop. He was going to sue his neighbor, the marina, the manufacturer of the sandpaper, etc.

I was familiar with the "orange" boat. I had often noticed the poor upkeep—it didn't appear to have been washed in the last 10 years. Ever the diplomat, I tried to calm him down and we went down on the docks together and talked to his neighbor. The accused agreed to wash, buff, and wax the guy's "orange" boat and the proposed lawsuit was dropped. On the way back to the office, I noticed some "undesirables" working on a berther's boat. These were the same guys I had thrown off the dock on Thursday. In the latest "scam of the month," their "boss" had given some quotes to local boaters for varnish work that sounded too good to be true—because they were. But he had shown the nicest varnish jobs in the marina as examples of "his" work, collected some very large deposits, and then hired some drifters to do the work while he quickly left town with the money.

After telling the workers to get lost the first time, I'd notified one boat-owner about what was apparently going on. He had paid the con-artist $1,000 as a deposit. I reminded him that the longer the workers worked on his boat, the more money he would be liable for since the workers could put a lien on his boat if their "boss" didn't return to pay them. Friday, I received a call from the boatowner's lawyer who informed me that the good doctor now wanted to sue me. "Does he realize I saved him from more debt?" I inquired.

With the remainder of that unpleasant conversation running through my head, I once again confronted the "workers" and asked them to leave and not come back. This time one of the drifters, half-stoned and pissed off, weaved slowly up the dock toward me—and pulled out a gun.

Oh sheeeeitttt! The drifter had a gun! How I wished I was in southern California....I would probably be packing a gun as part of my job. All I was armed with was common sense, which dictated—no, demanded—that I run away as fast as I possibly could. Instead, for reasons unknown, I stood my ground and talked to the angry, armed young maniac. I don't remember what I said, but it made sense to him. After a few minutes, he handed over the weapon and I sent him and his buddies packing.

As I began walking back to the office, a strange feeling came over me. Maybe it was lack of sleep. Maybe it was the rush of adrenalin over the gun scare. Or maybe it was the sight of the flowerbox still sitting on the same finger of the dock after I had repeatedly told its owners to remove it. Whatever it was, something inside me must have snapped. I pointed the gun at the flower-box and pulled the trigger, spraying dirt, flowers, and crockery into the water.

Then, instead of heading back in to the office, I went over to where a couple of dinghies were perpetually pulled out onto fingers, another flagrant disregard of the rules. "Make my day," I muttered under my breath as I filled them full of holes and pushed them into the water to watch them sink.

Then I saw that big double-ender with the head-banging bowsprit overhanging the dock. I remember quite clearly asking this particular owner what kind of sailboat he had on the day he signed up for a slip. "A 38-foot sailboat," he had said. I guess he thought that: (1) I didn't know one boat from another or (2) it was none of my business what type of boat it was or (3) that once you subtracted the lengths of the boomkin and bowsprit, this particular 48-footer actually required a 38-foot slip! The result was a bowsprit overhanging the dock so far you had to practically turn sideways to get around it. I'd tried every diplomatic means to try to alleviate the situation. Now it became clear what I had to do.

I ran up to the maintenance shed, threw down the gun and picked up the right tool for this job. As I walked back down to the big double-ender, I pulled the cord and the chainsaw roared to life in a cloud of blue smoke. This guy said he had a 38-footer—I was just going to prove him right.

Just as the whirling teeth were about to bite into the varnished wood, somebody grabbed me from behind. Grabbing me from behind! Oh my God! They're pulling me away....

It was my friend Elizabeth!!! It was Saturday morning!!! When I regained my senses, I jumped up and peered out the forward hatch at a serene morning. No sunken boats, no gun-toting strangers. It was all a dream—or should I say, nightmare. I had a terrible headache. Ugh!!

"Come on," she said, already dressed and radiant from a good night's sleep. "Let's go to Albert's for breakfast. . . . You'll feel better after you get something to eat." And as I drank my coffee, Elizabeth reminded me of how much I have enjoyed working on the water and being with people who like boats and sailing. I'm going to miss it.

Sally Elizabeth Andrew

7
The Law

PUBLIC LAWS in our complex society reach into every nook and cranny of our lives. The liveaboard society is no exception. In return for living in such a unique environment, liveaboards are faced with equally unique laws over such items as search and seizure, plastic pollution, and vessel sanitation, to name but a few.

Probably the most volatile issue facing boaters—and liveaboards—in recent years is over searches and seizures conducted in the war against drugs. Regardless of one's position on drug use, the measures employed by enforcement officials have enraged, frustrated, and humiliated most boaters, especially liveaboards who naturally assume that their homes are also their castles.

An equally important, if no less volatile, issue is marine pollution. Marine pollution is rapidly becoming a major environmental public concern—whether over oil-tanker spills or medical wastes washed up on beaches. Boaters in particular are facing the prospect of having their beautiful and "limitless" environment befouled. Two specific issues that have raised the environmental consciousness of boaters, and of course, liveaboards, are regulations over plastic marine debris and vessel sanitation.

133

There is also the endless debate over guns, especially for those who cruise less settled areas. The question of whether to arm a boat for self-defense is arguable, but the law on this issue is clear.

A Brief History of Search and Seizure

A recent spate of highly publicized boat seizures by the U.S. Coast Guard under their Zero Tolerance program sent me to the library and a review of the history of search and seizure laws.

Gently with the Tides

In our democracy, an individual's right to protection from unreasonable search and seizure is a substantive right like that of free speech. It is also a procedural right protecting one from the improper use of evidence in a trial. Over the past seven centuries (see sidebar) this right has given lawmakers and judges great difficulty as society has become more complex and the interests of the individual had to be compromised against the good of society. In more recent times the concept of a boat as a permanent or temporary home and the government's right to protect society from illegal drugs and immigration have focused attention on the individual's protection from warrantless searches and seizures on the water.

The History of Search and Seizure

1215—King John bows to the will of the people and signs the Magna Carta in Runnymede, England. The 63 simply stated clauses in this document became a model for individual rights under a democracy. Clause 39 states, "No free man shall be arrested or imprisoned or disseized or outlawed or exiled or in any way victimized, neither will we attack him or send anyone to attack him, except by the lawful judgment of his peers or by the law of the land."

1628—Sir Edward Coke, an English jurist, coins the phrase, "A man's house is his castle." He codifies much of the English common-law, since the Magna Carta, into the British Bill of Rights. The judge-made common-law and the English Bill of Rights become the basis of our Bill of Rights.

1789—The First Congress of the United States passes the Bill of Rights for ratification by the States. The Fourth Amendment of the Bill of Rights states: "The right of the people to be secure in their persons, houses, papers, and effects, against unreasonable searches and seizures, shall not be violated, and no warrants shall issue, but upon probable cause, supported by oath or affirmation, and particularly describing the place to be searched, and the persons or things to be seized."

1790—The First Congress also enacts legislation which provides, "That every collector, naval officer, and surveyor, or other persons specifically appointed by either of them for that purpose, shall have full power and authority to enter any ship or vessel in which they shall have reason to suspect any goods, wares, or merchandise, subject to duty, shall be concealed, and therein to search for, seize, and secure, any such goods...and if they shall have cause to suspect a concealment thereof, in any particular dwellinghouse, store, building, or other place, they or either of them, shall upon application on oath or affirmation to any justice of the peace, be entitled to a warrant to enter such house, store, or other place (in the day time only) and there to search,...to seize, and to secure the same for trial...."

(Notice the specific distinction between vessel and dwellinghouse with regard to the need for a warrant.)

1925—In the case of *Carrol v. United States,* Chief Justice Taft notes, "...that the laws of the United States recognize a difference between the searching of structures such as houses and offices and vehicular instruments such as automobiles and boats because of the different uses to which they may be put in criminal activity."

1930—The 71st Congress enacts Title 19 U.S. Code Section 1581, which provides that "...any officer of the customs may at any time go on board of any vessel...at any place in the United States or within the customs waters...and examine the manifest and other documents and papers and examine, inspect, and search the vessel..."

1936—The 76th Congress enacts Title 14 U.S. Code Section 89, which states, "The Coast Guard may make inquiries, examinations, inspections, searches, seizures, and arrests upon the high seas and waters over which the United States has jurisdiction, for the prevention, detection, and suppression of violations of laws of the United States. For such purposes, commissioned, warrant, and petty officers may at any time go on board any vessel at any place and examine documents without any suspicion of wrongdoing."

1983—In the case of *U.S. v. Jose Reynaldo Villamonte-Marquez, et al.,* the U.S. Supreme Court decides 6 to 3 that the boarding of a 40-foot sailboat anchored in a ship channel in Louisiana, and the subsequent seizure of marijuana, is not unreasonable under the Fourth Amendment. The rights of the individual were not violated when officials acting under U.S. law, which authorizes customs officials to go on board any vessel at any place and examine documents without any suspicion of wrongdoing, boarded the vessel located in waters providing ready access to the open sea.

The Law

135

The logic behind warrantless searches of vehicles makes sense from a societal point of view because it is not practical to get a warrant if the vehicle may be moved quickly out of the jurisdiction in which the warrant is sought. This is especially true in the case of boats with almost limitless access to the open sea. Furthermore, it is impractical to set up highway-type roadblocks on the water that stop everyone for searches, safety checks, and registration compliance.

Smuggling, drug running, illegal immigration, environmental pollution, and public-safety offenses are understandable aspects of our complex society. With this complexity have come interpretations and, in the words of Supreme Court Justice Rehnquist, "modest intrusions" into an individual's protection from unreasonable searches and seizures. Unfortunately, when it comes to the subtle distinction between one's land-based house and a boat used as a temporary or permanent home, the "intrusion" can be frustrating, intimidating, and humiliating. But that's the law, at least for now.

A SHORT COURSE IN MARINE LAW ENFORCEMENT

The U.S. Coast Guard, charged with the responsibility to interdict drug smuggling and enforce the law on drug use on the water, has an active campaign to "explain" and promote the U.S.C.G. mission. Captain R. D. Peterson, of the Coast Guard's Public Affairs office, contributed the following short course on marine law enforcement.

The chances of being boarded nationwide are extremely slim (about 1 in 100 boats gets boarded each year), but in the coastal areas of Florida and the Gulf or in the Caribbean passages, the chances are understandably much higher. The volume of narcotics and illegal aliens in that area necessitates a heavy boarding effort—and that effort has been quite effective in stemming the flow of contraband. In 1988 we seized 149 vessels and aircraft with 438,894 pounds of marijuana, 12,825 pounds of cocaine and other drugs, with 345 arrests, and interdicted 4,566 illegal aliens. The value of seized drugs was more than $1.3 billion.

Even though nobody likes to be boarded, I believe most people's experience is that boardings are conducted in a professional and courteous manner. If this is not the case, the local Coast Guard District Commander should be notified, with the particulars, by letter.

A boarding officer does have the unquestionable right to come aboard. Most will ask permission, but they do not require the master's permission. That right has been repeatedly upheld by the courts. Also, a vessel must stop when ordered. Failure to stop can be a felony and the commanding officer has the authority to fire both warning shots and, if necessary, disabling fire if a vessel refuses to stop when ordered. Unfortunately, this has occasionally been necessary.

There are no boardings specifically for just safety inspections or just Zero Tolerance or other drug matters. All boardings are to inspect for conformance to *all* applicable federal law. All applicable federal law includes: safety, required equipment, environmental issues, drugs, licensing, firearms, currency, FCC compliance, customs, or any number of other laws. In most cases, only an inspection is authorized, not a search, and the difference is significant. The boarding officer may look at those things covered by the law, including such things as wiring runs or fuel and sewage piping systems. The boarding officer may also look into any man-size space to account for all crew for his own safety. He may *not* search personal gear, people, closed areas, voids, drawers, or luggage without the master's consent or the development of probable cause.

Probable cause to believe a crime has been committed is developed at the scene based on the facts at hand, including perhaps what people have said, prior intelligence, smell of drugs, and other law violations. Border crossings are an exception. Under customs law a complete search, even a destructive search, may be conducted on a vessel entering the U.S. from a foreign country or the high seas.

All boarding officers are armed with side arms—no different from the state trooper who stops you on the highway. Shoulder weapons are not carried aboard unless there is reasonable suspicion or unusual conditions. In general, shoulder weapons are common in Florida and the Caribbean, and uncommon elsewhere.

If a boarding officer is greeted by hostility, verbal abuse, and an uncooperative attitude by the master or crew, our officers are taught to be courteous— but firm. The uncooperative attitude will be noted on the boarding form, and will be considered in the determination of any fines for violations. Assault against a federal law enforcement officer is a *very* serious crime and results in immediate arrest.

For most safety or other minor violations, the hearing officer generally disposes of the case with a letter warning, with assurances that the violation has been or will be corrected. Fines, however, can sometimes be significant—particularly for repeated violations.

The Zero Tolerance Policy

If you use drugs, or allow others to use them aboard, you are liable for heavy penalties and you risk forfeiture of your boat. There have been over a hundred Zero Tolerance seizures—in virtually all cases, the drugs or paraphernalia were in plain sight and not the result of a search. In all cases, the boats were not forfeited, but most did have heavy fines imposed. The "innocent owner" is protected by the law if he is in fact innocent, but he had best take special precautions to ensure that drugs are not on board. If the owner is aboard, he has very little defense. Hopefully there is no sympathy for drug users.

(Late in 1989, the Coast Guard revised its policy regarding boat seizures in the case of "personal use" quantities of drugs. Instead of immediate seizure, the person in charge of the vessel will be given a written summons by the boarding officer.)

The standard boarding process is as follows:

- A signal to stop, or commonly to slow on a safe heading, may be made by loud-hailer, VHF radio, flag-hoist, flashing light, or rotating blue light and siren. It should be noted that ships on patrol generally avoid radio use and will generally identify themselves by the prominent hull number on the bow rather than by name.
- A boarding party from a ship will be transported by small boat, generally an inflatable. The size of the party varies with the size of the boarded vessel.
- Generally all crew will be requested to gather together, either forward or aft, before being boarded. Boarding teams are very "antsy" about this...they are very vulnerable while actually boarding.
- Generally, boarding ladders or fenders complicate the situation and should be avoided. Except for very large vessels, boarding will be directly from the boat (with perhaps a bit of scrambling).
- The first question will generally be: "Do you have any weapons aboard?" The intent is not to confiscate, but simply to identify where they are.
- The boarding officer and the master generally start the paperwork with registration or documentation, while one boarding team member remains with the crew and one or two make a quick sweep through the boat to see if others are aboard.
- Identification for all crew will be requested. Before boarding, the vessel will have been checked against a data base for past history. Individuals will also be checked, again no different from the state trooper who stops you on the highway.
- The boarding officer then goes down the list on a boarding form (Form CG-4100), checking all equipment and other items, with the master's assistance.
- Upon completion, the master is advised of the results, other concerns are discussed if needed, and the master is provided with a copy of the form. If you are boarded again fairly soon, be sure to present the form copy; it will likely speed up the second boarding (but won't necessarily prevent it).
- If there is any damage to your boat, the boarding officer will provide a claim form for you to get reimbursed for repair.

In the Caribbean and areas of Florida there may be some special techniques involved. A "boatscope"—a periscope affair—is often used to view the underwater body. Also, since hidden compartments are the normal way of smuggling, a lot of measuring may be done for space accountability, and a fiber-optic viewing device may be used to look into odd places. Sounding of all tanks is also common (a lot of cocaine has been found in fuel tanks). If probable cause has been developed, the search will include every conceivable hiding place—and we know them all!

Serious violations that most often result in arrest and/or seizure are generally: drugs (distribution quantities), outstanding warrants, operating a boat while intoxicated, reckless and negligent operation, illegal aliens or economic migrants, currency violations (more than $10,000 in cash without customs import/export currency report), illegal firearms (fully automatic weapons or sawed-off shotguns), other contraband (e.g., endangered species products).

The Law

To many people, law enforcement may seem to be a new mission for the Coast Guard, and one that perhaps tarnishes the normal "good guys" image of the Service. In reality, however, customs and tariff law enforcement was the reason that the Coast Guard was first established in 1790. Although we would prefer that it not be necessary, it is apparent that we will be doing extensive law enforcement work for a long time. We still pride ourselves most on our search and rescue, and in all cases, saving lives remains our highest priority.

Captain R. D. Peterson

PLASTIC POLLUTION: MORE THAN A LITTER PROBLEM
The widespread presence of plastics in the oceans is a global problem that will require international cooperation to solve. But the roots of the problem stem from local, individual human carelessness in disposing of a material that is part of our everyday lives. No one can point the finger at a particular country, region, industry, or group as the major contributor to the problem. The responsibility is shared by all.

Liveaboards as well as weekend recreational boaters are often accused of polluting the environment with vessel sanitary wastes and litter, particularly plastic debris carelessly tossed overboard. These accusations also lead to restrictive policies when it comes to allowing liveaboards in sensitive waters.

In 1989 the federal government ratified an international treaty on ocean dumping and outlawed plastic pollution within the U.S., including inland lakes, rivers, and bays. It is now illegal to dump overboard any plastic trash, no matter how small. This applies to all boats, from small recreational vessels up to ocean liners and commercial freighters. The law outlaws plastic trash from a single baggie or monofilament fishing line to a shipload of refuse. Since the treaty, referred to as MARPOL, is an international one, there are no territorial limits to this law. Dumping plastic trash is illegal from coastline estuaries, rivers, and bays to the deep ocean waters. The law also allows up to a $25,000 fine and imprisonment for violators. All ports are now required to have adequate trash-reception facilities for boats and ships.

In 1990 the U.S. Coast Guard required all vessels over 26 feet to post a placard prominently notifying all passengers and crew of discharge restrictions and penalties. For boats over 40 feet, the Coast Guard also requires a written waste management plan that describes procedures used for collecting, processing, storing, and discharging the vessel's garbage properly (in accordance with MARPOL Annex V laws) and designates the person in charge of carrying out the plan (see sample plans).

Strong action against plastic litter is now being taken because it is recognized as one of the most destructive and long-lived man-made products polluting the nation's waterways. It does not deteriorate after it is discarded, and it causes suffering and death to numerous species of marine wildlife. Water fowl and other marine animals become entangled in discarded fishing line or plastic six-pack ring holders and die of starvation or strangulation; seals, whales, and sea turtles ingest plastic bags they mistake for food and die.

Recreational boaters are a significant cause of marine litter, discarding millions of pounds of trash into our waters each year, according to the National Academy of Science. Merchant ships and commercial fishing ships are the other big sources of ocean trash.

And the pollution is not just in our bays, rivers, and along the coasts. In *Adrift,* author Steve Callahan writes of survival in a liferaft for 76 days across 1,800 miles of the Atlantic. He tells of drifting into a "highway of trash" stretching as far as the eye could see, of bottles, fishnets, plastic ropes, and polystyrene debris and thinking he must be near civilization. He was still more than 300 miles from land!

In 1988 and again in 1989, more than 47,500 and 65,600 volunteers, respectively, participated in beach cleanups in 25 U.S. states and territories. Volunteers used data cards to tally the quantities of debris, determine its source, and categorize the debris. The Center for Marine Conservation tabulated more than two million debris items, of which 62 percent were plastic products. The top six items collected were: plastic pieces or fragments; small Styrofoam pieces; plastic cups, spoons, forks, and straws; glass pieces; cigarette butts; and Styrofoam cups.

Twelve specific types of debris received the dubious distinction of being named the "Dirty Dozen" of items washed ashore on U.S. beaches.

Sample Waste Management Plans

Waste Management Plan for the vessel: _____

Person in charge: _____

Procedures: _____

All the garbage generated on this vessel is put in a garbage bag and disposed of in the trash containers at the harbor at the end of each trip (or is given to the tender vessel to take to shore for disposal).

All crew members have been oriented to the requirements of MARPOL Annex V by the captain and all new crew are specifically shown the MARPOL V placard and told to keep all refuse stowed on board. Passenger orientation to the vessel includes being shown the location of the trash receptacles and mention of refuse discharge regulations.

Waste Management Plan for the vessel: _____

Person in charge: _____

Procedures: _____

If the vessel is outside of 12 miles from shore: All the garbage with the exception of food materials and paper is put in a garbage bag to be disposed of in the trash container at the harbor at the end of the trip. Food materials and paper generated in the galley are collected in a bucket or paper bag and emptied over the side.

If the vessel is within 12 miles of shore: All the garbage generated on this vessel is put in a garbage bag and disposed of in the trash containers at the harbor at the end of the trip (or is given to the tender vessel to take to shore for disposal).

All crew members have been oriented to the requirements of MARPOL Annex V by the captain and all new crew are specifically shown the MARPOL V placard and told to keep all refuse stowed on board. Passenger orientation to the vessel includes being shown the location of the trash receptacles and mention of refuse discharge regulations.

Collectively, these 12 items constituted nearly 60 percent of all debris items recorded by the Center for Marine Conservation in the 1989 national beach clean-up campaign. In that campaign 860 tons of debris (3,013,778 items) were collected by 65,636 volunteers across the country. A breakdown of this list of marine debris in the ocean that eventually reaches the beaches is shown below. Recreational boaters and liveaboards can easily identify with these items and, hopefully, contribute toward making this problem go away.

The Dirty Dozen		
1.	Plastic pieces	242,119
2.	Small foamed plastic pieces	197,364
3.	Plastic eating utensils	170,805
4.	Glass pieces	167,657
5.	Cigarette filters (butts)	164,141
6.	Plastic caps and lids	145,938
7.	Paper pieces	142,110
8.	Glass beverage bottles	135,352
9.	Metal beverage cans	125,512
10.	Foamed plastic cups	106,301
11.	Miscellaneous plastic bags	98,078
12.	Plastic trash bags	93,184
	TOTAL	1,788,561

VESSEL POLLUTION

William Kenton, a professional engineer in California, tells of a unique study done in Newport and Avalon harbors in Southern California pinpointing recreational boats as sources of domestic waste leading to water pollution in environmentally sensitive waters.

Riddled with conflicting evidence and out-of-sight, out-of-mind attitudes, the vessel sewage issue is among the most contentious and confusing problems facing boaters, especially liveaboards. The amount of waste boaters pump overboard is small, compared with the millions of gallons of sewage discharged daily into coastal waters by municipalities and the natural runoff from urban and agricultural areas. But small as it may be, vessel sewage can be extremely unsightly and can raise bacteria counts to dangerous levels in poorly flushed bays and harbors and around important shellfish beds.

For a number of years it has been believed by many in the field that a substantial portion of the bacterial contamination of water pollution results from the flushing of heads and the discharge of holding tanks by boaters. To date, we have had little factual and conclusive proof; however, in the last few years, preliminary findings in Newport Harbor and Avalon Harbor, California, have given some very strong support to this issue.

Newport Harbor

Evidence has recently surfaced from routine random water samplings in various Newport Harbor locations. Coincidentally, a city-owned marina was closed for modernization and reconstruction over a 15-month period. Sampling was continued during this period and the bacteria count dropped dramatically. When the reconstructed marina was reopened, the counts returned to the elevated level.

These results gave the first hint of the degree of contamination resulting from marina activity. The conclusions were suspect and not beyond a reasonable doubt because of the random testing locations and the effect of storm-drain runoff in the immediate area.

Avalon Harbor

Further support for this theory came from the popular and world famous Avalon Harbor. Avalon Harbor is one of the primary recreational areas for marine activity in the southwestern United States. This harbor contains approximately 750 moorings in a protected half-moon-shaped harbor. Some of the moorings are privately owned; however, most are controlled by the city of Avalon and rented on a daily basis. These rentals provide the city with a substantial source of revenue. It is estimated there are from 5,000 to 10,000 visitors daily in Avalon each summer weekend. Many of these visitors arrive by private boat, and the balance by ferry or airlines. Swimming and water sports are the primary attractions enjoyed by the visitors.

This case study commenced early in the summer season of 1988, when the county health department was notified of a major sewage pipe failure and a spill in the area of the Casino of Avalon Harbor. Because of the break, the county health department and the city of Avalon decided to monitor harbor contamination closely. First reports of bacteria counts were so high that the health authorities threatened to close the beaches and prohibit water contact sports. Contractors quickly repaired the broken sewer line and the city and county health departments continued to monitor the water.

As the monitoring program continued for a number of days after the repair was completed, it was evident that the bacteria count was not diminishing substantially. Further investigation was deemed necessary to isolate the source of bacteria from among five suspected areas of contamination:

- boats moored in the harbor;
- runoff from several city streets;
- seagull and other wildlife defecation;
- additional undiscovered broken sewer lines; and
- contamination from the city's sewage treatment.

The problem of seagulls and other wildlife was eliminated when it was concluded that contamination from animal waste was undoubtedly minimal due to the rapid die-off of wildlife waste bacteria.

In order to ascertain if there were any unknown broken sewer pipes in the area, green fluorescent dye pills were injected in numerous locations throughout the city, saturating all of the sewer mains. Green dye did not appear on the harbor water, confirming that there were no other broken mains.

A study was initiated to determine the possibility of backflow of treated sewage into the harbor from the municipal treatment plant. The plant outfall was approximately 23 miles from the harbor entrance, and the treated effluent was discharged under 180 feet of salt water. The prevailing wind, tide, and current were away from the harbor entrance. There was little likelihood that the amount of contamination encountered was from this source.

Based on the elimination of the other variables, the city of Avalon concluded that the continued high bacteria counts must be from the recreational vessels using Avalon Harbor. The question was, how could this be proven and once proven, what was the solution? After some joint investigation, the city tested a dye pill which could be placed in the boaters' heads and holding tanks. If they were flushed into the harbor, the fluorescent red dye would remain visible from 12 to 24 hours.

A series of tests were performed using the marine heads on boats anchored in Avalon Harbor. The red dye pills were placed in the heads, and when the heads were flushed and discharged into the sea, the red dye became evident immediately. The pills were an added advantage because they tended to stain the hull at the point of discharge and remain visible underwater on the boat's bottom.

New Regulations

Based on these preliminary studies, the city of Avalon enacted legislation authorizing its harbor patrol to activate the plan of placing tablets in all heads and holding tanks of incoming vessels and providing warning notices of no discharging and the strict enforcement of the policy. The fine levied by the city of Avalon is $500 for the first violation and a requirement that the violator leave the harbor immediately and be banned from the harbor for one year!

The results of this enforcement program were spectacular. The bacteria counts dropped dramatically. Since enactment, several boaters have been fined under the terms of this law, and the quality of the water has returned to pristine condition.

The public's reaction to this program was, of course, of great concern to the city of Avalon because of the revenues derived from the tourist trade. More than 90 percent of the boaters surveyed have been in favor of this program and have encouraged the city to continue. Boaters enjoy water contact sports in the harbor and have in the past expressed concern about the health menaces. Only a small percentage of the boaters without holding tanks and who are accustomed to dumping in Avalon Harbor have indicated any concerns.

It has also been noted that, since this program has been initiated, and because of the continued monitoring program in effect, the cruise ships delivering large groups of passengers to Avalon Harbor on the weekend have ceased discharging their tanks while at or near the docks. The monitoring program has spotlighted the commercial ferries as an additional source of contamination. Commercial lines have now agreed to avoid discharging their holding tanks within one mile of the harbor entrance.

Regulations Around the Country

Federal authorities concluded early that boat sewage, particularly from small recreational vessels, did not constitute a serious national environmental problem. That is why federal laws governing vessel sanitation were passed in the early seventies, and as yet no federal agency has stepped in to actively enforce those laws. However, a number of states and communities, alarmed at economic and health issues associated with the well-being of these waters, are considering initiatives aimed at controlling vessel sewage.

In addition to these state initiatives, many local jurisdictions, such as the Avalon Harbor example, are taking matters into their own hands. What's at stake here for states and communities is clean water—a major reason why boaters are out there in the first place. Common sense says that all responsible parties—regulators, recreational boat owners, marina operators—have a vested interest in jealously protecting that resource.

William Kenton

The Law

YOU CAN'T ALWAYS CALL THE COPS

Steve and Lora Perry tackle a sobering and vexing question for live-aboards and cruisers—whether or not to have a gun aboard for protection. In many states the laws on guns, especially concealed weapons, are very explicit, and the boater needs to be informed or risk serious problems with the law!

It was 5 A.M. on Sunday, May 3. *Arabella* was alongside the town pier in the sleepy Maine village of Wiscasset—a luxury for us, available only because May is early in the yachting season that far north.

In the otherwise still morning, a roar of motorcycles woke us instantly. Steve jumped out of the V-berth and peered out the starboard port. Seven tough guys were climbing off choppers.

Steve watched the bikies step aboard a small open powerboat also tied to the pier.

"Yo! Way to go! Guy's got some beer here." The bikies swarmed over the runabout, helping themselves to breakfast and gear lying in the cockpit. It was obvious these men were in some kind of altered state: Their voices were slurred, their walk was unsteady. When the goodies ran out on the runabout, the bikies turned their attention to *Arabella*.

"Hey—maybe these dudes have something."

At this point Steve retrieved the two handguns we kept on board: an easily concealable .380 automatic (which he tucked in his pocket) and an intimidating Clint Eastwood–type Magnum .357 (which he hid beneath a jacket on the chart table).

The head bikie climbed aboard *Arabella*. Steve pushed back the companionway slide and popped his head out, feigning early-morning grogginess. His body was behind the boards.

"Oh—Good morning," Steve said pleasantly.

The bikie jumped. "Hey, man. Hey—didn't think anyone was aboard, you know? Sorry." But he continued to climb into the boat. He spied a small cooler under *Arabella*'s dodger. "Got anything to drink?" The bikie entered the cockpit, while his friends gathered on the dock expectantly.

Steve gripped the .380. "Just soft drinks."

The bikie flipped open the cooler and saw Steve was telling the truth. Then he tried to peer below. "What about down there—got anything down there? I never been in a boat like this before. Hey, can we come have a look?"

"Well, it's nothing special, and my wife is still in bed. It's pretty early, you know."

"Well, can't you cover her up, or something?"

Steve made a decision. If the bikie moved any closer, he'd have to brandish the gun. If the threat failed, he'd have to use it.

As it turned out, Steve avoided a dangerous confrontation through cautiously friendly conversation until 7:30, when the group decided gas stations—their primary need at the moment—were probably open. But it could have gone differently. Cruising liveaboards don't have the luxury of dialing the police or running out of the house when violated by an intruder.

Self-defense on a yacht is seldom necessary. For that matter, liferafts on yachts are seldom used but considered standard equipment. Whether you're in an isolated Caribbean cove, assisting a strange vessel in distress, or enjoying a remote early-season weekend, liveaboards should be as self-sufficient, knowledgeable, and experienced in personal protection as they are in everything else.

Firearms are one source of self-protection, but there are alternatives for people opposed to guns.

Who Should Carry a Gun?

The answer is simple and irrefutable: If you're not prepared to use a gun, don't carry it. The risk of an assailant seizing your gun or using his own during your moral or mechanical hesitation is probably greater than the odds of self-defense without a firearm. Law enforcement officials train exhaustively in the psychological, moral, and technical skills necessary for responsible gun use. Organizations like the National Rifle Association and other gun clubs teach not only how to use a gun, but, more importantly, how to assess a confrontation and avoid gun use if possible.

And this is important: Being prepared to use a gun should not be construed to mean you must use the gun. Proper assessment of the danger and persuasive threats are the first line of self-defense. Executed well, these skills make it possible to avoid gun use at all.

But if avoidance is not possible, a gun owner must have reconciled his conscience ahead of time. If you own a gun, be prepared to kill in self-defense.

What Firearms Should Cruising Liveaboard Yachts Carry?

Firearm regulations differ all over the world, but shotguns are more likely to be allowed into another country than handguns. They may also be a more dramatic psychological deterrent to an invader. A New York City cop once told us that wracking the action of a pump-action shotgun stopped 98 percent of the city's bad guys right in their tracks. If the shotgun is discharged, scattering pellets are more likely to reach the target than a solitary pistol or rifle round. The shorter barrelled 18-inch police riot pump-action shotgun is recommended over longer conventional bird guns for better maneuverability in close quarters.

The Law

The problem with a shotgun is it is not accurate beyond about 30 yards, and not lethal beyond 50 yards.

Rifles are accurate and lethal at greater distances than shotguns. But it's hard to assess a confrontation at rifle range. On the other hand, many yachters carry rifles to protect swimmers against sharks.

Finally there are handguns. Handguns are deadly accurate at short range, and inaccurate at long range. They are concealable, but because of this are much more subject to confiscation by authorities than shotguns or rifles.

Some yachters opt for handguns because they're concealable. They manage the risk of confiscation by hiding and not declaring them in foreign countries. While dozens of liveaboards we've talked to claim to have done this successfully for years all over the world, it is illegal. A firearms violation in a foreign country (or this one, for that matter) may incur harsh jail sentences. It is a risk we choose not to take aboard *Arabella.*

A Word About Flare Pistols

A while ago a movie was popular in which yachters defended themselves against an intruder by shooting him with a flare pistol. According to professionals, forget it! Flare pistols are inaccurate, don't have the power to penetrate the body, and will in all likelihood set the boat on fire.

However, at least one company makes a hefty stainless steel tube that fits in the nozzle of a 25mm flare gun and is designed to take a .410 shotgun shell. (It should be noted that separately these items are legal, but in combination the flare gun and the insert tube constitute a sawed-off shotgun, which is illegal under federal law.)

Coping with the Authorities—USA

Drugs are big business in Florida. In three months we got boarded three times by polite but vigilant Coast Guard and customs officials. Each time we declared our handguns, and used the opportunity to learn more about officialdom's view of firearms aboard boats.

According to the McClure-Volkmer Amendments to the Federal Gun Control Act of 1968, effective November 15, 1986, transportation of any legally owned firearm is allowed provided possession of the weapon is also legal in the state of destination. The firearms must be unloaded and not readily accessible. Guns must be stored in locked compartments, and ammunition stored in separate containers.

But be careful: According to the National Rifle Association, "U.S. laws apply to ships with a U.S. registry wherever the ship may be, including the high seas. U.S. territorial waters extend up to three miles offshore. State laws apply within this three-mile limit. You should contact [the NRA] regarding the laws of any state in whose waters you plan on sailing." (National Rifle Association, 1600 Rhode Island Avenue NW, Washington, D.C. 20036. Phone 202-828-6000.) In other words, if you're simply passing through, you're protected under the transportation guidelines in the preceding paragraph. If you're going to stick around for a while, comply with the state and local laws.

Firearm Identification Cards and Pistol Permits

The Second Amendment of the Constitution of the United States guarantees U.S. citizens the right to "keep and bear arms." Again, things get trickier distinguishing between handguns and other firearms. All guns were not created equal. In most states you can buy a rifle or a shotgun by proving you're a resident of the state via a driver's license, state ID, or firearms identification card.

To buy a handgun, however, a special pistol permit and waiting period may be required, depending on your state. Massachusetts has one of the toughest gun laws in the country: A license is required to carry a concealed or unconcealed handgun and the applicants are fingerprinted. The prints are filed and checked with the FBI. Technically, officials cannot withhold granting a license unless the applicant is a known felon. But they can make the process difficult by causing mysterious delays in the paperwork, or requiring gun training and examinations.

Since we have relatives in Massachusetts, we contacted the local police station there and were frank about our personal safety concerns as cruising liveaboards. The deputy chief understood our concern, and issued us permits to carry concealed weapons for protection of life and property using our relative's address. These permits have worked wonders smoothing things over with authorities in the U.S., Canada, and Bahamas. Before leaving Florida for the Bahamas, we decided to sell one of our two handguns and buy a pump-action shotgun. While the local gun dealer happily bought the .380, he could not sell us a shotgun without Florida identification. Following his suggestion, we went to the State Highway Patrol department. There, by presenting his Maine driver's license, social security card, and $3, Steve was photographed and issued a Florida state ID sporting the address "General Delivery, Key West, Florida." This is all we needed to buy the shotgun (or an unconcealed handgun), which we did the same day.

Firearms Abroad

The Law

Correspondence with the NRA indicated we should register our guns with customs before departing the U.S., to avoid having to secure an importation license for them when returning to the U.S. This involves physically bringing the arms to a local customs office, where the serial numbers are checked and recorded on a "Certificate of Registration for Personal Effects Taken Aboard," Customs form 4457. This registration has also helped during boardings by U.S. and Bahamian officials. The boarding officer simply asked to see the weapons, compared serial numbers, and recorded them. In the Bahamas we were also asked to itemize and count the ammunition on board.

Foreign gun laws vary greatly. To avoid possible problems, the NRA suggests contacting the legal officer at a country's embassy or consulate before visiting that country. Several things might happen:

- The weapons can be seized and not returned.
- The weapons may be seized and returned when you clear out of the country. The problem with this is it requires you to enter and leave the country at the same clearance port, which may be inconvenient. You will also be without the weapon for self-defense within that country.
- The weapons may be sealed in a locked locker. If the seal is broken, be prepared to do a lot of talking.
- The weapons may be allowed, but should be protected against theft in a locked, unsealed locker.

Danger at a Distance

A lot of yachters say a high-velocity rifle like the Mini 14 and other post-Vietnam assault rifles are useful protection not only against sharks, but from human danger at a distance. The rifle can fire meaningful warning shots, as well as accurately lethal ones at intruders.

But it's difficult to determine how truly dangerous a situation is at the longer rifle range. Not only is identification of the intruder hard to pinpoint, but you may be firing at someone with better artillery than you have. Or you may be firing upon a clandestine military patrol or drug interdiction boat, provoking a bureaucratic mess nobody wants to get involved in.

Danger Close Aboard

One of the riskier threats to personal safety at sea is the fake distress. Officials throughout the world stress such events are not common, but they can occur. Every good samaritan should approach distresses cautiously. If possible, local authorities should be radioed to assist.

If you're threatened during a rescue, the shotgun can be a very effective defense. Again, wracking the action may be the only deterrent necessary. If the invaders appear to be armed only with machetes, for example, a slug fired from a distance of 30 to 50 yards can put a hole beneath the offender's waterline sufficient to make a fake distress quite real. If you can determine the potential boarders have firearms as well, your defense will have to be against the people themselves. A round of bird shot will definitely let the target know he's been hit, but may not necessarily be lethal.

Danger Aboard

Nobody wants to kill another human being. But if this becomes necessary in the line of self-defense, steps should be taken to protect your own vessel from extensive damage or sinking when discharging the firearm. It's best to discharge above decks, but this may not be possible.

Again, forget the flare pistol. It is the surest way to start a fire below, short of setting one deliberately. Discharging a handgun or high-powered rifle below may not only hole your own boat if you miss the target, but there's the risk of accident to yourself or family due to ricochet as well. It is perhaps the shotgun that is the best firearm to discharge below. Its scattered projectiles are less likely to hole the boat, but are still lethal to an assailant at such close range. It is also less likely to ricochet.

Alternatives to Firearms

One of the best alternatives to firearms on a yacht is a crossbow. Crossbows are not subject to confiscation, are highly accurate at short range, do not require licensing, will not hole the boat, and are inexpensive compared to guns. They can be purchased at any store that sells archery equipment. The disadvantage to a crossbow is if you miss, you've got to reload. You may have only one chance at defense.

Pets may also provide some protection. We have two cats that were raised on the boat. People have asked us if they're trained "attack cats," but the truth is Oreo and Dreyfus are just plain ornery to strangers—hissing, spitting, and biting. Had they been aboard *Arabella* that Sunday in Wiscasset, the situation may never have escalated to the point it did in the first place. Other liveaboards have enjoyed the protection of a loyal dog.

Mace or other tear gases are available, as are shock weapons. These may require permits in some areas. They're also defenses that mean you're already in hand-to-hand combat with the assailant.

Noise can be a weapon. We have a hand-operated emergency evacuation siren that sounds exactly like a S.W.A.T. Team screaming through New York City. We've never had the opportunity to use it. But our hope is, if it's necessary, an invader will think law enforcement officials are on their way. At worst, perhaps the noise will create confusion.

But the most effective form of self-protection is prevention. Be sure you can lock the companionway and all hatches from the inside. We installed a simple barrel bolt on the top inside of our sailboat's companionway. When engaged, the bolt prevents the companionway slide from moving, and the boards cannot be removed. To maintain ventilation we leave the bottom board out. This opening is too small for anyone to crawl through. To prevent an intruder from coming down the forward hatch, and still maintain ventilation, we place two lengths of 1 x $^3/_{16}$-inch aluminum across the opening, secured by wing nuts. The wing nuts are quickly released for an emergency exit through the forward hatch if necessary. The risk of someone intruding aboard a yacht is probably less than the risk of someone invading your home ashore. In the case of an anchored boat, the crooks have to work at it. Like everything else with yachting, it's good to be prepared.

The Law

Steve and Lora Perry

THE END OF THE CRUISE

Not everything about the boating lifestyle is idyllic. One of the realities of the liveaboard life, as for life in general, is that it must come to an end. Long ago I recall Thomas Colvin, in his book Cruising Wrinkles, *taking on the unpleasant subject of burial at sea. More recently, George Hostetter, writing for* The Ensign *and the* Living Aboard Journal, *updates us on the rules covering this eventuality.*

When the "long trick" is over, and it's time to move on to whatever destiny awaits us, there's the inevitable question of what to do with the physical evidence that we've been here. Burial and/or cremation are acceptable alternatives, but there's always the question of where.

To many who have spent their most enjoyable hours afloat, the choice, in one form or another, is burial at sea. The emotional appeal might be strong, but the government regulations can be daunting. For instance, if survivors are asked to toss your ashes from your favorite bridge into your favorite "river to the sea," the action could be expensive if they're caught. Burial at sea, either the scattering of ashes or full-body type, is regulated by state and federal laws, and none of those laws permit it inside U.S. territorial waters (or randomly over the land, for that matter). To be more specific, here are some quotes from the Code of Federal Regulations:

"Burial at sea of human remains which are not cremated shall take place no closer than three nautical miles from land and in water no less than 100 fathoms (600 feet deep)....All necessary measures shall be taken to ensure that the remains sink to the bottom rapidly and permanently."

Weighing and the required "suitable shroud" must be taken care of by a licensed interment service.

Cremated remains must also be scattered outside the three-mile territorial limit, though it may be "without regard to the depth limitations specified above."

Before you write in disputing that statement—yes, we know the U.S. extended its territorial waters to 12 miles on December 28, 1988. (Note that almost every other country bordering on the world's oceans claims 200 miles.) Burials at sea, however, are one of the few exceptions that will remain under the "old" territorial limit.

Along our ocean shorelines there are many charter boats and yacht clubs offering burial at sea services. They require special licenses. Sea burials may also be conducted from private boats or, for that matter, from chartered planes. Most state regulatory boards and the U.S. Environmental Protection Agency have "open" permits for this. That means there are no formal applications or licenses needed prior to disposition. You are just on your honor to obey the law, and now you all know what it is.

After the burial, the boat (or plane) owner must file a formal letter with the EPA within 30 days, addressed to the nearest Regional Administrator. The letter should state the date of burial, the latitude and longitude, the number of remains (how many people) and/or number of burials (if there were more than one), and a sentence stating, "I certify that these scatterings occurred at a distance greater than three miles from land." No paperwork is required beyond a notation on the permit for disposition (which is required for any body disposal) that the burial was "at sea."

Incidentally, if you are caught burying someone illegally, the fine is $50,000. The Coast Guard in California says that no such busts have yet been made there, and they hope the occasion never arises. They don't want to crash someone's funeral.

The owner of a charter boat licensed for both cremated and non-cremated sea burials indicated to me that ash-scatterings, considered straight charters, might cost about $200 an hour and could be expected to last about three hours. The potential $600 charge presumes a single disposal and up to 30 passengers. Obviously there are cost adjustments for multiple disposals and/or fewer guests. Full body burials, because of distance and water depth requirements, are considered special charters and usually require a full day. The cost, about $2,500, includes shrouding and weighing the body. Further informal chats with funeral directors reveal that, for a lesser charge, they will charter a plane to fly out far enough for a legal scattering. Any figures quoted here, of course, should be checked against local customs and conditions.

Whether or not you favor one of these options might depend on your sense of fitness and dignity. Note that burials at sea are written into the Code of Federal Regulations—under the Ocean Dumping Act.

George Hostetter

The Law

8
Voyages

BEING A liveaboard doesn't necessarily mean that you're a bluewater, distant ocean voyager or an adventurer headed for Cape Horn. Many of us never leave the pier, at least not with our homes. Others, however, have combined their home life with a love for leisurely travel and adventure. Some dally along the Intracoastal Waterway slowly keeping up with the seasons. Others sail across oceans to visit new continents and explore remote islands. Still others take short hops to the Bahamas, Bermuda, Caribbean islands, Mexico, or Canada just to relish the adventure of sailing into a foreign port. Then there are those who set sail late in the evening and drift a mile or two to a quiet evening anchorage.

With all of these voyages, whether long or short, comes a sense of serenity, maybe a few harrowing moments, beautiful scenery, tedium, frustration, bonding relationships with crew and passing boaters, loneliness, a sense of accomplishment—but always an adventure worth telling others about.

A young 60-year-old lady wrote me some time ago from Fiji. She had set sail from the east coast of the U.S. with the company of a gentleman friend. By the time they reached the Panama Canal, he had had enough of the seagoing life and jumped ship. She continued, sailing singlehanded to the South Pacific!

Another liveaboard acquaintance enjoys his beautifully appointed Krogen trawler tucked away on a creek near Annapolis. On weekends, for a change of pace, he and his wife motor three miles to Annapolis Harbor, where they moor in the company of weekend revelers and a constant parade of boaters.

A young couple joined the cruising race division of the popular Antigua Race Week on their way around the world. Their small sailboat boasted no hailage. As they explained it, "We are citizens of the world." The day following the race, their motorless sailboat was seen gliding out of English Harbour for parts unknown.

Charles Villas was the publisher and editor of *Cruising Club News,* the journal of the Cruising Club of America. He passed away late in 1988 after a lifelong commitment to the cruising lifestyle. He and his wife, Margaret, had sailed the legendary cutter *Direction* for more than 40 years. He once said: "Rare is the man with total commitment to the cruising life. Rare too is the man, once tasting of that life, who does not dream of total commitment for some time in the future." There are even clubs that demand a degree of commitment of their members (see sidebar on page 156).

Villas went on to say: "The rewards of the cruising life are directly proportional to the degree of commitment a person is able or willing to give. We are all programmed for land orientation and indoctrinated with the work ethic—slaves to the clock and calendar. The experienced cruising man (and woman) learns to be ruled by the tides and the wind. And here lies the basic conflict. How wisely you resolve it has an important bearing on how much you get out of your cruising."

The following is an account of a modest commitment to the cruising lifestyle—a liveaboard voyage with an emphasis on the unhurried, small pleasures of touring by boat.

THE LIVEABOARD TOURIST

I have always viewed my boat as a platform from which I can satisfy my travel itch. Traveling with your home, not unlike the Wally Byrum Air Stream caravans, avoids the hassles of planes and airports and the homogenized atmosphere of Holiday Inns. In return you get a chance to go slow and smell the roses.

The Northeast Corridor from Washington, D.C., to Boston is one of the most traveled routes in the U.S. Millions of people commute this corridor daily in airplanes, buses, trains, and cars. The entire trip may take anywhere from $1\frac{1}{2}$

CRUISING CLUB OF AMERICA—was launched in 1921 by a group of yachtsmen interested in cruising and the development of cruising-type yachts. In the words of a founding member: "By gathering into a group all who are fond of offshore work, we sow the wilderness of the sea with a host of acquaintances, for whose houseflags we shall always be expectantly watching. Let us refuse stoutly to accumulate an on-shore contingent; let membership in the Club be a mark of achievement. This policy will give us standing at home and abroad such as no American yacht club ever has had." CCA, Box 2396, Short Beach, Connecticut 06405

SEVEN SEAS CRUISING ASSOCIATION—was formed in 1952 by a small group of seagoing sailors. They merged and formed a worldwide association for the purpose of sharing cruising experiences through the medium of a monthly bulletin. Associate members are not required to live aboard or even to own their own boat. However, commodores of SSCA must be persons who are (or have) cruised in their own seagoing sailboat and whose only home is their boat. Commodores, when recommending new members, ask themselves the question, "Do I want to follow in his or her wake?" The Golden Rule of the association is "Leave a Clean Wake." SSCA, Box 1256, Stuart, Florida 34995

THE JOSHUA SLOCUM SOCIETY—founded in 1955, is open to all persons who have an interest in smallboat voyaging or the lore of bluewater sailing on the oceans of the world. Ownership of a boat is not necessary, nor is actual sailing experience. "In an age when mass society has rendered obsolete the qualities of individual courage and independent thought, the oceans of the world still remain, vast and uncluttered, beautiful but unforgiving, awaiting those who will not submit. Their voyages are not an escape but a fulfillment." The Joshua Slocum Society, Box 76, Port Townsend, Washington 98368

OCEAN CRUISING CLUB—founded in 1954, to foster and encourage ocean cruising in small craft. The club keeps records of voyages made around the world as well as "port captains" who can provide local assistance to visiting members. Qualification for membership in OCC is the completion of a port-to-port ocean voyage of 1,000 miles or more as skipper or member of the crew in a vessel under 70 feet. OCC, Siscowit Road, Pound Ridge, New York 10576

BLUEWATER CRUISING ASSOCIATION—founded in 1977 to band together Canadian and Pacific Northwest cruisers for the purpose of sharing cruising experiences and furthering safe seamanship. The association publishes voyage accounts, hosts seminars and lectures, and arranges rendezvous for its members. They are "Doers, Donners, and Dreamers" of the cruising lifestyle. Bluewater Cruising Association, MPO Box 4492, Vancouver, British Columbia V6B 3Z8

GREAT LAKES CRUISING CLUB—founded in 1934 for the promotion of cruising on the Great Lakes among fellow yachtsmen. The club fosters the promotion of marine safety, the establishment and improvement of harbors and anchorages, the preservation of the natural beauty of traditional cruising areas, and the dissemination of cruising information. The hallmark of the club has been the *Port Pilot and Log Book*. In the past 55 years, this publication has grown to 2,250 pages describing—in charts, photographs, and narrative—1,102 harbors, bays, and channels in the Great Lakes region. GLCC, 20 N. Wacker Drive, Chicago, Illinois 60606

Voyages

hours by jet to 10 hours by car. Most commuters never see much of the landscape beyond the "fasten your seat belt" and "toll booth ahead" signs. Places along the way are often labeled with nothing more than exit numbers. New Jersey is a classic example. When someone admits to being from this state, they're often asked "Oh, what exit?"

I planned a different kind of commute. I was taking *Sabra,* my 32-foot Chinese junk-rigged schooner, from Washington, D.C., to Boston for the summer and returning in the fall. The boat was to be my vehicle and my home for this adventure.

Many years ago, in the days when aerospace companies were looking for something to do that was socially redeeming, I worked on plans for high-speed, high-tech alternatives to Northeast Corridor transportation. Twenty years later, the number of commuters has increased but commuting speeds have not. As a matter of fact, the true door-to-door speed has decreased due to congestion, which often approaches gridlock at airports, bridges, and tunnels. But all this concern over speed seems irrelevant when commuting by sailboat. Somehow, back then, the choice of sailing never entered my multimodal computer simulations of Northeast Corridor travel.

Departing Washington, D.C.
The sailing "commute" to Boston took seven days almost to the hour. We could have done it in four, but the object was to go slowly and see the sights. Even our departure from Washington, D.C., was unhurried, starting with a leisurely breakfast at the Happy Harbor Cafe in Deale, Maryland, a lowdown eatery favored by watermen and recreational fishermen. Friends brought us to the boat so that I wouldn't have to leave a car parked unattended for the two

months at the marina. *Sabra* was already loaded for the voyage, including all my business files, laptop computer, and the cutest little 12-volt, battery-operated printer. The forepeak was to serve as my office. I intended to do a lot of writing over the summer.

The first leg of the commute was to Rock Hall Harbor, a few miles north of the Chesapeake Bay Bridge. As we passed under the bridge we saw thousands of holiday bound tourists creeping across the bay towards the Atlantic shore for the Fourth of July weekend. We took pleasure knowing that we were already enjoying the sun and wind while the motorists still had three or four hours of tedious bumper-to-bumper driving ahead of them before they could start vacationing. We sailed on in moderate winds and glorious sunshine for most of the day before turning on the engine for the last hour or so to enter the harbor. We tied up at a restaurant pier for a well-deserved seafood dinner to celebrate a very pleasant first day. The next morning we rose at a civilized hour and after coffee continued the sail northward toward the Chesapeake and Delaware Canal, which links the two bays. It was another beautiful sailing day. When you get two great days in a row on the bay, you're definitely on a roll. In the early afternoon we turned on the engine to time our arrival in Chesapeake City with a favorable tide and before nightfall. As we moved northward, tides became a bigger scheduling factor. A sailboat under sail isn't much of a match against the inexorable force of the tide.

Tying up at Shaeffer's Restaurant in Chesapeake City was a bit tricky due to the strong tidal current in the canal. Fortunately, they have a lengthy pier and many helpful hands to catch lines. The restaurant is located right along the canal. As you dine, large freighters and barges pass within feet, providing constant entertainment. We had a comfortable berth for the evening and retired early for the next day's lengthy run to Cape May.

Delaware Bay and Cape May

Delaware Bay is far less attractive than Chesapeake Bay. It seems to turn frequently into a monotonous day-long motor trip from the C&D Canal to the mouth of the bay and the Cape May Canal. The only distractions from the flat, shallow expanse of water are the numerous lighthouses and the frequent passing of freighters, tankers, and tugs pushing or pulling barges. We were traversing these waters just a week after the most recent oil tanker accident in the Delaware River, which flows into the bay, but saw none of the oil that had spilled. The hyped-up images conjured by press releases are often quite different from reality. Environmental damage is often subtle and largely unseen with the naked eye. Unfortunately, getting the public's attention often requires a little shrill reporting. The sound will continue to get louder and more insistent as tankers continue to spill their cargoes in rivers and along shorelines. For most of the day we slowly motored southward from one lighthouse to the next to the accompaniment of the loud thumping diesel. I have tried to insulate the engine box with the latest high-tech sound insulation, but nothing seems to mute the incessant drone of a diesel. Thankfully, by late afternoon our course changed eastward, and we were able to hoist sail and shut off the unpleasant noise.

For several hours we sailed on toward the Cape May Canal, which cuts off the tip of the New Jersey peninsula and offers a protected rest stop before entering the Atlantic Ocean. We approached the canal under sail just at cocktail hour. With a setting sun, a glass of wine, some cheese and crackers, and the quiet surroundings of the wetlands on either side, we slowly sailed into the canal. Unlike more picturesque, rugged, rocky shores, or the energy of pounding surf, wetlands provide a quiet, peaceful beauty. The serenity is all the more impressive when you see birds feeding and visualize in your mind the unseen frenzy of billions of creatures that make wetlands such important nurseries for the rest of the marine environment. The visual impressions at the surface are soothingly attractive, but they don't begin to convey the life energy and true importance of wetlands as pollution filters and nurseries.

The sails were full, we had a beautiful orange sunset at our back, and the water was rushing by the hull as we marveled over life in the canal. All seemed perfect until I noticed that the same unusually shaped tree trunk was crossing our beam, again! *Sabra* was sailing backward, away from our destination. The tide was exerting its influence and winning. It was back to the engine and on to Cape May.

Ever since I started sailing, I've had the desire to someday cruise the French canals. After this passage in the Cape May Canal, I can't imagine how European canals can be any more attractive. The grass can't be any greener over there.

We finally made it to Cape May only to be turned away from the first marina we approached because it was fully occupied. It was full of sport fishing vessels, the type with the tall, shiny tuna towers and expensive-looking fishing chairs. The next marina was equally full of fishermen, but they managed to squeeze in another boat. By then we were too tired, and too full of snacks, to look for a restaurant. The supposedly quaint town of Cape May was too far from the marina, so we showered and went to sleep looking forward to the next day's sail in the ocean.

Atlantic City

We had a gentle southeasterly breeze along the New Jersey coastline toward Atlantic City. The weather forecast was good, so we sailed close to shore for a better view of the hotel and casino skyline. Naturally, the Trump Plaza casino was the most prominent and the first we were able to identify. There must be a direct relationship between ego and size of lettering used to display one's name.

Sabra was tied up in a rundown part of town, but only a few hundred feet from the elegant *Trump Princess*. It turned out that most of the town was rundown, the marina was no exception. This was our first encounter with the inconsistency of opulent hotels and casinos in the midst of seedy neighborhoods. It was the Fourth of July and we were expecting a fireworks display from our waterfront vantage point, but New Jersey had recently outlawed fireworks. Instead we did the obligatory walk on The Boardwalk but found it depressing and tacky. Equally depressing were the football-field-size gambling halls and the thousands of patrons, mostly retirees, pumping slot machines, playing cards, and shooting dice. It's hard for me to relate to all those people plunking down $20 and $50 bills on the throw of a card when you know that the odds are against you. And with all that money coming in, you would have thought that the city fathers could have extracted a small percentage to beautify the neighborhood—all that cash and squalor side by side!

We walked to a restaurant, recommended by the marina's dockmaster, through a very seedy neighborhood and were amazed by the number of homes and buildings with broken windows and decaying paint. Afraid to walk back in the dark, we called a cabby who assured us that the whole town stinks and so do the politicians who run it.

We didn't stay for the night. At about three in the morning we slipped our lines and headed out to sea for the Big Apple. With all the alleged marine pollution off the New Jersey coast, the ocean seemed a lot cleaner than Atlantic City.

New York City

The only bad weather on this trip occurred on the leg to New York City. After a pleasant morning sail we encountered several squalls and a terrific rain storm. Visibility was near zero and our anxiety was rising because we were in the approach channels for one of the world's busiest harbors. Fortunately, the storms passed in a few hours, but then the winds died entirely and we motored, again!

I had envisioned a glorious, unlimited-visibility entrance into New York Harbor and a "victory lap" sail around the Statue of Liberty. The last time I was in this harbor was about 40 years ago, coming to America as an immigrant on the U.S.S. *Marine Carp,* a converted troop carrier. As is the case more often than not, it was overcast, damp, with little wind, and nighttime rapidly approaching. But nothing can dampen the excitement of sailing into this city in a small sailboat alongside dozens of large foreign vessels and local ferries crossing every which way. We threaded our way carefully under the lower Manhattan skyline towards the South Street Seaport Museum piers. There we tied up alongside the restored *Peking,* a century-old clipper ship, and a fleet of modern J-boats raced by the Manhattan Yacht Club.

After tying up to the constantly rolling, floating pier, we made a beeline for the nearest New York pizza parlor. No trendy Lower East Side food for this hungry boat crew, just hot, freshly baked pizza, thank you. Satiated, we returned to the bouncy pier. The wake of every passing barge going up the East River tossed *Sabra* around like a floating cork on a tether. But I went to sleep exhilarated, knowing that I had sailed successfully into New York City. I didn't even mind the large junkyard dog prowling the marina grounds and "protecting" the inhabitants.

Next morning it was off to a New York deli for breakfast and a search for a small block of ice. The Fulton Fish Market right next to the marina was the perfect place for the ice. They had a bewildering array of fish, all packed in ice chips. With all the chip ice, there had to be block ice somewhere. We finally located a guy, and after a "Whaddaya want, Buddy," we had a small block for the exorbitant price of $3. But that's New York.

We headed slowly and apprehensively up the East River toward Hell's Gate. The waterway guidebooks are filled with horror stories about the tide rips in this channel between the East River and Long Island Sound. We had planned well, reading and rereading *Reed's Nautical Almanac* to time our entrance into Hell's Gate at slack water before the flood tide into the sound. The planning paid off, there were no problems, and it turned out to be an uneventful passage.

The ride up the East River was another one-of-a-kind experience as we slowly motored past stalled rush-hour traffic on the FDR Expressway, ogling the elegant East Side apartments and the U.N. building. We raised a cup of coffee to all the frustrated commuters as we slowly glided upriver.

Block Island

Once in Long Island Sound, we realized that this is no place for a sailboat. It was as flat as a pond, and so still you could read a newspaper in the reflection. For the next 20 hours we motored toward Block Island at the mouth of the sound. During the night a heavy fog descended, reducing visibility to a few yards beyond the bow. We had one scary moment when out of nowhere a strong beam of light suddenly appeared, periodically sweeping our very small horizon. Seconds later, awash in the glare of a spotlight, we heard and saw a large tug towing a huge black hulk of a barge. We passed safely, but it was unnerving to have the beast materialize so quickly and without warning. The only good thing about the experience was that the tug's skipper must have seen us on radar and then used the searchlight to identify the "target" on his radar screen. Hooray for radar reflectors. *Sabra* has carried her reflector prominently atop the foremast ever since a similarly frightening experience in the Florida Straits.

Block Island looks like a good place to escape to and write a lengthy book. There isn't much to do after you've seen the landscape. It's probably an attractive destination for a ferry ride and a lunch or dinner before sleeping over or heading back to the mainland. We had arrived in the early morning in time for breakfast and a short walking tour; and by afternoon we were getting restless. The wind had picked up, and we were eager to take advantage of it after so much motoring. We cut the visit short and headed for Buzzards Bay and the town of Marion.

Buzzards Bay and Cape Cod Canal

The passage from Block Island started out with a good sail, but halfway there the winds died. We motored into the night and finally tied up around midnight to a spare mooring at Burr Brothers Marina in Marion. We slept very well after two nights of catnaps, had a healthy breakfast, visited with friends, did some odd chores on the boat with the help of a local chandlery, and made plans to enter the Cape Cod Canal at slack water. We were now eager to make for Boston, our destination.

Experience breeds expertise, and by now I had a good handle on the tides. You don't get much tidal experience in Chesapeake Bay with its 6-inch tides. The sunset passage through Cape Cod Canal, also noted for strong tidal currents and cruising guide admonitions of "sailors, beware," was very pleasant. We slowly motored along gazing at the attractive summer homes lining the banks and the many shoreside onlookers strolling the pathways along the canal. By the time we had made it all the way through it was dark, and we proceeded up the Cape Cod Bay coastline past the sleeping towns of Plymouth, Scituate, Hingham, and on to Boston.

At sunrise, just as the first rays reflected off the Boston skyline, we entered the outer harbor. It was glorious. By the time we got to the inner harbor the Aquarium, Faneuil Hall, and the rest of the restored waterfront were awash in the early morning light.

We tied up at the Constitution Marina just 4 hours short of one week after our departure. It had taken us 164 hours, or 100 times slower than the Trump Shuttle, but it was infinitely more interesting and rewarding.

The crew left, and I was ready to experience Beantown, the Athens of the New World, the Hub of the Universe, home of the world champion Celtics, the Boston Pops. . . .

Boston's Quincy Market and North End

I am sitting at my favorite parkbench office in Boston's historic Quincy Market as I type this portion of my journal. Most mornings I take a 20-minute walk across the Charles River for my daily fix of Colombian, Mexican, Sumatran, Celebese, or Costa Rican coffee at the Coffee Connection's C.O.D.—Coffee of the Day—club. I then buy a poppyseed bagel or indulge in an outrageous pastry from the next stall before settling down with the morning paper. After a daily saturation of Dukakis' financial woes, I take out my laptop computer and do a couple of hours of work. On the weekends I spend a little more time because of the added attractions of a fatter paper and a piano player at a nearby outdoor café.

Besides the pleasant surroundings, the parkbench has a side benefit in the people I meet. The computer attracts a lot of stares and several people stop to chat about computers, the weather, Boston's tourist sights, my living on a boat, the polluted state of the harbor....There was the time when I finished the *Sunday Times* and offered it to a fellow benchsitter. She asked if I was a *Times* reporter because of the computer and my reading of an out-of-town paper. It turned out that she was a reporter for the *Globe*. On another occasion, around lunch time, a well-dressed couple sat by me with their carryout lunches. The gentleman noticed my computer and notebook and said, "Must be nice working outdoors." I learned that they worked for a local clean-harbor coalition, and we had a lively conversation on marine pollution and the fate of the proposed Stellwagen Bank marine sanctuary in Cape Cod Bay.

After my morning read and work session I slowly walk back to the marina. The path takes me directly through the North End's Italian district. I enjoy walking by the old men sitting at their doorsteps in animated discussions of what I assume are world-shaking events, judging from their gesticulations. I also pass by the outdoor green grocers, pastry stalls, and Old World specialty shops like the bonbon store. I usually leave the boat with a relatively empty backpack and return with a load of fruit, candies, a bread, and maybe a bottle of wine and a hunk of cheese—the necessities. Saturday evenings there is always a fund-raising street festival for some saint. Fortunately, there are plenty of saints and no shortage of feasts. Standard fare is fried calamari, hot and spicy sausage, classic Italian ice slushies, and of course, a Holy Cannoli. In between eating binges one can enjoy the stand-up comedians on the corner bandstands who seem to have gotten their start and joke material on the Catskill circuit.

Constitution Marina

The Constitution Marina is located alongside the 200-year-old U.S.S. *Constitution,* "Old Ironsides," the oldest active-duty vessel in the navy. There are 200 slips at the marina and about half of them are occupied by liveaboards. During the harsh Boston winter, the liveaboard population drops to about 30 percent of that, but no one is worried about keeping their boats in the water. They say the water is so polluted that it can't freeze. Summer is the peak season for transient boats like *Sabra.* A new boat coming into the marina is always an occasion. It's like watching the moving van unload in a small neighborhood. Here the onlookers are curious about the captain's ability to dock the vessel safely, and the ship's complement of wife or girlfriend, children, and pets.

Last week I was standing on the marina office's veranda when a 137-foot, gleaming white "yacht" slowly backed into a channel that I thought was tight for *Sabra*'s 32 feet. The captain did a masterful job with two massive engines and a pair of bow thrusters. After the boat was safely tied up, the assembled onlookers shouted, "Well done, Cap'n," and gave him a rousing hand. From my perch on the veranda, I noticed nine young, attractive, and well-dressed crewmembers on *Halcyon.* They all wore neatly pressed white shorts and green knit shirts with the boat's logo. One resident, who popped out of his boat cabin, bare-chested, to see what all the commotion was about, saw the nattily dressed crew and shouted over to the dockmaster, "Does this mean we'll have to dress up?"

When all the lines were secured, two of the female crewmembers went around the cabin replacing the objets d'art—Tiffany lamp, vases, ships models, glass ash trays—from storage locations back onto the various end tables, mantles, and shelves in the elegant saloon. Then, finally, the captain, a gray-haired Cary Grant type, sauntered down the gangway, probably feeling full of himself, toward the marina office to register and pay by the foot! As the onlookers departed, one was overheard wondering what would happen if the wind picked up, "Would this large vessel take the entire marina out to sea?"

Janet, the dockmaster (or is it "dockmistress"), is a young, friendly woman who manages a staff of four and oversees a 200-slip marina grossing about $1.2 million annually. She had worked for her father in a boat business before being tapped for this job. There's definitely a woman's touch to the marina, a flower garden in front of the office, an herb garden for the residents, clean shower facilities and laundry room, and a well-groomed staff. It's not often you see a dockmaster scampering around in a dinghy, wearing a skirt.

The marina's laundromat is a great gathering place and a good source of news and gossip. I met a fellow off a 53-foot powerboat in the charter business, based four months in the Boston area and the remaining time in Ft. Lauderdale. The boat charters for about $5,000 to $8,000 per week, and according to this guy there is no shortage of clients. The interesting thing about this fellow is that while on charter he acts as the cook and doesn't let the guests know that he is the owner of the boat. He says that this reduces complaints and results in tips that might otherwise not be given. Once, on a week-long charter, he received a $1,000 tip which, incidentally, he did not share with the captain and crew because he feels that they are paid well enough for their services. He is currently eyeing a 70-foot vessel for his charter business. It won't hold more than the eight guests he can now accommodate, but he says that people will pay more for the spaciousness of the bigger boat. The rates don't seem so outrageous when you consider the fact that the boat burns $35 an hour in fuel. A typical trip from Florida to Massachusetts costs about $4,000 for diesel fuel alone!

Rebecca and Michael are docked about 10 boats down from *Sabra*. They came over the other day to compare notes on unstayed masts. They have a 39-foot Freedom schooner with unstayed, carbon-fiber masts and had noticed *Sabra*'s aluminum masts as we came in. People definitely notice you. It's like noticing your neighbor's azaleas or crab grass. I noticed that their boat was called *Rebecca Anne*. It's dangerous to name a boat after your friend or spouse. It's like getting a tattoo with your current girl's name. I saw a tattoo once with the words YOUR NAME HERE across a heart shape. How would that look on a boat's transom? Michael and Rebecca are getting married soon; hopefully, the boat's name will survive.

Michael is completing his residency at a nearby hospital and is thinking of settling in the Washington, D.C., area. Rebecca drives a tour bus and has promised me a special V.I.P. tour anytime I want to see the sights. They have lived at the marina for several winters, and Michael said I should come back and take photos of all the boats in their winter shrink wrapping. He says that people make frames out of bent electrical conduit and then help each other install shrink-wrapped plastic over the entire boat with a small cutout for an entryway. They claim that the greenhouse effect makes for a cozy cabin even when the temperature drops into the teens. Rebecca says the winters are trying, but it's fun to unwrap the boat in the spring, like opening a summer cottage.

The marina residents are very friendly, and you can't pass anyone on the docks without a hello or a nod. Everyone is interested in each other's boats, either out of simple curiosity over the boat brand or style or out of a feeling of helpfulness in time of need. When someone pulls into a slip there are always helping hands to catch a line. The weather, the tides, and the unrelenting forces of water band these people together. As neighbors pass by other boats, they instinctively notice mooring lines, always making sure that everything is snug and as it should be.

Between *Sabra* and *Rebecca Anne* lives Dotty, the self-proclaimed "game warden" of the dock. In her charge are several very tame ducks and a pair of dogs, including a three-legged one. They all live in and around *Travesty*, a houseboat with a large lighted goose in the bay window. Dotty feeds her "children" and constantly washes down the dock to clean off the droppings. Pretty ducks can be very messy.

Sabra is docked on an outside pier facing the Charles River. From the cockpit, I have an unobstructed view of the endlessly fascinating Boston skyline. The floating dock is a bit rolly because of the wake of passing boats headed up the Charles, but the inconvenience is well worth the constant parade. On weekends there is always some activity around the U.S.S. *Constitution,* which draws a wide variety of boats, including some very old classics under sail. Last weekend there was a parade of old, wooden boats led by a fireboat under full spray. The parade was so close to me that I got showered by the fireboat as it passed.

Rain and Other Hardships

Don't get the idea that everything is wonderful and idyllic all the time. For example, when it rains, life in a marina can get depressing very quickly. One is confined to a small boat, which gives new meaning to the phrase "cabin fever," and when one ventures out, the normally bobbing docks are all the more dangerous when wet and slippery. The pay phones are uncovered, so one stands there trying to take notes while talking in a downpour. I nodded to the man next to me on the telephone and said, "Ah, the joys of living aboard." He replied from under his dripping foul-weather hood, "Try it with kids!"

Boats, which are made virtually leak-proof below the waterline with a minimum of well-sealed through-hull fittings, generally have an abundant number of unintentional openings above deck through which rainwater eventually seeps in. If drops don't actually hit you in the face as you lie in your bunk, then they simply add to the close, damp, clammy, miserable atmosphere.

Normal boat noises like slapping halyards, creaking lines and rigging, and the lapping of water against the hull can peacefully lull you to sleep. But strange and especially loud noises can also frighten and annoy. One night an enormous foghorn blasted the late-night stillness with its characteristic moan, "oooohaaaayh." It sounded as though it had gone off right in my cabin. The next day the dockmaster said that someone had accidentally triggered the *Nantucket Lightship* foghorn. This horn was designed to be heard at a distance of 5 miles in heavy fog, so you can image what it sounded like from 200 yards away, where it was tied up as a museum ship next to the *Constitution*. And if you like to sleep late in the mornings, forget it. At 0800, every day with naval precision, a large cannon blasts off the deck of the *Constitution*. I guess it's their way of saying, "Good morning, world."

One morning I made it to the *Constitution* just before 0800 to watch them prepare for this cannon ritual. While a group of sailors ignited the powder in the cannon below deck, a young deckhand stood at attention in his 1790s "sailor boy" outfit, saluting the Union Jack while another sailor played the "Star Spangled Banner" on a large, modern-day boom box. I was particularly amused by the attention to historical detail alongside the up-to-date sound system.

If you're trying to conduct business off a boat, as I am, then you're dependent on messages taken by the marina office and on the ubiquitous pay phones around town. My favorite pay phone is a booth in the elegant Bostonian Hotel. It offers large, well-appointed, and soundproof booths complete with note pads and sharpened pencils. Unfortunately, called parties aren't always in, and then I have to depend on the marina office staff to relay returned calls. I spent several days on the boat waiting for messages before I realized that they deliver phone messages by dinghy rather than walking the docks. The messages, in the form of small, crumpled wads of paper, are stuck to the tiller under a small bungee cord. It was quite a while before I noticed the wads of paper and by then the "CALL, ASAP!" messages were very old. If you think it's frustrating to play telephone tag with secretaries or answering machines at either end, try it with a dinghy at one end. Life's tough in the slow lane.

Labor Day was fast approaching, and with it the end of my summer stay in Boston. It was time to get *Sabra* ready for the return commute to Washington, D.C.

Peering through the murky water at the hull, I noticed that the colder, brackish water environment of Boston Harbor had encouraged a healthy colony of barnacles on the propeller. This was going to slow *Sabra* down, especially while motoring during the return transits of the Cape Cod, Cape May, and C&D canals, so I made arrangements with the marina to have a diver scrape off the barnacles. Fortunately, my two-year-old, poisonous, antifouling bottom paint (applied before the EPA ban) had successfully discouraged these pesky mollusks from attaching themselves to the hull. But the propeller was thoroughly encrusted and looked like some ancient archeological artifact dredged out of the deep.

Two days before the diver was due, my son arrived on his way to college. He was telling me about his recent SCUBA lessons as he studied the propeller from dockside. He stuck his toe in the harbor water and said, "C'mon, Dad, we can scrape the propeller ourselves with the snorkeling gear." Well, that was all the goading I needed, and the next thing I knew we were both in the polluted Boston Harbor taking turns diving under the boat and scraping the propeller blades. Afterward, we stood on the dock hosing ourselves off as neighbors shook their heads in disbelief. "Nobody swims in Boston Harbor," said one boater. "You've probably shortened your life by a few years," said another.

Well, the job was done, and we were proud of it. Actually, the water didn't seem as bad as it had a few weeks earlier after a rainstorm, when all the upstream sewage plants in the area overflowed and raw sewage came down the Charles River. At that point there definitely was some powerful stuff in the water, and in the immortal words of Amie Carter, who would have found the water as obnoxious as nuclear power, "It was yukkie."

Provincetown

On the way back I took a 50-mile detour across Cape Cod Bay to Provincetown at the tip of Cape Cod. *Sabra* was going to participate in a promotional event highlighting the proposed designation of Stellwagen Bank as a marine sanctuary. Stellwagen Bank is one of several sites proposed as a national marine sanctuary program, which now has eight such sanctuaries in U.S. coastal waters. Stellwagen is the summer feeding ground for several thousand of the estimated 10,000 remaining and endangered Atlantic humpback whales. Since I had participated earlier in the year in a similar event off the Dominican Republic's north coast, where the humpbacks breed and spend the winter months, it seemed only natural to close the loop on this magnificent creature's annual migration.

Sabra pulled away from the Constitution Marina at 6 A.M. The early morning silence was broken with the thump, thump, thump of the diesel as I motored out of the harbor with the help of an ebb tide. It was a crisp and clear autumn morning with the sunrise reflecting off the gleaming glass and

metal buildings along the waterfront. In the harbor, fishing boats and tugs were already busy with their daily chores. Fortified with a thermos of hot tea, I made my way past Logan Airport, where planes were lined up for their commutes to New York, Philadelphia, Washington, and other busy places. From my sea-level vantage point all I could see were the high tail sections, bearing the familiar TWA, Northwest, Delta, and Trump logos, slowly creeping toward their take-off point. Inside I imagined briefcases being snapped open for a last-minute perusal of the day's agenda, power lunch appointment, or the latest *Wall Street Journal* takeover news.

I, on the other hand, was busy dodging thousands of lobsterpot buoys and the fishermen working the inner harbor. Who's eating these lobsters? I wondered. With all the recent publicity over Boston Harbor pollution, it was hard to believe that people were paying good money for a New England lobster dinner and then scrumptiously devouring a bottom-scavenging resident of Boston's Inner Harbor. Maybe the restaurants put these creatures in a tank filled with imported Maine water and call them Maine water lobsters!

It was a perfectly still morning as I motored around the outer harbor islands frequently staring back at the fiery sunrise. I wondered nostalgically what the Coffee-of-the-Day would be at Quincy Market.

Although I was feeling full of myself on this singlehanded passage to Provincetown, I still wanted someone aboard to turn to and to be able to say, "Wow, look at that sunrise!" I enjoy singlehanded sailing as a test of my seamanship, but it is lonely. There's no one to get in the way in a small cockpit, but there's also no one to share the experience.

The 12-hour trip was uneventful, and by late afternoon I was tied up in Provincetown waiting for *Gift Horse,* a 60-foot schooner that was also coming here for the sanctuary festivities. Earlier in the day I had contacted *Gift Horse* by radio, and we planned to rendezvous at the pier. Along with *Fin II,* a 50-foot motor cruiser, the three boats, making up the marine conservation fleet, were to shuttle guests to the Stellwagen Bank area northeast of Provincetown to take part in some serious whale watching.

In between whale watching we sampled some of the area's seafood restaurants, hopefully not serving Boston lobster, and walked the town's main shopping street. The boutiques are disappointingly similar in their wares, but the shoppers are the real show. The town is justly famous for its eclectic lifestyles. As one of our hosts remarked, "Where else can you find a major transvestite convention every fall?"

Atlantic City Revisited

I returned briefly to Boston to pick up a crewmember and then headed south to the Cape Cod Canal. There was very little wind, and we motored all the way. But with the lack of wind came another one of those endlessly fascinating ocean phenomena.

Hurricane Gabriela had recently bypassed this area but in her wake had left very large swells—12 feet or more. The swells were running about a minute apart, and it felt as though the boat was rising and falling on a smooth elevator. The sea looked glassy, but you could feel the steady rise and fall, and you could see nearby boats virtually disappear as you moved up and they moved down. It was a gentle reminder of an awesome force.

About halfway between Buzzards Bay and Atlantic City, we suddenly found ourselves in company with hundreds, or at least dozens, of houseflies. It was as though they had spontaneously generated to annoy us. The faster we killed them, the more numerous they became. At one point a small, tired bird landed on my chest as I rested in the cockpit, and quickly scrambled around the deck looking for a footing and a breather before heading on. It proceeded to catch and eat the flies, but unfortunately we needed a flock of birds to make a dent in the fly population. Later the flies disappeared as mysteriously as they had appeared.

The 150-mile crossing to Atlantic City was strangely empty of commercial traffic, considering that we were crossing three ship-traffic lanes to the busy New York Harbor. We did see one of those sewage barges on its way back from Site 106. I had thought of visiting this area, 106 miles east of Cape May, because *Newsweek* magazine called it "the filthiest place in America." Actually, I was told by a researcher who had been to the area, that to the naked eye it looks no different than any other part of the Atlantic in spite of the fact that millions of New Yorkers literally give of themselves daily to this remote part of the ocean. Seeing the barge was enough for this trip.

Atlantic City wasn't my first choice for a stopover on the return trip, but it is undeniably convenient for the ground and air connections serving this gambling mecca. The bus-loading area under the Trump Castle Hotel looked as busy as New York's Port Authority and certainly busier than Washington, D.C.'s bus station. In back of the bus-loading zone and facing the front of the 20-story hotel and casino is the Senator Frank Bradley Marina.

The marina is owned by the state of New Jersey and operated by the hotel management company. Since it is the home port of the *Trump Princess,* it recently received a total face lift, making it one of the cleanest and best-designed marinas I have seen on this trip. The marina has 640 slips plus one very large dock for the 248-foot *Princess.* It also will fit Trump's newest boat acquisition plans, a 420-footer currently under construction. Trump's recent financial troubles may make this slip unnecessary.

The marina management claims that during the summer season about 50 percent of the boats are liveaboards enjoying the status of "hotel guests" at a fraction of the normal room rates. I was introduced to this guest privilege when I went to the hotel deli and found two lines—one moving slowly, with about 30 or 40 people waiting patiently to be seated, and another labeled "guests," with only two persons in line.

The marina has excellent shower and laundry facilities and, like all marinas, this is where you meet your neighbors and gossip about boats and places. I met a retired Detroit-area policeman and his wife. They had left Lake Michigan bound for Florida, the Bahamas, the Caribbean, and eventually the Venezuelan coast. He told me that he visited the police office near the marina to ask some fellow officers directions to a good fish restaurant. Their reply was that it wasn't safe to leave the hotel/marina grounds. He said he felt right at home after his 29-year career in the Detroit area. I passed on lots of tips about the relatively crime-free Chesapeake Bay area, and we promised to call on the radio if we saw each other's boat en route. His wife refuses to do any night sailing, so we'll probably be ahead of them most of the trip, but it's always a pleasant diversion to hail a recognized boat.

Trump Castle

Apart from the plush marina, I was also looking forward to classy hotel surroundings. At first I was overwhelmed by the glitz and gloss, but as time wore on I became increasingly uncomfortable. I realized that the hotel exists for only one reason and that is to get people into the gambling area as quickly and for as long as possible to gamble.

One morning I was early for the deli and had to wait a few minutes before it opened. I found a paper to read and was sitting on a marble shelf, part of a large planter box, in front of the hotel restaurant. A guard came by and told me that there was no sitting allowed in this area. I looked around for a lobby chair or couch when it hit me that there was no seating in the hotel lobby other than in the gambling area at the tables. I have never been to a hotel without lobby seating. I also noticed that all of the flat stones in the lobby that could be used as benches had chrome-plated spikes running the length of the surface to discourage sitting. In Washington, D.C., they use this technique to discourage the homeless from taking up residence.

The actual gambling area is located slightly below the lobby level, and there are wide, ramp-like corridors leading to the slot machines and card tables. I wouldn't be surprised if the entire hotel were built on an imperceptible incline to encourage people subliminally into the casino. The philosophy is to keep 'em moving into the gambling pits. What makes this so troubling is that most of the people are retirees, and from the looks of them they're not rich retirees. I understand that the hotels charter buses to haul people from surrounding retirement communities for a day of "fun"—box lunch included. Looking at it on the bright side, it's a day away from the boredom of shuffle board and pool gossip.

Disaster Strikes

We left Atlantic City around midnight with a new crew and high hopes for some ocean sailing before Delaware Bay. Unfortunately, the little wind we had was on the nose and there was a schedule to keep, so the "iron sail" was called to duty.

As evening approached we were carefully picking our way from one lighted buoy to the next toward the Chesapeake and Delaware Canal. We were only a hundred yards or so from the Canal entrance when we became disoriented by what later proved to be a mislabeled buoy lighting sequence on the chart. My charts are only five years old, but apparently a change had been made and I wasn't up-to-date. We cautiously backtracked to our last known position for another try when the engine died. Before we had a chance to even think of our next move, a powerboat came by and asked if we were in trouble. They had noticed our erratic movements over the past few minutes. We explained our difficulty, and they offered to tow us to a marina and a diesel mechanic on the New Jersey side of the bay. What looked like a painless solution to our problems turned out otherwise.

The powerboat owner turned out to be the owner of a marina on the Salem River. The water near the dock wasn't deep enough for *Sabra* so he let us off in deeper waters where we dropped anchor for the night. The tidal currents were very strong in this area, and it took several attempts to secure the anchor for a much needed night's sleep.

After breakfast I bled the fuel system, and the engine mysteriously started. We quickly hoisted the anchor and set off. About a mile up the narrow passage on the Salem River the engine quit again, and we quickly lowered the anchor. This time we were "parked" in a very narrow passage used by ocean-going freighters that had to maneuver around us very delicately. I radioed for another tow, and this time we were taken to a deepwater marina dock where we awaited the mechanic. In the towing process, we managed to lose both the anchor and the anchor chain, which had become hopelessly entangled on a large piece of concrete construction debris.

At the second marina we were tied up next to an 87-year-old Nova Scotia schooner being restored by yet another ex-policeman and current liveaboard. Living aboard must be a good antidote to the stresses of police work.

The mechanic arrived close to midnight and fiddled with the engine, which again mysteriously started. He couldn't explain it, and I decided to try again the next day after a long warm-up period. One anchor and 100 feet of chain later, we were off again.

Baltimore

We made it to Baltimore and tied up at the Inner Harbor Marina to let off the crew. The marina is beautifully situated for a visit to this much underrated city. The Inner Harbor is less than a mile across and ringed by a redeveloped commercial district including the National Aquarium, the tall-ship *Constellation*, a World War II submarine, and a host of eateries and shopping boutiques. I recalled a previous visit to Baltimore, sailing into the Inner Harbor on a perfect late-afternoon breeze to the watchful eyes of thousands of people strolling the wharf and sitting at the outdoor cafés. I dropped *Sabra*'s distinctive tan-bark-colored sails and tied up to the wharf, whereupon someone shouted down from the embankment, "Isn't that a Chinese junk rig?" I was really taken aback, not expecting an inner-city resident to recognize this unique rig. When I replied that it was, he said, "We used to chase those m—— f——- all over Nam!"

Baltimore is definitely on the list for another liveaboard tourist visit. But for this season it was a brief visit and the next-to-last stop on the way home. Two days after arriving in Baltimore, I set sail, again singlehanding, for Herring Bay and home port. The winds were well over 20 knots for the entire 40-mile trip. The sailing was exhilarating, and it reminded me of a bad game of golf that ends by shooting par on the 18th hole—an ending designed to bring you back for more.

There is always another season and many more places to visit with my floating home.

9

The Liveaboard Gourmet

LIKE THEIR land-based brethren, liveaboards also need and enjoy good food, well prepared, at home. The ship's galley presents some unique opportunities, problems to some, in provisioning, preparing meals, and sometimes in the simple act of serving foods. Along with all the other technical expertise needed by the liveaboard, being an accomplished gourmet and nutritionist helps.

The boat galley may not be the ideal kitchen, but it's surprising what culinary wonders are possible in small cramped quarters without the help of a Cuisinart or microwave oven. After a day of soaking up the sun, or a bone-chilling sail, even simply prepared meals can have a banquet impact to a hungry crew.

The boat offers some unique challenges to the cook and provisioner. First, there is the problem of space, not only for meal preparation but also for food storage. Second, there is the constant concern for power. Unless the boat is connected to shore power or carries extensive generating capacity, the energy for cooking and refrigeration is limited. Last, there is, for those that leave the slip, a constant motion about the boat that can make it difficult to cook, and on some occasions, even difficult to eat.

Along the way several readers have submitted suggestions and the occasional recipe. The emphasis here is on simplicity and wholesomeness rather than elegantly prepared, Martha Stewart spreads. Oftentimes the conditions are abysmal or the energy requirements—human and otherwise—make cooking and eating a challenge. But don't get me wrong, liveaboards don't suffer. There is nothing like sipping your favorite brew in the cockpit to the accompaniment of freshly caught fish and a magnificent sunset over water, or enjoying a hot bowl of oatmeal with raisins and honey to start a chilly day.

Plenty has been written on the subject of onboard cooking. If you're looking for a recipe to make a warm, hearty meal for a ravenous crew coming off a cold watch, or if you need to bring something special to a potluck dock party, or the ice has melted and you're searching for some non-refrigerated food preparation ideas, or you're planning a seductive meal in a secluded anchorage, or you're in charge of making the provisioning list for a long passage, or the captain wants to know what you're going to do with that guava paste he's found in the bottom of the locker left over from a Caribbean shopping spree, you're in luck. Someone has probably written the perfect galley cookbook for you.

The interest in cooking aboard is amply demonstrated by at least four dozen cookbooks currently found in boating libraries and chandleries (see list below). These range from tips on growing your own sprouts and foraging the sea to the enticing title, *Sex at Sea: How to Put Romance in Your Recipes*. Maybe you're interested in assembling your own favorite recipes and galley hints and are looking for a suitable title.

The large selection of seagoing cookbooks demonstrates an interest in the galley every bit as important as the attention showered on the engine room, deck layout, hull lines, and sailing rigs. Here is an assortment of a few tasty samplings from liveaboards.

GALLEY COOKBOOKS

The Bareboat Gourmet: Creative Cooking with Standard Provisions by Doris Colgate
The Beaufort Scale Cookbook by Jane Raper
The Best of People and Food by Barbara Davis
The Boat Cook, 2nd Edition, by Donna Marxer
The Boat/US Members Choice Cookbook by Erica Lowery

Bottoms Up Cookery by Robert B. Leamer, Wilfred H. Shaw, and
    Charles F. Ulrich
Can-to-Pan Cookbook by Lynn Orloff-Jones
The Captain's Cookbook by Walter Kaprielian
The Care and Feeding of the Offshore Crew by Lin and Larry Pardey
Catch of the Day by Ginny Lentz
The Charter Cookbook by Reba E. Shepard
The Complete Galley Slave by Gillian Morgan
Cooking Afloat: On Any Size Boat by Beverly Fuller
Cooking on the Move by Rika Gingell
Cooking Under Pressure by Lorna J. Sass
Cooking with Canned and Packaged Foods by Mary Boone
The Cruising Chef by Mike Greenwald
The Cruising Cook by Shirley Deal
Dehydrated Cookery by Becky Johnson
Dining on Deck: Fine Foods for Sailing & Boating by Linda Vail
Fish and Shellfish by Charlotte Walker
The Galley Cookbook by Janet Groene
Galley Cuisine: A Shortcut to Gourmet Cooking
    by Sandra Homer & Ritta Ullman
Galley Goop by Allan "Doug" Douglas
Galley Gourmet III by Ferne Raveson
Galley Gourmet by Gail and Nancy Scherer
Galley Ho! Boat Cookbook by the *Yachtsman's Wife Quarterly*
The Galley K*I*S*S Cookbook by Corine C. Kanter
Galley Proof by Gail Swanton
The Gimballed Gourmet by Kathryn Farron
Gimballing Gourmet: Galley Guide by Marcia Grosvenor
Good Food Afloat: Every Sailor's Guide to Eating Right
    by John Betterley
The Gourmet Galley: Fine Cooking on Small Boats
    by Terrence Jenericco
Gourmet in the Galley by Katherine Robinson
The Happy Ship Cookbook by Marion Berick
Heavy Weather Cooking by Jan Silver
The Mariner's Cookbook by Nancy Hyden Woodward
Maverick Sea Fare: A Caribbean Cookbook by Dee Carstarphen
Meals on Keels by the Bluewater Cruising Association
The Nautical Gourmet by Sandra Arnold Hartley
The Perfect Galley Cookbook by Deane Taylor
The Racing Galley: The "How To" Book by Goldie Joseph
The Sailing Chef: How to Prepare 150 Simple Elegant Meals Afloat
    by Ty Harrington

Seacook: Guide to Good Living Afloat by Bob Heppel

Sex at Sea: Put Romance in Your Recipes by Allan "Doug" Douglas

Ship to Shore: Virgin Islands Charter Yacht Recipes by Jan Robinson

Ship to Shore II: Caribbean Charter Recipes by Jan Robinson

Simple Seafood: Seafood Cookery Made Easy by Vicki Emmons

Sip to Shore: Cocktails and Hors d'oeuvres by Jan Robinson

Son of a Sea Cookbook by Kenneth R. Tolliver

Two Burners and an Ice Chest by Phyliss Bultmann

Windjammer World: A Down East Galley-Eye View
    by Dee Carstarphen

The Women's Guide to Boating and Cooking by Lael Morgan

Yachting Cookbook by Elizabeth Wheeler and Jennifer Trainer

ICE: NECESSITY OR LUXURY?

Margaret Roth is an accomplished liveaboard and world cruiser. With her husband, Hal, she has taken several extended voyages, including a circumnavigation of the Pacific, a rounding of Cape Horn, and a complete circumnavigation of the globe—all with no ice. Here she tells of her secrets for provisioning and healthy fare.

During 20 wonderful years of living aboard our 35-foot yacht *Whisper,* Hal and I sailed to a hundred distant parts of the world. We had no refrigeration at all. Now in 1990, we are aboard a new and larger yacht, but we still get along quite nicely without the complexities and problems of refrigeration. Our friend, the famous Argentine sailor Bobby Uriburu, once told us: "All the talk about iced drinks comes down to the few inches between the lips and the throat."

For refreshing drinks, we find that limes or lemons with a little sugar and water will quench our thirst just as well as an iced beverage. There are half-pint cartons of fruit juices that have a shelf life of six months and are much tastier than canned juices.

Many fresh foods keep well without refrigeration. It is important to buy first-quality items that preferably have never been refrigerated. The shelf life of potatoes, for example, can vary from one week to several months depending on the quality. The same is true for onions. Fresh farm eggs will keep much longer than refrigerated supermarket eggs. However, even store-bought eggs are usually good for several months if greased with petroleum jelly. Squashes with hard outer coverings keep well, carrots are usually good for a couple of weeks, and cabbage will last up to a month. Good-quality grapefruit, oranges, lemons, and limes will keep three or four weeks, and longer if you wrap each piece of fruit in aluminum foil.

I never refrigerate jams, pickles, or mustard. Mayonnaise is a little trickier, but a small jar is good for several weeks. Cheeses with heavy waxed coatings—Gouda, Tillamook, Edam, Bonbel—keep well until the wax is broken. Cooking oil and Crisco don't require refrigeration at all. Butter, margarine, and Nestle's cream can often be bought in cans. Instead of powdered milk, you can now buy long-life milk in cartons that lasts for months if kept unopened. The containers are usually one quart, but it's possible to buy half-pint sizes that are more convenient if you are not a big milk-drinker.

Besides fresh food there are dried items such as rice, pasta, dried beans, lentils, and TVP (textured vegetable protein) that keep for long periods. TVP is not only a substitute for ground beef in spaghetti sauce (particularly if you add a bouillon cube), but almost always brings calls for second helpings. I often use lentils in curry sauces and in rissoles.

The Liveaboard Gourmet

Fresh meat is generally frozen for long-term storage, but you can buy small cans of roast beef, corned beef, chicken, turkey, and tuna. A favorite aboard our yacht are small cans of chunk chicken. This is handy on crackers for quick meals during crises or at night. It can also be served in a white sauce.

Something new—developed for astronauts—are pouch meals. You drop a sealed foil pouch into boiling seawater or fresh water for 10 minutes, slit open the pouch, and the food is ready to eat. (While the pouch is heating, you can cook rice or a pasta to go with the main course.) I particularly like the Yurika brand, which has such entrees as trout almandine, chicken breasts in wine sauce, sweet-and-sour pork, Swiss steak, beef Burgundy, beef stew, beef stroganoff, chili with beans, chili con carne, clam chowder, and so on. There are a number of brands of pouch meals that vary quite a lot in quality; by all means buy a few samples and try them before you purchase them in quantity.

We also carry some freeze-dried foods, often used by hikers, but in general these are not as tasty as pouch meals. However, the Mountain House freeze-dried chicken and beef stews are old favorites. They seem to keep forever, are excellent and tasty for quick meals, and we always have a couple of giant cans aboard. Freeze-dried garden peas and green beans are much better than canned varieties and look good because of their bright green color. Again buy a sample of various kinds and try them out.

Here is one of my favorite recipes:

PINEAPPLE CORNED BEEF SWEET-AND-SOUR

1 12-ounce can of corned beef

1 egg

1 cup flour

$1/2$ teaspoon of monosodium glutamate (MSG), optional

2 cups vegetable oil
18-ounce can of pineapple chunks
1 medium green pepper (nice, if available)
1 teaspoon soy sauce
$^{1}/_{2}$ cup sugar
$^{1}/_{4}$ cup catsup
$^{1}/_{2}$ cup vinegar
2 tablespoons cornstarch

Gently with
the Tides

Cut the corned beef into thumbsize squares. Dip each square into the beaten egg. Then coat the pieces with a mixture of flour and MSG. Bring the vegetable oil to a boil, and slowly spoon in the pieces of coated beef. Fry until golden brown on all sides—about five minutes. Remove the chunks of cooked meat and drain on a paper towel.

Put the soy sauce, sugar, juice from the can of pineapple, catsup, and vinegar in a deep skillet, stir well, and bring to a boil.

Separately, mix the two tablespoons of cornstarch with two tablespoons of water to make a paste. Gradually add this paste to the sauce. Continue to boil the sauce and stir until it thickens. Add the cooked beef, pineapple chunks, and sliced green pepper. Keep mixing everything for about five minutes or until all the ingredients are very hot. Serve with steamed rice. My recipe is supposed to be enough for three or four portions, but this dish disappears fast!

Margaret Roth

GALLEY PROOF

Gail Swanton's friends gave her a blank notebook when she and her husband set off for the Caribbean. The instructions were that she was to write down her recipes as they wandered from place to place. The result was the Galley Proof *cookbook. I bought a copy of the book to learn more about her travels and her culinary secrets.*

Gail and her husband, Jack, lived aboard a 1929 wooden classic, William Atkins–designed motorlaunch for more than 10 years, setting out from New England for the Bahamas, Mexico, and the Caribbean islands as far south as the Grenadines. She wrote down recipes as she cooked and added notes about the people, the sea conditions, and all the little things that made their memorable voyage. The longer they stayed in the islands the more time she had to refine the recipes and the travelogue.

Galley Proof turned out to be a handy little cookbook that won't take up much shelf space in the cabin, and it fits easily into a small duffle bag if you're off on a friend's boat. It's chock-full of quick and simple as well as some slightly more involved recipes designed to keep the crew well fed and guests dazzled. All the recipes are practical and can easily be prepared in a small galley. Equally as interesting as the recipes are the vignettes of their years of living aboard and cruising from Maine to the sunny Caribbean.

Gail's recipes are a reflection of what can be done with a mix of basic ingredients and local fish, fruits, or vegetables. The book begins with a good listing of basics to outfit the galley and includes a number of unique but very practical suggestions—purchase whole wheat berries to grind into flour, and brewer's yeast to sprinkle on popcorn instead of salt and butter.

We all know the importance of using fresh goods. Yet no matter how vigorously one searches for those fresh supplies whenever available, a solid supply of canned goods is essential for extended cruising. Gail has suggestions for interesting canned combinations for several soups and salads. Her seafood recipes, including how to open and clean a conch, would be particularly helpful for island cruising where fresh foods can be scarce. Also included is a fine variety of breads, cookies, and other baked goods, as well as canning and preserving recipes for those who can't resist the urge.

The stories of their travels add another interesting dimension to this book. In a series of brief paragraphs sprinkled like a garnish throughout the book, she conveys the joys and frustrations of long-term living aboard and cruising. You'll find yourself chuckling over stories of lost refrigerator doors and accidents with rising bread dough in the warm engine room.

Most importantly, *Galley Proof* is a small package with a full array of menus that could serve as the only cookbook in a cramped galley. Amusingly illustrated by Olivia Cole, the book is clearly a labor of love.

THE PRESSURE COOKER

Given a choice, I will always prepare and eat "one-handed sandwiches," fresh fruits, raw vegetables, and a cookie even when at anchor or tied to a dock. Friends have encouraged me to broaden my culinary horizons. They suggested a pressure cooker as an alternative, especially for easy, no-fuss cooking while cruising.

Several years ago I read an article about the advantages of a pressure cooker for preserving leftovers. The image of a witch's brew-like concoction of foods collecting over several days and smoldering away didn't make me rush out to buy a cooker. But the holidays rolled around, and the captain found a sleek, high-tech, Porsche-black, Hawkins Futura Cooker under the tree. This compact little unit, and I emphasize compact, would be right at home in any spaceship. The advertised features of this little wonder include:

- Saving cooking energy and cooking time;
- Preserving the volatile vitamins and adding to the nutritional value of the meal;
- Containing the meal—even if the cooker is thrown off the burner the contents don't end up on the floor or ceiling;
- Using the cooker as a steamer for clams, shrimp, crabs, and lobster.
- The finished meal, if left in the unopened cooker, can sit for long periods without spoiling—just reheat and serve.

Here is a recipe for an Indian-flavored lentil soup prepared in a pressure cooker. Remember, when fresh foods are scarce, spices can provide a variety of tastes to basic foodstuffs.

INDIAN LENTIL SOUP

$1/2$ cup lentils
14-oz can Italian-style tomatoes, drained and chopped
1 tablespoon lemon juice
1 medium onion, chopped
1 clove garlic, minced
$1/4$ teaspoon ground cinnamon
$1/8$ teaspoon ground cardamom
$1/8$ teaspoon ground coriander
$1/4$ teaspoon ground ginger
$1/2$ teaspoon ground turmeric
$1/4$ teaspoon ground cumin
$1/2$ teaspoon ground cayenne
2 tablespoons butter
$1/2$ teaspoon salt/pepper

Wash and drain the lentils. Melt the butter in a saucepan, add blended spices, and cook over low heat for one minute to bring out the flavor. Add onion and garlic and sauté until clear. Add all the ingredients, except the salt and pepper, to the pressure cooker. Add water so that the pressure cooker is half full. Cook 15–20 minutes after pressurized (time may depend on the cooker unit instructions). Allow pressure to drop normally. Add salt and pepper just before serving.

For more information on pressure-cooker techniques read *Cooking Under Pressure* by Lorna J. Sass.

THE SANDWICH

Sandwiches are the least publicized and often the most appreciated goodies in a gourmet chef's repertoire. They lack the pizazz or the mystery of more elegant dishes like Le Filet de Poison Dore au Vermouth. But it is the lack of complexity—the utter simplicity and practicality—that make the sandwich so right for a boat. Remember, "One hand for the meal and one for the boat."

When one becomes tired of the tried-and-true sandwich standbys—ham 'n' cheese or PB & J—browse through the recipes in the four Deadly Sin mysteries by Lawrence Sanders. The main character, Detective Edward X. Delaney, is a sandwich freak. He classifies sandwiches into wet, which he eats over the kitchen sink, or dry, which he often consumes with a beer. Some of his favorites are:

The Liveaboard Gourmet

- smoked fish, onion slices, and mayonnaise on a croissant;
- cold sliced pork, German potato salad, scallions, and horseradish on an onion roll;
- corned beef, sauerkraut, potato chips, and dijon mustard on sour rye bread;
- cold sliced chicken, tomatoes, onions, and Russian dressing on an onion roll;
- smoked turkey, dill pickles, and tiger sauce on a hard roll; and
- roast beef, pickles, relish, sliced onion, and horseradish on sourdough bread.

Pita bread is a useful device for holding a variety of ingredients. Pita bread is especially good for sandwiches because when you cut it in half, you have two natural pockets to stuff. One fast-food lunch counter in Washington, D.C., calls pita bread sandwiches "kangaroos" because of their obvious similarity to kangaroo pouches.

The following recipe was adapted from *Gourmet* magazine and features a curried turkey chutney salad in cantaloupe halves topped with condiments.

CHICKEN CURRY KANGAROO

2 chicken breasts
1 cup thinly sliced celery
1 cup mayonnaise
2 teaspoons curry powder
$^3/_4$ cup drained and chopped chutney

Salt 'n' pepper to taste
Pita bread cut in half to form two pockets

Poach the chicken breasts in a broth. Cool, discard skin and bones and cut the chicken in ¹/₂-inch cubes. In a bowl, combine the chicken, celery, curry powder, mayonnaise, chutney, and the salt 'n' pepper. Stuff each pouch for a delicious curry kangaroo sandwich.

When it's damp and chilly and you're dreaming of far away places, there is nothing better than the following sandwich adaptation from Arabella Boxer's *Book of Elegant Cooking*.

STUFFED PITA WITH MEAT OF ARAB INSPIRATION

2 tablespoons oil
2 tablespoons pine nuts
1 onion, chopped
1 lb. ground beef
2 tablespoons golden raisins
1 teaspoon cinnamon
¹/₂ teaspoon allspice
Salt 'n' pepper to taste
Small bunch of parsley, finely chopped
Pita bread cut in half to form two pockets

Fry the pine nuts in oil until lightly browned. Remove the pine nuts and fry the onions until softened. Add the meat, raisins, and flavorings and stir until meat changes color. Take from the heat and add parsley and pine nuts.

Put two tablespoons in each pouch and wrap in foil. Warm up in an oven or barbecue. The Arab meat combination can be prepared well ahead of time and saved for use later, either as a sandwich ingredient or over a bed of rice. You'll amaze your friends and crew with a truly gourmet meal prepared in less time than it takes to douse the jenny and reef the main.

NON-REFRIGERATED MEALS

Most liveaboards never venture far from a well-stocked supermarket, delicatessen, bakery, and reliable refrigeration or supply of ice. However, for those who do take ocean voyages for longer than it takes a block of ice to melt or who find themselves in distant countries offering a limited selection of canned goods and very few fresh fruits or vegetables, provisioning and meal preparation offer special challenges. Let me offer some suggestions for the non-refrigerated voyage of a small boat, that is one without a full-time cook and bus boy.

First of all we should keep in mind that during an ocean voyage of more than two or three days there's a tendency to do more "grazing" than sticking to a regular meal schedule. Therefore, all sorts of munching foods are needed. Secondly, there's the urge not to spend too much time in a pitching, rolling galley to cook or to clean up afterward. Lastly, the boat's constant motion makes it difficult to set a table, and one usually resorts to eating out of a single bowl or anything that can be clutched in one hand.

The Liveaboard Gourmet

Let's start with breakfast. Dry cereals keep indefinitely, but milk is a problem without refrigeration unless you turn to powdered milk or those long-life milk cartons. On shore I'm an ice-cold-milk freak, but on a voyage it doesn't take me long to get accustomed to room temperature milk. I also think that warmish milk goes better with non-sugary cereals, especially the natural granola types. Raisins are a good addition to cereal, and they make an excellent snack food during the day. Another interesting innovation is mixing the cereal with a bowl of canned fruit. There's enough liquid with the fruit to wet down the cereal.

In colder weather, I like hot oatmeal. Sometimes I throw in some raisins, granola, and grits to add variety to the oatmeal. I then top off the serving with a squeeze of honey. Look for honey in plastic squeeze bottles with a pouring spout. It avoids breakable glass and the need to ladle it out. Leaving honey on the edge of a jar is a good way to keep cockroaches healthy, strong, and sexually active. (Remember not to throw empty plastic containers overboard. It's against the law!)

On to lunch. I'm a big fan of one-handed, not too sloppy sandwiches. Depending on the type of bread and the weather, bread may last 5 to 10 days. Toward the end it takes some trimming to avoid the mold. When you trim more than you save, you can turn to basic soda crackers, which last indefinitely when packed in tins, plastic jars, or moisture-proof packets.

Inside the sandwich the choice of ingredients is almost limitless. Some of my favorites are:

- Non-refrigerated hard beef salami (it probably contains lots of harmful chemicals, but it's tasty). Look for a Danish product called "DAK Smoked Salami."
- Peanut butter and jelly or jam. Look for plastic containers for both

the peanut butter and the jam. Welch's "squeezables" offer a variety of jellies and jams in plastic bottles with pouring spouts.

- Canned sardines, chicken, or tuna fish.
- Small rounds of cheese packaged in wax keep for a very long time, especially the smoked cheeses.

We can't forget Happy Hour. The British Navy had the right idea when it instituted the policy of offering every sailor his daily dram of rum. As with cold milk, I generally prefer my drinks on-the-rocks. But it's surprisingly easy to get used to a room temperature gin 'n' tonic with plenty of fresh limes. Remember, the British invented this drink for the tropics without ice. The limes keep for quite a while, and when they do give out you can turn to lime juice. Pretzels, kept in air-tight containers, vacuum-packed mixed nuts, and crackers and cheese all make excellent hors d'oeuvres.

Finally, the dinner hour. I have had the pleasure of introducing my crews to a variety of what I call "gruels." Strictly speaking, the meals aren't thin and soupy, but they do have that prison quality of something ladled into a bowl. There's my ordinary one-pot gruel, the super gruel (three ingredients), and when more than one pot is involved in the cooking—the megagruel. The principle is to have a basic ingredient like rice, pasta, or beans and then add canned meats, canned fish, and/or canned vegetables. When you can stand standing in the galley, fry up some fresh onions (which last for a very long time) in vegetable oil and mix them with canned corned beef in a pan. At the same time you can be cooking rice or pasta in another pot. When the pots are combined you have a tasty megagruel.

Another of my favorite one-pot meals is a package of Lipton's Deluxe Chicken Noodles & Sauce augmented with canned chicken. Also Hickory Farms stores carry an excellent dried and sealed package of tortellini that is simply added to boiling water. Be sure to have plenty of Parmesan cheese, ketchup, and barbecue sauce on hand.

When I read that Spam was celebrating its golden anniversary, I was reminded that this "miracle in a can" is another favorite lunch or dinner ingredient. That's what Alan Green called Spam in an article for Eastern Airline's June 1987 *Review* magazine. He goes on to salute this piece of quint-essential Americana with the following facts:

- Spam was born in 1937.
- Vacuum-sealed Spam cans have a seven-year shelf life.
- Hormel was going to call it BRUNCH, but later opted for the SPiced hAM acronym.
- The ad campaign for Spam was the first-ever singing commercial on radio.

- In the last five decades Hormel has unloaded four billion tins of their compressed pig parts on the public.
- Thirty percent of American households are Spam devotees.
- Hormel currently turns out one million cans a week.

Is there anything else you wanted to know about Spam?

Grazing. For those in-between meals, I love to "graze" throughout the day. I have lots of munching foods in wide-mouthed plastic jars that make it easy to reach into and at the same time keep the foods fresh. My favorite items are M&Ms, GORP (made with granola, nuts, raisins, M&M's, and dried fruit), cookies, crackers, unshelled sunflower seeds, pretzels, and hard candies.

Finally, for drinks, other than at Happy Hour, I recommend powdered iced tea, powdered lemonade, tea bags, coffee made with Melitta filter paper, single-serving cans of fruit juice, and just plain water.

All this emphasis on non-refrigerated foods, plastic containers, single-pot meals, and no-hassle preparations may sound dull to those who enjoy gourmet cooking and fine dining. But believe me, in a small boat underway in a big rolling ocean, being a gourmet cook is definitely a secondary hobby.

ONE OF NATURE'S PERFECT FOODS

Rice is one of nature's perfect foods, and doubly so for liveaboards with special concerns for long-term provisioning. Rice provides important vitamins and fiber, it is cholesterol free (with only a trace of fat), low in sodium, non-allergenic, easy to digest, and only 82 calories per half-cup serving. And, at only four cents per half-cup serving, rice allows you to splurge on the rest of your ingredients.

Rice was introduced into the U.S. in the seventeenth century, when a trading ship en route to Europe from Madagascar got slightly off course and ended up in Charleston, South Carolina. There the colonists were given rice in return for the repair bill on the ship.

Long, medium, and short grain are the three main types of rice. Long-grain rice remains separate when cooked. Cooked medium- and short-grain rice are the most moist and tender and cling together more than long grain.

Regular-milled white rice has been completely milled; most has also been enriched. It takes only 15 minutes to cook on top of the range, and because of enrichment, it is similar in nutritional value to brown rice.

Parboiled rice, which cooks in 25 minutes, has undergone a special process that makes the cooked grains extra fluffy and separate. Precooked rice is the fastest-cooking rice of all. Completely cooked and dehydrated, precooked white rice takes only about 5 minutes to prepare, while precooked brown rice requires about 10 to 15 minutes. Brown rice's tan color comes from the natural bran layers left on the grain. This form of rice has a nutty flavor and a slightly chewy texture. It takes about 45 minutes to cook.

Uncooked milled rice (white, parboiled, and precooked) keeps indefinitely without refrigeration. Once opened, rice should be stored in air-tight containers. Because of the oil in its bran layers, brown rice has a shelf life of about six months.

Gently with the Tides

ONBOARD HERBS

What better place to learn about herbs than from the curator of the herb garden at the National Arboretum, Holly Shimizu. On his long sailing voyages, the famed circumnavigator Sir Francis Chichester cultivated bean sprouts between sheets of damp toweling paper to give his meals a fresh, home-grown taste. Had he known Holly, he would have welcomed her advice on growing herbs aboard a boat. She offers the following gardening advice to liveaboards who want to add a dash of fresh flavor and garnish to their meals.

Herbs are easily cultivated on board in pots and flower boxes. They require at least six hours of direct sunlight, good air circulation, a moderately rich soil, and frequent pruning to keep plants from becoming too leggy. Specific considerations for growing herbs on a boat include protecting the tender leaves from heavy salt spray and from sun scorching. Concentrated salt on the leaves could cause burning and yellowing. Herbs suddenly subjected to intense sunlight will become brownish gold because the cells actually get sunburned and die. Plants must be given relatively constant lighting conditions either by exposure to consistent natural sunlight or by supplying supplemental lighting in boat interiors.

Watering herbs in pots and boxes rather than in the ground can be a bit tricky. The rule is to keep them moist—not too wet and not too dry. The rate at which water is taken up will depend on the quantity of roots and the type of soil. Judge each herb independently. Also, the water requirements will vary depending on the amount of sunlight, air circulation, and temperature. Strive to give the herbs relatively consistent conditions and avoid any severe stress. Be sure to use a sterile soil medium free of weeds and disease-causing organisms. Potting mixes are available at reputable garden centers. Set the pots on a tray of gravel so that excess water will be sitting in the gravel. This will keep the humidity higher around the herbs as well as prevent water runoff problems.

The best way to get started is to select the herbs you want to grow, then pot them together in one larger planter. Give each plant adequate room to grow so that they won't get too crowded. As the plants put on growth, feel free to harvest the leaves. To encourage more rapid growth, a liquid fertilizer (20-20-20) can be applied every two to three weeks. Most of the commercial soluble fertilizers will suffice (e.g., Miracle-Gro, or Peter's). Certain herbs such as dill and coriander are annuals (living for one year) and have an extremely short life cycle. So do not be alarmed if these plants die quickly.

It is necessary to know the types of herbs and a little bit about them to get the full enjoyment out of this project. Holly has selected the following herbs for their culinary popularity and the ease with which they can be grown on board.

Basil (Ocimum basilicum). Considered the king of herbs, basil is best known for its use in Italian food—its association with tomatoes goes back centuries. Basil is a tender annual, which means that it will not withstand any frost and has a one-year life cycle. It prefers to grow in plenty of sunlight and should be pinched regularly. In fact, never let the flowers form on basil because flowering and seeds mean less flavor in the leaves. Pinch off leaves as needed for cooking. Never cook basil too long (no more than 15 minutes) because you will cook the flavor out of it.

Use fresh leaves on salads, for pesto sauce or spaghetti sauce, or just experiment. Basil is one herb you rarely have too much of. There are other interesting types of basil including lemon, cinnamon, holly, and spice basil, which can be used in many creative ways.

Chives (Allium schoenoprasum). An easily grown, hardy perennial, chives are valued for their onion-like flavor. The bright green, hollow leaves are chopped fresh and added to salads, sauces—especially sour cream for potatoes—and soups. To harvest, simply cut leaves on the outside of the clump back to the base and new leaves will develop quickly. The leaves and flowers of chives can be added to vinegar to impart their flavor for a salad vinegar.

A closely related plant known as garlic chives (*Allium tuberosum*) can be used in similar ways, although its flavor is stronger and more garlic-like. Especially popular in oriental food, garlic chives have flat green leaves and ornamental white flowers.

Coriander (Coriandrum sativum). Also known as Chinese parsley, coriander has recently become more common in American cuisine. The basal leaves have distinctive flavor and are well known in Mexican cooking as cilantro. The seeds are an ingredient in curry as well as in other spice mixtures. Since coriander is a short-lived annual, it is best to sow seeds every three to four weeks to have a constant, fresh supply of leaves. Once the plant goes into bloom, the basal leaves disappear and seeds develop. Chew the seeds after a meal to enjoy their flavor and as an aid in digestion.

French tarragon (Artemisia dracunculus *var.* sativa). French tarragon is an essential culinary herb. The fresh leaves are useful for salads, sauces, fish, chicken, and soups. It is important to obtain true French tarragon rather than the weedy and flavorless Russian tarragon that is sometimes sold by nurseries. The French tarragon can be propagated only by cuttings or division and never from seed because it never sets seed. Plants should not be allowed to bloom. Keep them well trimmed—using tips as you cut back the plant. Although French tarragon is a hardy perennial, it does need a dormant or rest period; otherwise, the plant will use up all of its energy and die. Every one or two years the plants need to be divided to keep them young and vigorous.

Dill (Anethum graveolens). Best known for its seeds, which are used for pickling, dill is gradually being recognized as an important herb for its leaves. Actually the young leaves give superb flavor to sauces, salads, fish, and soups. Since it is a short-lived annual, seeds should be sown every three to four weeks and the plant harvested progressively.

Lemon thyme (Thymus citriodorus). The unique lemon thyme combines the refreshing lemon flavor with the piney thyme flavor to produce a delightful fragrance. The leaves make a delicious tea or can be added to meats, chicken, fish, vegetables, and dips.

Lemon thyme is easy to grow, and it loves being pinched back. Keep plants cut back so they stay full and attractive. The golden form of lemon thyme is a lovely yellowish form of this plant.

Parsley (Petroselinum crispum). Parsley does not get enough credit for being the marvelous herb that it is. Parsley is one of the most nutritious herbs as well as being nature's best breath freshener. In ancient times parsley was always eaten after consuming garlic to improve the breath.

The flat-leaved Italian parsley is the best for cooking. Its flavor is a bit stronger, and it is easier to work with. Use the fresh leaves in almost any foods because their gentle flavor will complement most meals. The curly-leaf parsley is more attractive and makes a beautiful garnish. Parsley is a biennial plant (living two years) but it should be treated as an annual. It grows well during cool weather and resents extreme heat. When harvesting the leaves, always cut the outer leaves back to the base.

Rosemary (Rosmarinus officinalis). Rosemary grows beautifully in a pot as long as it never totally dries out. It loves to grow near the sea and should be quite happy on a boat as long as it is not neglected.

The spicy leaves are a great addition to lamb and for making herbal teas. Just rubbing its leaves to release the essential oils is reason enough to include this ancient treasure in your boat's herb garden. Because its flavor is strong, large quantities are rarely needed.

Your key to success in cultivating herbs on board is to experiment. Find a place where you can accommodate the needs of the plants and expect to replace them periodically. They will bring great pleasure in their fragrance, flavor, and health-enhancing freshness.

Sources of information on herbs:

Carroll Gardens, Box 310, 444 East Main Street, Westminster, Maryland 21157.

Johnny's Selected Seeds, Foss Hill Road, Albion, Maine 04910.

Logee's Greenhouses, 55 North Street, Danielson, Connecticut 06239.

The Sandy Mush Herb Nursery, Route 2 Surrett Cove Road, Leicester, North Carolina 28748.

For further reading, check out:

Park's Success with Herbs by Gertrude B. Foster
and Rosemary F Louden
The Complete Book of Herbs and Spices by Sarah Garland
Herbs, How to Select, Grow and Enjoy by Norma Jean Lathrop

Holly Shimizu

GYOTAKU

Here's something you can do between the time you catch a fish and prepare it for the evening meal. It's called gyotaku *(pronounced ghio-ta-'koo).*

Gyotaku is a Japanese fish-printing art that has been around since the seventeenth century, recording catches of sport fish. It is believed to have been practiced by samurai warriors who were required to be skilled in fishing and the fine arts, as well as martial arts.

Here's how to do it in six easy steps:

1. Clean the fish with detergent and water (or salt water alone if it's to be eaten) and allow to dry.

2. Position the fins artfully with the help of pins.

3. Brush ink (watercolor, acrylic paint, or tempera—be sure to use something that's non-toxic) with a soft brush, sponge, or a tampon (avoid the eyes—not yours, the fish's).

4. Very carefully place newsprint or rice paper on top of the fish and gently rub the entire fish with your fingers. Try not to move the paper.

5. Gently lift the paper from one end and peel it off quickly.

6. Paint in the eyes and let the print dry. Wash off the ink and enjoy a good meal.

You can keep a picture record of your favorite catches like bottle labels from fine wines.

10
Marine Environment

WHEN ASKED what they liked most about living aboard, many boat residents responded with some positive reference toward the environment—"living with nature," "communing with nature," or "back to nature." Others described their liveaboard lives more passively as being made more peaceful and serene by their closeness to natural surroundings.

It is safe to assume that a unique relationship exists between the water environment and living aboard. I think this can be explained partly by a dependence on, and a healthy respect for, the elements. Liveaboards need to survive comfortably in a seemingly fragile home often only a fraction of an inch from a hostile world. Liveaboards are also closer to wildlife than their city neighbors, even when docked at a marina. Most would agree that ducks, fish, and the occasional sea turtle that swims by are far more desirable neighbors than roaches, pigeons, and raccoons.

The unique relationship with the environment may also be explained by some subconscious desire to return to a watery world where, after all, life starts. The rocking motion, gurgling sounds, and gentle undulations of a boat home are physical descriptions that may convey a deeper psychological relationship.

Protecting the environment and its inhabitants also receives a great deal of attention from liveaboards. Sometimes this is translated directly into laws and regulations as were discussed earlier in connection with vessel wastes and littering. Here a few of the wonders of the marine environment are explored, but always with a special concern for its protection and conservation. Marine sanctuaries, endangered species, coral habitats, illegal trade in endangered species products, and the ubiquitous barnacle all contribute to concerns for the liveaboard neighborhood.

Gently with the Tides

MARINE SANCTUARIES

As the boat slides down the launching ramp, I can hear the fish saying, "There goes the neighborhood." It's true that too many boaters, careless manners, accidents, and greed can spoil the neighborhood. Protected areas such as marine sanctuaries are one answer.

The United States is blessed with more than two million square miles of ocean under its jurisdiction with an unrivalled diversity of marine life and habitats. From underwater oasis-like boulder patches of Alaska's Beaufort Sea to the colorful coral reefs of the Florida Keys, the United States possesses an underwater legacy equal to its most spectacular mountain ranges, canyons, and forests of our terrestrial landscape. However, human activity within this vast marine area is accelerating, particularly in near-shore waters, and some areas are already being damaged.

Boaters can and do regularly enjoy the many moods of our nation's waters. Even so, many boaters are unaware of the rich, living seascape beneath them. To increase our awareness of these marine treasures and to ensure their protection for generations to come, the government has set up a marine sanctuaries program similar to our national park program. The sanctuaries harbor a fascinating array of plants and animals, from huge whales to tiny, brightly colored sea snails. In many cases these protected waters provide a secure habitat for species close to extinction.

Marine sanctuaries are to this nation's ocean resources what the national parks are to our terrestrial landscape. Yellowstone Park, our first national park, was designated in 1872. The U.S.S. *Monitor* Marine Sanctuary, designated in 1975 to protect the wreck of this Civil War ironclad, was the first designated U.S. historic marine sanctuary. And since 1975, seven additional biological marine sanctuaries have been designated, protecting other outstanding marine areas (see sidebar).

The primary purpose of the national marine sanctuary program is to conserve unique and significant marine areas through careful management, con-

192

Designated Marine Sanctuaries

U.S.S. *Monitor* National Marine Sanctuary. This sanctuary is an area 1 mile in diameter southeast of Cape Hatteras, North Carolina. It protects the wreck of the Civil War ironclad, the U.S.S. *Monitor.* The sanctuary provides an excellent opportunity to increase public awareness of an important American historical and cultural resource.

Key Largo National Marine Sanctuary. This sanctuary is a 100-square-mile coral reef area south of Miami, Florida. It contains coral reefs, hard and soft corals, seagrass beds, commercial and recreational species, a lighthouse, and sunken ships with associated artifacts.

Channel Islands National Marine Sanctuary. This is a 1,252-square-mile area surrounding the northern Channel Islands and Santa Barbara Island off California. The area supports one of the largest and most varied assemblages of marine mammals and seabirds in the world.

Looe Key National Marine Sanctuary. This sanctuary consists of a 5-square-mile area of the Florida reef southwest of Big Pine Key. The area supports a beautiful coral formation and a diverse marine community.

Gray's Reef National Marine Sanctuary. This site is approximately 17 square miles located on the Atlantic continental shelf due east of Sapelo Island, Georgia. This is one of the largest near-shore hard-bottom reefs supporting a diverse community of temperate and tropical species.

Point Reyes-Farallon Islands National Marine Sanctuary. This sanctuary is a 948-square-mile area off the coast of California north of San Francisco. This area supports one of the largest seabird rookeries in the U.S. The area also supports whales, porpoises, and seals.

Fagatele Bay National Marine Sanctuary. This sanctuary is located 2,300 miles southwest of Hawaii in American Samoa. This coral ecosystem was formed in recent geologic time when a volcano crater collapsed.

Cordell Bank. This site is located five miles north of the Gulf of the Farallones Marine Sanctuary. This submerged mountain supports lush biological marine communities, including slow-growing, endangered California hydrocoral. Upwelling of nutrients caused by the underwater topography attracts fish, marine mammals, and seabirds.

Marine Environment

tinued research, and public education. Rather than focusing upon one particular resource or activity, a marine sanctuary seeks to elevate the conservation of all resources in an area through the various marine and coastal programs of state and federal agencies. The sanctuary program does not close down an area to all human activity, but rather encourages uses that are compatible with protection of its resources.

Implementation of the national marine sanctuary program has been fitful. With very little fanfare, the program designated two sites in 1975 and then languished without an official government office or funds. In the early eighties, six additional sites were designated in a sometimes heated political atmosphere over oil and gas development vs. the environment.

In 1989 Congress reviewed the national marine sanctuary program and renewed its commitment to protecting outstanding marine resources. As a result of this renewed commitment, the list of active candidates for sanctuary designation has grown to include the following sites:

Stellwagen Bank is located between Cape Cod and Cape Ann just east of Boston, Massachusetts. It consists of 605 nautical miles of physical and oceanographic features resulting in unusually high productivity and supports large populations of fish and marine mammals. Included are three species of endangered large whales, the humpback, the fin, and the right whale. In addition, the plentiful food supply at Stellwagen attracts a diverse group of pelagic and coastal birds.

Flower Garden Banks is located 115 miles south of Galveston, Texas, and supports the northernmost shallow-water tropical coral reef in the Gulf of Mexico. Associated with this reef system is an abundant and diverse collection of life forms.

Monterey Bay is located off the central California coast and includes a great diversity of habitats, such as kelp beds, sandy beaches, and several submarine canyons. The Monterey Canyon, which begins less than one mile from shore, is the largest submarine canyon on the North American continental shelf and is deeper than the Grand Canyon of the Colorado River. The area is an important breeding ground for five species of seals and sea lions.

Outer Coast of Washington is a near-shore area adjacent to Olympic National Park, which borders one of the least developed shores in North America. The earlier recognition of Olympic National Park as an international biosphere reserve and World Heritage Site attests to the uniqueness of the area. Spectacular offshore rock formations provide haulout areas for seals and sea lions and breeding areas for 50 percent of the state's marine birds.

Puget Sound includes the rocky marine habitats surrounding the San Juan Islands where turbulent tidal currents provide a unique and productive marine system. The area provides a refuge and feeding grounds for a large population of killer whales, or orcas, sea birds, bald eagles, marine invertebrates, marine mammals, and seaweeds.

Norfolk Canyon is located about 60 miles off Virginia. It is a deepwater submarine canyon that contains large tree corals and "pueblo villages"—assemblages of large invertebrates and finfish that dig burrows in the canyon sides.

There are many other potential sanctuary sites waiting in the wings to be reviewed. The Atlantic and Pacific coasts as well as the Great Lakes and the Caribbean have many marine areas of unique value to Americans. Only relatively recently have we as a people accorded our marine heritage the level of care and protection that we have given our national parks and wildlife refuges. Hopefully, many of these candidate sites will join the ranks of protected marine sanctuaries and thereby enlarge our legacy of ocean resources for future generations.

Marine Environment

Boaters enjoy a unique opportunity to visit these sanctuary resources as many already do when diving and snorkeling the coral reefs of Key Largo and Looe Key sanctuaries. But with increased access to these sensitive areas comes a responsibility to protect the "neighborhood" as noted in the next article.

CORAL REEFS

In the waters off the Florida Keys and the Caribbean islands, many boaters enjoy the underwater coral gardens and their varied and brightly colored wildlife. These areas are the equivalent of terrestrial rain forests for their abundance of vivid life forms. But like the rain forests, these areas are also in danger from man.

Coral reefs are an underwater fantasy garden of rainbow-hued fish, swaying sea fans, and coral splashed with vivid color. For thousands of years the reefs have grown and withstood natural stresses, only to face the most devastating threat of all: boat groundings, boat anchors, anchor chains, and careless divers.

Though plant-like in appearance, corals belong to the same group of animals as anemones and jellyfish. In fact, corals are composed of hundreds of individual animals called polyps. Successive generations of polyps remain attached to the original polyps and by constant additions of new buds, colonies are formed. For some species these colonies can reach several meters in diameter and live up to a thousand years.

195

There are two main types of corals, soft corals and reef-building corals.

Each polyp in reef-building corals constructs a limestone cup around its body for protection. Over thousands of years, the calcium carbonate skeletons of previous polyp generations accumulate from the sea floor and raise the base of the reef closer and closer to the water's surface. This results in various architectural structures, including fringing and barrier reefs, atolls, and coral islands. Reefs are generally found in clear, tropical waters within 22 degrees latitude north and south of the equator.

Soft corals, including sea whips and sea fans, have flexible inner skeletons that support the colony while allowing its branches to move gracefully with the underwater currents. The skeletons of the black and red corals are considered precious and thus commercially exploited for jewelry.

Corals owe much of their survival to microscopic plants called zooxanthellae. These plants, packed within each polyp's tissue, give corals energy and oxygen while carbon dioxide and nutrients from the coral support the zooxanthellae—a perfect symbiotic relationship.

Coral reefs are important habitats for many species, including the beautiful and, unfortunately, endangered hawksbill sea turtle. In addition to serving the foundation on which an entire undersea ecosystem thrives, coral islands and atolls provide sanctuary for terrestrial creatures, while fringe and barrier reefs act as breakwaters, protecting coasts from the ravages of storms and erosion.

Unfortunately, a reef's beauty and bounty can contribute to its own demise. The seemingly abundant supply of reef commodities, including shells, sand coral, and fish, attract commercial developers whose actions can result in great damage to the reef. Well-meaning tourists also harm reefs with anchors, bodily contact, and by taking coral souvenirs. Even casual reef walking, an activity for which there is even a specialty shoe advertised in sailing magazines, can damage delicate polyps. Finally, pollution can subtly but significantly disturb a reef's fragile ecological balance. Corals can be devastated by any foreign materials that alter the water's salinity, temperature, or clarity. For example, deforestation and subsequent land development close to shore can cause soil runoff to cloud the waters and dramatically effect the health of corals.

Due to a slow growth rate of inches or fractions of an inch per year, corals cannot be considered a renewable resource. When black coral "trees" are constantly harvested for jewelry, the species is destined to disappear forever. Fortunately, there are ways to conserve corals. Mooring buoys for recreational and charter boats are one of them. Hundreds of years of coral growth can be destroyed in a few hours as boats dig in and swing about their anchors. Mooring buoys can prevent this needless damage.

Protecting the beauty of the reefs of Florida and the Virgin Islands has already started, with a few mooring buoys installed at strategic points, for use by charter and dive boats as well as cruising tourists and locals. These anchoring buoys allow those of us who enjoy the reefs to continue visiting them without damaging the coral and sea grasses. Key Largo and Looe Key National Marine Sanctuaries have already established regulations, including stiff fines, for boatowners whose anchors damage any part of the sanctuary. Buck Island Reef National Monument and Coral Reef State Park are two of the state parks and local areas that have passed regulations to protect coral. There are still, however, many reefs unprotected by such laws.

Although coral reefs are extensive, ranging more than a thousand miles in Australia, they grow very slowly. What you actually see when diving is the thin layer of live coral on top of the nonliving skeleton. Recent research indicates that it takes 150 to 500 years for the coral heads of a reef to grow 7 feet high. Thus, an irresponsible skipper can easily wipe out 500 years' worth of growth by knocking down the castle-like coral heads in one shattering encounter. If a boat drifts or swings on its anchor, the chain will grind on the ocean floor, destroying any coral or sea grass in its path.

Marine Environment

In addition to coral damage, valuable sea grasses are also easily damaged by inconsiderate anchoring practices. A comparison of 1960 maps of sea grass beds with grass beds today near anchoring sites shows that grasses have been greatly reduced. The disruption of this ecosystem is devastating to endangered sea turtles, fish, and other organisms dependent on the grasses for survival. The state parks, the national marine sanctuaries, and national monuments of Florida and the Virgin Islands are beginning to act on the anchoring problem. Mooring buoys and anchoring regulations are coming into widespread use to protect the sea grasses and coral, to regulate the carrying capacity of the area by limiting the number of visitors at any one time, and to educate the boating public about its impact on the beautiful yet fragile reefs.

Another way to help protect coral reefs is to discourage the harvest of coral for jewelry and other decorative products. Black coral hand-crafted jewelry is a major export item in many Caribbean islands. It is also listed by an international convention on endangered species trade (CITES) as a species that might become threatened if commercial trade is not controlled. Tourists can help discourage the harvesting of coral by not buying coral jewelry.

Snorkeling and diving among coral reefs is an easy way to visit some of our more dramatic marine neighbors. But the ease of access for boaters can also bring about the danger of losing these beautiful neighborhoods if we are not careful.

RETURN OF THE PREHISTORIC CREATURES

Marydele Donnelly, or MAD, as she's known to her friends, has had a five-year affair with sea turtles, and especially their protection. Sea turtles, with their uncanny ability to navigate the oceans, have been around for ages, but man is doing his best to make it difficult for these wondrous crea-

tures to survive. She promises boaters who are lucky enough to encounter sea turtles an unforgettable experience and offers some advice.

Have you ever wanted to see a prehistoric creature up close? Do you regret being born tens or hundreds of thousands of years too late? Well, take heart. Survivors of the Age of the Dinosaurs are alive and reproducing among us.

Imagine, if you will, an anchorage by a dark and quiet beach. Stars fill the night sky. Palm fronds rustle in the breeze. Waves crash on the shore. A village dog barks in the distance. You have beached the dinghy and have been sitting quietly for more than two hours waiting for them to come. There are tracks in the sand, indisputable evidence that some were here last night and the night before that. Your hands and legs are covered with fine, black sand, and the ubiquitous sand fleas are beginning to bite. You stare at the place where the waves come in and recede. There is nothing. You wonder if you're ever going to see one. And then ... it happens.

As the last wave washes in and goes out again there is a creature bigger than the wave ever was but you didn't see her until the wave was gone. She must have made one enormous lunge from the sea. She pauses for a very long moment. Slowly, she begins to drag herself up the beach. You hold very still. You pray that she won't notice you. That she'll just follow her instincts and do what she came ashore to do, just as two million generations before her have done. She doesn't know it, but she's one of the lucky ones. This female has come ashore on a safe beach; she will survive the night.

Each year this scene is repeated thousands of times on tropical beaches the world over as sea turtles come ashore to nest. These ancient reptiles have survived more than 65 million years, but today their very existence is threatened by man. Man hunts turtles for their meat and skin and oil and shell. He steals their eggs. He pollutes the ocean and alters their nesting beaches and foraging areas. Now seven of the world's eight species of sea turtles are considered to be in danger of extinction.

To watch a primitive and vulnerable turtle, weighing hundreds of pounds, drag herself up the beach to lay her eggs is an unforgettable experience. By observing just a few "rules," you will ensure that the turtle is not disturbed and you and future observers will fully enjoy this wonder of nature.

Sea turtles are fascinating creatures, in large part because we know so little about them. The mystery begins when a hatchling turtle emerges from its nest and disappears into the sea. After probably spending its first year in the sargassum weed, the young turtle may move to a coastal area for foraging. The juveniles of some species, such as the leatherback and the olive ridley, are rarely seen. On reaching reproductive age (estimates vary from 15 to 50 years), turtles will return to the beach on which they hatched to nest. The ability to find this beach, which may be hundreds or thousands of miles away, is a mystery. Like other long-distance migrants, sea turtles probably depend

Gently with the Tides

on a combination of abilities. Whatever factors are involved, sea turtles are among the earth's greatest ocean navigators.

The beaches of the southeast United States from South Carolina to Florida are prime nesting habitat for the loggerhead sea turtle and, to a lesser extent, for green and leatherback turtles. Most female sea turtles breed every second or third year, but during a season a female can lay several clutches of eggs at about two-week intervals. From May through August it is possible to watch sea turtles nest. In July, about eight weeks after the first nests are laid, the tiny hatchlings begin to emerge. Hatching continues through the end of October.

Should you be lucky enough actually to observe an emergence from the ocean, I guarantee that you will be impressed. Watching a loggerhead or green turtle weighing several hundred pounds come from the surf is tantamount to seeing the arrival of the creature from the deep. Even more impressive is the 800 to 1,200 pound leatherback, which is likened to a VW Beetle coming from the sea.

Marine Environment

Please remember that sea turtles are protected by the U.S. Endangered Species Act, and it is a violation to "take, harass, harm, pursue, hunt…" marine turtles, their nests, and/or eggs. The penalty can range up to $20,000 and one-year imprisonment. Sea turtle nesting takes place in several stages: emergence, excavation of the body pit, excavation of the egg chamber, egg laying, covering of the nest, and return to the sea.

Exceedingly vulnerable on land, sea turtles are quite skittish when they emerge from the ocean to nest. To avoid frightening a potential nester away, it is advisable not to be too close to the shoreline. Remain still and at a distance as the female emerges and chooses her nesting spot. Nesting takes place over an hour or two. First the female will excavate a body pit—beware of flying sand. Some species, such as the green turtle, dig a pit up to 2 feet deep. The next stage is the preparation of a flask-shaped egg chamber. To accomplish this, the female digs with her hind flippers, alternating one and then the other flipper until they can reach no more. You can approach quietly from behind as she digs the egg chamber. After the chamber is complete, the eggs are released in small clusters of two or three at a time from the female's cloaca.

Approximately the size of Ping-Pong balls, the shells are white and leathery. The average clutch size is 120 eggs, but that number can vary considerably. It is recommended that you leave your flashlight off at all times. If you do want to see the eggs more clearly, briefly turn your light on and off again. Your eyes will adjust rapidly to the dark. Remember not to touch the turtle or her eggs. Beware again of flying sand as the turtle covers the eggs and returns to the sea. With luck, the eggs will incubate for 50 to 60 days.

Turtle nests fall prey to a number of predators such as raccoons and ghost crabs and, in many areas of the world, to humans. Predation is generally highest in the first few days after the nest is laid and right before the hatchlings emerge. The little turtles hatch several days before they emerge from their nest. Activity within the nest causes the sand overhead to fall, slowly raising the level of the nest. When the sand temperatures are cool, the hatchlings break out.

They find the sea by heading in the direction of the brightest light, which on a naturally dark beach is the light reflected from the water. Once again the cycle begins as the hatchlings swim away. Hopefully some will return one day to nest. If you should see hatchlings struggling on a beach, please remember that it is illegal to touch them and that hatchlings have managed on their own for millions of years. Probably only one in 1,000 will survive to reproduce, but they have been doing that successfully for countless generations. If we leave them alone and stop befouling their habitat, they will continue to survive.

I like to think that with good will and good science sea turtles and people can use and enjoy the beaches together.

Marydele Donnelly

LIVING WITHOUT **TBT**

In 1989 the Environmental Protection Agency banned TBT (Tri-Butyl Tin) based anti-fouling paint. Jim Chamblee, a former EPA official, a longtime sailor, and a tireless warrior against barnacles, reflects on life after TBT.

Imagine the end of a spring day on which you have just finished sanding your boat's bottom in preparation for antifouling painting. You pause a moment to look around your dockyard at the many boats bathed in the late afternoon sun. While a delicious supper of expensive and smallish oysters is steaming, you idly read the label on a can of bottom paint that will be slopped on your boat tomorrow morning. It's the same paint you used last year; and you were very pleased that this paint did an excellent job in keeping growth off your hull. The label says that your paint contains a compound called TBTF.

TBT compounds are extremely toxic, wide-spectrum substances used as anti-fouling agents. TBT is short for Tri-Butyl Tin. This compound is usually chemically coupled with another atom, such as fluorine. The result when fluorine is coupled is called TBTF; but 19 other TBT compounds also exist. Sometimes they are called "Organotin," because of the organic nature of the molecules coupled to the tin atom in the chemical structure. TBTs are all deadly killers of living things.

Without your knowledge, you have been exposing yourself to TBTF all day long in your hull-sanding work. The oysters you are cooking are laced with TBTs that were absorbed in the marine environment. You will be exposing yourself to TBTF tomorrow when you paint your hull. Your use of anti-fouling paints with TBTs can be hazardous to both your health and the health of every living creature in the water near your boat. Multiply the number of boats that use anti-fouling paints with TBTs and you get serious environmental damage.

TBTs have significantly improved the performance of anti-fouling paints. In most cases, they prevent all hull growth, and they last a long time. TBT was originally developed for the military, and the U.S. Navy has estimated that TBT paints keep their hulls clean for seven years.

At the same time, TBTs have contributed to the poison of our waterways. Minute concentrations of TBTs have a pronounced impact on the ability of aquatic life to reproduce and survive. Particularly impacted are shellfish such as crabs, lobsters, and oysters, whose hard shells are fabricated from the elements of the surrounding water. When that water contains toxic levels of TBTs, shellfish can't survive. TBT effects on finfish are not yet fully known, but some initial laboratory tests have shown TBTs to be very toxic to freshwater fish in concentrations from 1 to 24 parts per billion.

Laboratory tests by the U.S. Environmental Protection Agency have shown a kill rate of 50 percent for one species of mollusk after 15 days at TBT concentrations of only 100 parts per trillion (ppt). This concentration is roughly equal to 1 pound of TBT released in a harbor uniformly 12 feet deep, 2,000 feet long, and 2,000 feet wide. A researcher at Rutgers University has found that a TBT concentration of 0.5 part per billion is toxic, resulting in limb deformities in 17 percent of fiddler crabs after just two weeks. These are concentrations that couldn't be measured just a few years ago, so historical data on TBTs is sparse. There is very little data on the long-term effects of TBTs on humans or aquatic species.

The TBT problem is the problem of all chemical pesticides. As far as boatowners are concerned, barnacles and algae are pests. We want our boats to have barnacle-free, clean hulls. Chemical and paint companies respond with products that meet those needs. Since time began, copper was recognized as a reasonably effective anti-fouling substance. The best sailing ships were sheathed in solid copper sheeting. The reason that our bottom paints have traditionally been red is that it was very hard to produce any other color given a large dose of copper oxide in the paint. In the 1970s, our bottom paints improved, to include both copper and other compounds as anti-fouling ingredients. Some of these other compounds were banned or ineffective, and since copper is not well suited to steel or aluminum hulls, paint manufacturers and the U.S. Navy sought an alternative. TBT was the result. We pay big bucks for anti-fouling paints that contain pesticides such as TBT, and we frown when the first barnacle appears on our hull. It is estimated that 250,000 to 300,000 pounds of TBT are used annually in anti-fouling paints in the U.S.

By their very purpose, anti-fouling paints prevent hull growth by releasing small doses of toxic substances into the water next to the hull, thus discouraging new growth over a long period of time. If the cycle only stopped there, everything would be fine, but the story and the TBT go much further.

TBTs and other anti-fouling compounds are designed to kill living things over a long period. As TBTs are released from bottom paint, they accumulate in the marine environment, often in bottom sediments and as part of the shell of an invertebrate such as an oyster or a crab. This kills crabs and oysters, and the harvests of these prime seafood delicacies are reduced, driving up prices and reducing quality. That is why the oysters you were cooking were small and expensive.

Shellfish and boats like to concentrate in the same protected and shallow waters. Boats congregate in marinas and yacht clubs and spend most of their time closely packed together, while shellfish live very close by. Shallow bays, estuaries, and harbors are where the most significant TBT damage is found, and measured TBT concentrations are highest in the waters around marinas and boatyards.

In San Diego Bay, for example, concentrations peaking at 930 ppt were measured near the Shelter Island Yacht Club. Hamilton Harbor on Lake Ontario had TBT concentrations as high as 840 ppt, and the state of Virginia found toxic concentrations of TBTs widely dispersed in the Elizabeth River estuary near Norfolk.

The major TBT danger to humans is thought to be through inhalation, not consumption. When you sanded some of last year's paint from your hull, you could have inhaled enough TBTs to make you very sick. TBTs don't differentiate among life forms. Therefore, TBTs try to kill you too, lungs first. You probably aren't in much danger from eating TBT-laced shellfish, but nobody knows for sure yet. It is believed that TBTs can be absorbed through the skin with harmful effects.

Like many of society's environmental and technical issues, TBTs presented a dilemma: Society could have had cleaner boat hulls or a healthier marine environment, but not both. Society opted for the environment, and most of us would probably support that decision. For the boatowner, this means that the first barnacle will appear a little sooner. Don't frown when you see that first little mollusk. Think instead of the crabs and oysters you like so much. As an alternative, perhaps we should develop an appetite for barnacles.

Jim Chamblee

SAILING WITH GREAT WHALES

On several occasions I have felt fortunate to have sailed close to a great whale. Once off Cape Cod I encountered one of the most endangered of all whales, the right whale. On Silver Bank off the Dominican Republic I was treated to the acrobatic displays of humpbacks. Each encounter was awesome because the animal was so graceful, yet so threateningly large. A two-story giraffe loping by a small pup tent might be a close terrestrial counterpart.

Cruising sailors generally are of one of two minds when it comes to whales— poetically awestruck or scared to death. There is no middle ground between these extremes when confronted at close range by such graceful beauty yet such powerful enormity.

While making a routine sailing pilgrimage from Chesapeake Bay to New England, I encountered my first whale at sea. The word *awesome* does not do justice to the experience. The sighting took place about 50 nautical miles southwest of Montauk Point. It was timed perfectly because it took place during cocktail hour, and the entire crew was on deck and in good spirits.

Two whales glided by silently about 50 feet from our 32-foot boat in a soft, undulating motion, exposing only a small fraction of what we imagined to be their full size. They blew and dove, breaking the surface every 50 yards or so while we waited hopefully, yet nervously, for them to leap out of the water in one of those Sea World photo poses. They never did. It wasn't until much later that I realized that they were probably fin or sei whales and not humpbacks, which frequently do leap completely out of the water.

I did not poll the crew at the time, but my guess is that some were definitely nervous, if not frightened, after recalling horror stories of sailboats being holed by whales. As captain, I was trying to project an air of respectful apprehension, while at the same time being thrilled at the sight, and also recalling the horror stories. They were so much larger than the boat and so much stronger than a half inch of fiberglass. As their 40-plus-foot bodies slid by, it occurred to me that they were taller than the average depth of Chesapeake Bay, and they were only half the size of blue whales!

Our fascination with the cetacean world is endless. We listen to humpback whale song albums; we read miles of newsprint on "wrong-way" Humphrey's progress down the Sacramento River; we crowd out international news coverage to watch the plight of three gray whales caught in an ice pack; we are entertained by performing orcas at Sea World; we peer through aquarium windows at the smiling faces of beluga whales; we attend lectures by survivors of life-and-death whale encounters; we study the literary character of Moby Dick; we donate to "save the whale" movements; we set quotas on international whale hunting; we pay money to go on whale-watching expeditions....

Small-craft sailors, especially those who do extensive offshore cruising, share these fascinations along with sharing the same ocean neighborhood with these gentle giants.

Marine Environment

203

CARIBBEAN TOURIST TRAPS

*When voyaging liveaboards, as well as other tourists, visit the
Caribbean isles, they are enticed to buy many exotic items made from
endangered species. Inadvertently these well-meaning tourists contribute to
the continued exploitation of the species. Amie Brautigam, an official with
the International Union for the Conservation of Nature (IUCN), cautions
the unwary tourist.*

*Gently with
the Tides*

Going to the Caribbean? Watch out for tourist traps. Tortoise-shell bracelets, stuffed sea turtles, parrots, corals, orchids—these are just some of the many traps vendors lay for unknowing visitors seeking the perfect souvenir of their Caribbean vacation. Not only do these vendors often neglect to inform their customers when the wildlife offered for sale are endangered species, they also fail to warn prospective buyers about national and international laws prohibiting their buying and bringing them home.

Island ecosystems are not only exotic, they are fragile. Many island animal and plant species are unique and have evolved without predators, including—until recently—humans. They are therefore highly vulnerable to introduced animals and plants, over-exploitation, and habitat modification.

Wishing to protect their natural heritage, many Caribbean countries have passed laws prohibiting the taking, sale, and/or export of many wild animals and plants that are rare or otherwise considered vulnerable to exploitation. Importing countries such as the United States are also bound by domestic and international laws to deny importation of such items.

Many an American tourist returns home from a Caribbean island resort only to see the perfect memento of lazy days on the beach seized by U.S. Customs or Fish and Wildlife inspectors. Seizure is not the only penalty: if federal officials can establish that the tourist was aware of import prohibitions they may levy a fine exceeding $10,000. On vacation in the Caribbean? Enjoy. But watch out for the wildlife tourist traps.

Probably the most common Caribbean wildlife items lost to U.S. Fish and Wildlife and Customs inspectors are stuffed sea turtles and tortoise-shell jewelry. Sea turtles, while once prevalent in the Caribbean, are becoming less so due to centuries of exploitation for local and international markets. Once sought for their calipee, the yellowish, jelly-like material inside the lower shell that is used for making turtle soup, green turtles are now hunted primarily for their meat. Hawksbill sea turtles are prized almost exclusively for their colorful shell, which is made into jewelry and other luxury products largely for international markets. Juveniles of both species are stuffed and sold as souvenirs. As a result of this exploitation, in many areas of the Caribbean, sea turtles are considered to be in danger of extinction.

Parrots and other birds are also a temptation to many tourists, as their colorful plumage and lively character make them endearing pets. Because of the limited range and population size of many Caribbean bird species, many restrictions have been established at national and international levels to protect them from undue trade pressure. Importation of many Caribbean bird species into the United States is restricted by various government agencies, including the U.S. Department of Agriculture, which sets rigorous quarantine requirements to guard against disease. In addition, importation of stuffed birds and items made with bird feathers is largely prohibited. Caribbean plant species, like birds and reptiles, are also characterized by limited range and population size, making them especially vulnerable to collection for international trade. Imports of orchids, cacti, and other plant species are subject to the same restrictions as those of birds, including inspection by U.S. Department of Agriculture agents.

Marine Environment

Coral is another popular item among tourists to the Caribbean, but unbeknownst to many of us, import of coral items may also be illegal. Many Caribbean countries protect corals from collection, sale, and/or export, and international trade in some coral species is restricted. Stony corals and black coral jewelry are among the items which, due to these restrictions, may best be avoided.

U.S. tourists are more often than not unaware of the various laws governing importation of wildlife products into the United States. U.S. membership to the Convention on International Trade in Endangered Species of Wild Fauna and Flora (CITES), an international treaty adhered to by 96 countries, obligates it to prohibit trade in listed endangered species. Major U.S. regulations controlling trade in endangered species are authorized by the U.S. Endangered Species Act, while the Marine Mammal Protection Act fundamentally prohibits trade in marine mammals and their products. The U.S. Lacey Act prohibits the importation of any wildlife taken or exported in violation of laws in the country of origin. The CITES treaty and U.S. laws work together to ensure trade does not threaten the continued survival of wildlife. Remember these laws—and don't get trapped.

Amie Brautigam

205

11
More Reading

SOMEONE ONCE said that he wanted to set a new world boating record by sailing around the world and not writing a book about it. Fortunately, for both the armchair sailor and the practicing liveaboard, not everyone shares that philosophy and many fascinating books have been written about life afloat. Many of these books are highly specialized in subjects like self-steering, diesel mechanics, 12-volt doctoring, canvas work, offshore cooking, and other useful and essential topics. A small group of books deals with the total immersion into life aboard. For the liveaboard these books have become guidelines for the final break with land and the continuing comfort and safety afloat. Many of the books deal with offshore cruising in sailboats, a popular theme for both the dreamer and the practitioner. Very few books have been published on coastal cruising in powerboats and houseboats. Fortunately, most of the quiet charm as well as the little annoyances and frustrations of life afloat are universal for all boaters and not dependent on the specific type of vessel. The theme that binds these books is their emphasis on going slowly and in comfort to be able to enjoy the floating lifestyle.

The following is a list of books about the liveaboard lifestyle. They cover the personal stories, the voyages, and the how-to of living aboard. Some of the books are readily available at bookstores, others can be ordered through nautical book catalogs, and still others can be found with the patient help of a librarian.

After 50,000 Miles by Hal Roth, W.W. Norton 1977
Always a Distant Shore by Hal Roth, W.W. Norton 1988
Atlantic Circle by Katheryn Lasky Knight, W.W. Norton, 1985
Blown Away by Herb Payson, *SAIL* Books 1980
Blue Water Dreams by D. H. Clark, David McKay 1981
Bluewater Handbook by Steve and Linda Dashew, Beowulf 1984
Children Afloat by Pipa Driscoll, International Marine 1989
The Circumnavigator's Handbook by Steve and Linda Dashew, W.W. Norton 1983
The Complete Live-Aboard Book by Katy Burke, Seven Seas 1982
The Complete Yachtsman: A Cruising Manual by Bobby Schenk, Ziff-Davis 1977
Cruising by J. D. Sleightholme, Granada 1977
Cruising as a Way of Life by Thomas E. Colvin, Seven Seas 1979
Cruising for Fun: Power and Sail by Tom Batlomley, 1977
Cruising in Comfort by Jim Skoog, International Marine 1986
Cruising in Seraffyn by Lin and Larry Pardey, Seven Seas 1986
Cruising Under Sail by Eric Hiscock, International Marine 1981
Cruising with Children by Gwenda Cornell, Sheridan House 1992
Deep Water Cruising by Gordon and Nina Stuermer, David McKay 1980
First Crossing by Malcolm and Carol McConnell, W.W. Norton 1983
Floating by Hugo Leckey, W.W. Norton 1982
Handmade Houseboats: Independent Living Afloat by Russell Conder, International Marine 1992
Houseboating by Eileen Rzecinski
Houseboats by Mark Gabor, 1979
How to Live Aboard a Boat by Janet Groene, Hearst Marine 1982
Living Aboard: A Cruising Sailboat as a Home by Jan and Bill Moeller, International Marine 1977
Managing Your Escape by Katy Burke, Seven Seas 1982
Ocean Cruising on a Budget by Anne Hammick, International Marine 1991
On Board with Bradley by Dick Bradley, Hearst Marine 1983
Sail Far Away: Reflections on Life Afloat by Robert S. Carter, W.W. Norton 1978
Sailing the Farm: Guide to Homesteading on the Ocean by Ken Neumeyer, Ten Speed Press 1981

More Reading

207

The Sailing Lifestyle: Sailing and Cruising for Pleasure by John Rousmaniere, S & S 1985

Seattle's Unsinkable Houseboats by Howard Droker, Watermarine Press 1977

The Self-Sufficient Sailor by Lin and Larry Pardey, W.W. Norton 1982

Sell Up and Sail by Bill and Laurel Cooper, Stanford Maritime 1987

Sensible Cruising: The Thoreau Approach by Don Casey and Lew Hackler, International Marine 1990

Setting Sail: How to Buy a Boat and Cruise the World on $300 a Month by Laurence Taylor, B&L 1982

Shantyboat: A River Way of Life by Harland Hubbard, University Press of Kentucky 1953 and 1981

The Small World of Long Distance Sailors by Ann Carl, David Mead 1985

Two on a Big Ocean by Hal Roth, W.W. Norton 1972

Unlikely Passages by Reese Palley, Seven Seas Press 1984

Voyaging Under Power by Robert Beebe, Seven Seas 1984

Waterhouses by Ferenc Maté, Albatross Publishing 1977

Wind Off the Dock by Marjorie Cahn Brazer, McMillan 1968

Wind Shadow West by Ralph J. Naranjo, Hearst Marine 1983

World Cruising Survey by Jimmy Cornell, International Marine 1989

Yacht Cruising by Patrick Ellam, W.W. Norton 1983

The Yachtsman's Mate's Guide by Margie Livingston, Ziff-Davis 1980

Appendix A
The *Living Aboard* Survey

BETWEEN 1975 and 1990 more than 2,000 liveaboards, those planning the liveaboard lifestyle, and dreamers responded to the following survey. A surprisingly large percentage of folks responded (about 25 percent) with facts, figures, and, more often than not, a humorous anecdote.

LIVING ABOARD SURVEY
(Everything we've wanted to know about you and aren't afraid to ask)

Please feel free to complete as much or as little of this survey as you like. But do respond, completing the sections which are applicable to you, then detach, fold, staple and mail. We'll be reporting the results in upcoming issues of Living Aboard.

Remember that the reason we want all of this information is in order to know WHO WE ARE - for an accurate public profile; WHERE WE ARE - in terms of needs and goals for the Association; and WHERE WE WANT TO GO - with the organization and its present and future membership.

The boat and marine products section of this survey assumes that among the things we seek are the benefits of our collective experiences. Other questions have been designed to pretty much cover the waterfront, hoping we'll come up with some interesting and insightful sentiments or statistics in some unexpected area. There is a great deal not known about the liveaboard phenomenon - perhaps with this periodic mini-census we'll begin making some discoveries that can help to inform us all.

Thanks for your help.   *Michael and Ryp*

SHIP'S COMPANY (Please indicate with a big "X" in front of your name if you wish anonymity)

CAPTAIN'S NAME _____

AGE   20-29 ☐ 30-39 ☐ 40-49 ☐ 50-59 ☐ 60-69 ☐ over 70 ☐

OCCUPATION _____ RETIRED ☐

FIRST MATE'S NAME _____

AGE   20-29 ☐ 30-39 ☐ 40-49 ☐ 50-59 ☐ 60-69 ☐ over 70 ☐

OCCUPATION _____ RETIRED ☐

CHILD'S NAME _____ AGE _____

_____ AGE _____

_____ AGE _____

_____ AGE _____

PET'S NAME _____ TYPE _____

_____ TYPE _____

FAMILY INCOME   UNDER $24,999 ☐ $25,000 - 69,999 ☐ OVER $70,000 ☐

DO YOU SUPPLEMENT YOUR INCOME WITH CRUISING JOBS OR HOBBIES YES ☐ NO ☐ IF YES, DESCRIBE

_____

LICENSES HELD (USCG, Ham, etc.)

_____

COURSES TAKEN (USCG, Navigation, Sailing, CPR, etc.)

_____

HOW LONG HAVE YOU LIVED ABOARD (YEARS)

PART TIME _____ FULL TIME _____ DREAMED ABOUT IT _____

ARE YOU   MOORED ☐ ANCHORED ☐ DOCKSIDE ☐ RENT MOOR/SLIP ☐ OWN MOOR/SLIP ☐

ARE YOU PLANNING TO LIVE ABOARD YES ☐   IN ____YEARS NO ☐

YEARS OF BOATING EXPERIENCE _____   DO YOU CRUISE YES ☐ NO ☐

GIVEN A CHOICE, WOULD YOU CIRCUMNAVIGATE ☐ OR STAY CLOSE TO HOME ☐

CRUISE THE BAHAMAS AND CARIBBEAN ☐ CROSS THE ATLANTIC ☐ OR FIND A PACIFIC ISLAND & SIT ☐

IS YOUR CRUISING CONFINED TO INLAND WATERWAYS ☐ DO YOU ENJOY OFFSHORE SAILING ☐

LONGEST VOYAGE TO DATE _____ MILES _____ DAYS

HOW MANY DAY TRIPS OR WEEKEND JAUNTS DO YOU TAKE PER YEAR _____

LIFESTYLE

THREE REASONS YOU DECIDED ON THE LIVEABOARD LIFESTYLE _____

_____

_____

YOU ENJOY BEING A LIVEABOARD MOST WHEN _____

_____

_____

MOST SIGNIFICANT DRAWBACK TO THIS LIFESTYLE _____
_____
_____

WHAT DO YOU MISS MOST ABOUT LIFE ASHORE _____
_____
_____

WHAT ARE THE THREE MOST IMPORTANT LIVEABOARD SKILLS_____
_____

WHAT IS THE MOST IMPORTANT SKILL YOU DON'T POSSESS _____
_____

WHAT IS THE GREATEST SOURCE OF CONFLICT_____
_____

WHAT IS MOST REWARDING ABOUT LIVING ABOARD _____
_____

WHAT HAS BEEN THE SCARIEST MOMENT SO FAR _____
_____

WHAT DO YOU ESTIMATE TO BE THE LIVEABOARD COSTS PER MONTH INCLUDING FUEL, FOOD, MAINTENANCE, SLIP, INSURANCE, BOAT MORTGAGE, MEDICAL AND INCIDENTALS $ _____ PER MONTH

YOUR BOAT

(IF YOU DON'T OWN A BOAT, PUT AN "X" HERE ☐ AND TELL US THE FEATURES OF YOUR DREAM BOAT)

BOAT NAME _____

BOAT TYPE SAIL ☐ CRUISER ☐ HOUSEBOAT ☐ TRAWLER ☐ MOTORSAILER ☐ MULTIHULL ☐

LENGTH_____ BEAM _____ DRAFT_____ DISPLACEMENT_____

MAKE_____ MODEL_____ YEAR_____ OWNER BUILT ☐ COST $_____

FIBERGLASS☐ STEEL ☐ WOOD ☐ ALUMINUM ☐ FERROCEMENT ☐

NO ENGINE ☐ DIESEL ☐ GASOLINE ☐ FUEL CAPACITY _____WATER CAPACITY_____

NUMBER OF BERTHS_____ REFRIGERATION ☐ FREEZER ☐ FOOD PROCESSOR ☐ MICROWAVE ☐

SOLAR PANELS ☐ WIND GENERATOR ☐ GAS/DIESEL GENERATOR ☐ WATER GENERATOR ☐

WASHER/DRYER ☐ TV ☐ VCR ☐ COMPUTER ☐ HEATER ☐ AIR CONDITIONER ☐

SATNAV ☐ LORAN ☐ RADAR ☐ VHF ☐ SINGLE SIDE BAND ☐ RDF ☐ GPS ☐ SEXTANT ☐

DO YOU PERFORM YOUR OWN MAINTENANCE YES ☐ NO ☐ ONLY SMALL REPAIRS ☐

HOW MANY HOURS ARE SPENT ON MAINTENANCE PER MONTH _____ HOW MANY $_____

HOW OFTEN IS YOUR BOAT HAULED_____ PER _____

HOW MUCH DO YOU SPEND IN PARTS AND SUPPLIES PER YEAR $_____

PLEASE LIST THE LAST 6 MARINE PRODUCTS YOU HAVE PURCHASED AND PROVIDE A COMMENT ON WHAT WORKED WELL AND WHAT YOU HAD PROBLEMS WITH

1. _____   _____

2. _____   _____

3. _____   _____

4. _____   _____

5. _____   _____

6. _____   _____

Index

Discover *Living Aboard* magazine!

Other boating magazines tell you to spend, spend, spend.

Living Aboard helps you *enjoy* the time you spend on your boat . . . whether a weekend, a month, or a lifetime. Learn from people who have actually made the move and how you can reinvent your life to live in a style most people only dream of.

Subscribe today and start working toward the dream.

A reader-written magazine covering power and sail.

"I drop everything when I get your magazine and read it cover to cover." — B.W., Brooklyn Park, Minn.

L·I·V·I·N·G
A·B·O·A·R·D

To read a sample copy online or to subscribe visit: **www.livingaboard.com** or call toll-free in the U.S. and Canada

1-800-927-6905

outside U.S. & Canada call (512) 892-4446

fax (512) 892-4448 / e-mail: info@livingaboard.com

The Best of *Living Aboard*

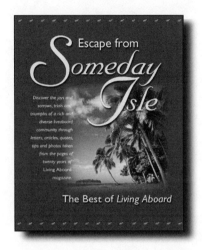

With this book you can learn what it's like to simplify your life to live aboard a boat. It's a "how-to" guide, but also a manual on recognizing and setting life's true priorities.

There are dreamers and there are doers in this world — and there is joy in both. Whether you are an armchair adventurer or a seasoned sailor, you'll enjoy reading this book.

If you've ever said to yourself, "Someday, I'll . . .," read this book. Here you'll meet people who have broken away, changed their lives, and discovered the joys and challenges of living aboard a boat.

Discover the highs and lows, tricks and triumphs of a rich and diverse liveaboard community through letters, articles, quotes, tips and photos taken from the pages of the past decade of *Living Aboard* magazine.

The world doesn't end when you decide to follow your dream — it begins. Make your own personal escape from Someday Isle.

ISBN 0-9741991-0-9

To order call 1-800-927-6905
or order online at www.livingaboard.com